CGP
– books
like no others!

CGP

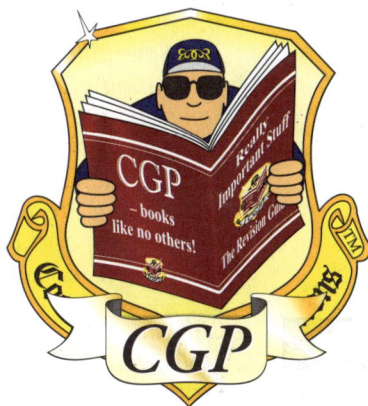

IVYBRIDGE COMMUNITY COLLEGE
SCIENCE DEPARTMENT

SCIENCE TEXT BOOK NO......**S6**..............

Name	Set	Date
Caitlin Banning.	High!	All the time...
Brittaney O'Reilly		

A...............ce

This book is for anyone doing **GCSE OCR Gateway Additional Science** at higher level.
It covers everything you'll need for your year 11 exams.

GCSE Science is all about **understanding how science works**.
And not only that — understanding it well enough to be able to **question**
what you hear on TV and read in the papers.

But you can't do that without a fair chunk of **background knowledge**. Hmm, tricky.

Happily this CGP book includes all the **science facts** you need to learn,
and shows you how they work in the **real world**. And in true CGP style,
we've explained it all as **clearly and concisely** as possible.

It's also got some daft bits in to try and make the whole
experience at least vaguely entertaining for you.

What CGP is all about

Our sole aim here at CGP is to produce the highest
quality books — carefully written, immaculately presented
and dangerously close to being funny.

Then we work our socks off to get them
out to you — at the cheapest possible prices.

Contents

MODULE B4 — IT'S A GREEN WORLD

MODULE C4 — THE PERIODIC TABLE

MODULE P4 — RADIATION FOR LIFE

Published by CGP

From original material by Richard Parsons.

Editors:
Katie Braid, Emma Elder, Edmund Robinson, Helen Ronan, Lyn Setchell, Hayley Thompson, Jane Towle, Karen Wells, Dawn Wright.

Contributors:
Lucy Muncaster, John Myers, Sophie Watkins.

ISBN: 978 1 84762 756 8

With thanks to Barrie Crowther, Ben Fletcher, Ian Francis, Helena Hayes, Sue Hocking and Rosie McCurrie for the proofreading.
With thanks to Jan Greenway, Laura Jakubowski and Laura Stoney for the copyright research.

Data used to draw graph on page 19, source developed by the National Center for Health Statistics in collaboration with the National Center for Chronic Disease Prevention and Health Promotion (2000). http://www.cdc.gov/growthcharts

Data used to construct stopping distance diagram on page 51 from the Highway Code.
© Crown Copyright reproduced under the terms of the Click-Use licence.

Groovy website: www.cgpbooks.co.uk

Printed by Elanders Ltd, Newcastle upon Tyne.
Jolly bits of clipart from CorelDRAW®

Photocopying — it's dull, grey and sometimes a bit naughty. Luckily, it's dead cheap, easy and quick to order more copies of this book from CGP — just call us on 0870 750 1242. Phew!

The Scientific Process

You need to know a few things about how the world of science works — both for your <u>exams</u> and your <u>controlled assessment</u>. Investigate these next few pages and you'll be laughing all day long on results day.

Scientists Come Up with Hypotheses — Then Test Them

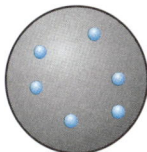

About 100 years ago, we thought atoms looked like this.

1) Scientists try to <u>explain</u> things. Everything.
2) They start by <u>observing</u> or <u>thinking about</u> something they don't understand — it could be anything, e.g. planets in the sky, a person suffering from an illness, what matter is made of... anything.
3) Then, using what they already know (plus a bit of insight), they come up with a <u>hypothesis</u> — a possible <u>explanation</u> for what they've observed.
4) The next step is to <u>test</u> whether the hypothesis might be <u>right or not</u> — this involves <u>gathering evidence</u> (i.e. <u>data</u> from <u>investigations</u>).
5) To gather evidence the scientist uses the hypothesis to make a <u>prediction</u> — a statement based on the hypothesis that can be <u>tested</u> by carrying out <u>experiments</u>.
6) If the results from the experiments match the prediction, then the scientist can be <u>more confident</u> that the hypothesis is <u>correct</u>. This <u>doesn't</u> mean the hypothesis is <u>true</u> though — other predictions based on the hypothesis might turn out to be <u>wrong</u>.

Scientists Work Together to Test Hypotheses

Then we thought they looked like this.

1) Different scientists can look at the <u>same evidence</u> and interpret it in <u>different ways</u>. That's why scientists usually work in <u>teams</u> — they can share their <u>different ideas</u> on how to interpret the data they find.
2) Once a team has come up with (and tested) a hypothesis they all agree with, they'll present their work to the scientific community through <u>journals</u> and <u>scientific conferences</u> so it can be judged — this is called the <u>peer review</u> process.
3) Other scientists then <u>check</u> the team's results (by trying to <u>replicate</u> them) and carry out their own experiments to <u>collect more evidence</u>.
4) If all the experiments in the world back up the hypothesis, scientists start to have a lot of <u>confidence</u> in it.
5) However, if another scientist does an experiment and the results <u>don't</u> fit with the hypothesis (and other scientists can <u>replicate</u> these results), then the hypothesis is in trouble. When this happens, scientists have to come up with a new hypothesis (maybe a <u>modification</u> of the old explanation, or maybe a completely <u>new</u> one).

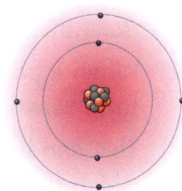

Scientific Ideas Change as New Evidence is Found

Now we think it's more like this.

1) Scientific explanations are <u>provisional</u> because they only explain the evidence that's <u>currently available</u> — new evidence may come up that can't be explained.
2) This means that scientific explanations <u>never</u> become hard and fast, totally indisputable <u>fact</u>. As <u>new evidence</u> is found (or new ways of <u>interpreting</u> existing evidence are found), hypotheses can <u>change</u> or be <u>replaced</u>.
3) Sometimes, an <u>unexpected observation</u> or <u>result</u> will suddenly throw a hypothesis into doubt and further experiments will need to be carried out. This can lead to new developments that <u>increase</u> our <u>understanding</u> of science.

You expect me to believe that — then show me the evidence...

If scientists think something is true, they need to produce evidence to convince others — it's all part of <u>testing a hypothesis</u>. One hypothesis might survive these tests, while others won't — it's how things progress. And along the way some hypotheses will be disproved — i.e. shown not to be true.

Evaluating Hypotheses and Scientific Information

In everyday life (and in your exams unfortunately) you'll encounter lots of scientific information. It's important that you know a few things about how to evaluate any evidence you're given.

Some Hypotheses are More Convincing Than Others

1) You might have to evaluate hypotheses that give different explanations for the same thing. Basically, this just means you need to say which one you think is better, and then explain why.

2) The most convincing hypotheses are based on reliable evidence (e.g. data that can be reproduced by others in independent experiments, see p.5) — not opinions or old wives' tales.

3) Reliable evidence comes from controlled experiments in laboratories (where you can control variables to make it a fair test — see p.4), studies (e.g. of a population), or observations (e.g. of animal behaviour).

4) Evidence that's based on samples that are too small doesn't have much more credibility than opinions. A sample should be representative of the whole population (i.e. it should share as many of the various characteristics in the population as possible) — a small sample just can't do that.

Scientific Information Isn't Always Very Good Quality

When you're given some scientific information, don't just believe it straight away — you need to think critically about what it's saying to work out how good the information really is.

1) Scientific information can be presented by a person who is biased.

2) When a person is biased, it means that they favour a particular interpretation of the evidence for a reason that's incorrect or unrelated to the scientific information.

3) This can be unintentional — the scientist might not realise they're being affected by something which makes them biased.

4) It can also be intentional — a scientist might give a particular interpretation on purpose because they have a personal reason for doing so.

5) A person who is intentionally biased might misrepresent the evidence — give the true facts, but present them in a way that makes them misleading. This might be to persuade you to agree with them...

EXAMPLE

Scientists say 1 in 2 people are of above average weight

Sounds like we're a nation of fatties. It's a scientific analysis of the facts, and almost certainly true.

But an average is a kind of 'middle value' of all your data. Some readings are higher than average (about half of them, usually). Others will be lower than average (the other half).

So the above headline (which made it sound like we should all lose weight) could just as accurately say: **Scientists say 1 in 2 people are of below average weight**

6) A person who is intentionally biased might also give scientific information without any evidence to back it up. This might be because there's no evidence to support what they're saying, or it could be that the person is just ignoring the evidence that exists (e.g. because it contradicts what they're saying).

7) Information that isn't backed up with any evidence could just be an opinion — you've got no way of telling whether it's true or not.

EXAMPLE

"Global warming is just something that ice cream sellers have made up."

There's no evidence to back up this claim so it could just be completely made up.

It's a scientific fact that the Moon's made of cheese...

Whenever you're given any kind of scientific information just stop for a second and ask yourself how convincing it really is — think about the evidence that's been used (if any) and the way that the information's been presented.

Scientific Development, Ethics and Risk

Scientific developments have a bit of a bumpy ride and yep, you guessed it, you need to know why this is.

Society Influences the Development of Science

1) You might think that scientific and technological developments are always a good thing. But society doesn't always agree about new developments.

2) Take embryo screening (which allows you to choose an embryo with particular characteristics). Different people have different opinions on it. For example:

> Some people say it's good... couples whose existing child needs a bone marrow transplant, but who can't find a donor, will be able to have another child selected for its matching bone marrow. This would save the life of their first child — and if they want another child anyway... where's the harm?
>
> Other people say it's bad... they say it could have serious effects on the new child. In the above example the new child might feel unwanted — thinking they were only brought into the world to help someone else. And would they have the right to refuse to donate their bone marrow (as anyone else would)?

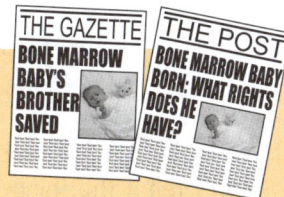

THE GAZETTE — BONE MARROW BABY'S BROTHER SAVED

THE POST — BONE MARROW BABY BORN: WHAT RIGHTS DOES HE HAVE?

3) The question of whether something is morally or ethically right or wrong can't be answered by more experiments — there is no "right" or "wrong" answer.

4) In an ideal world, the best decision about any moral or ethical dilemma would have the best outcome for the majority of people involved.

Other Factors Can Affect Scientific Development Too

There are other factors that can influence the development of science and the way it's used:

Economic factors:
- Companies very often won't pay for research unless there's likely to be a profit in it.
- Society can't always afford to do things scientists recommend (e.g. investing heavily in alternative energy sources) without cutting back elsewhere.

Social factors: Decisions based on scientific evidence affect people — e.g. should fossil fuels be taxed more highly (to invest in alternative energy)? Should alcohol be banned (to prevent health problems)? Would the effect on people's lifestyles be acceptable...?

Cultural factors: Cultural feelings can sometimes affect whether research is carried out or given funding, e.g. some religious groups are against testing on human embryonic stem cells.

Scientific Development Has Benefits and Risks

1) Like most things, developments in scientific technology have both benefits and risks.

2) There often needs to be a balance between personal risk and the overall benefit to society. For example, building a nuclear power station poses a risk to the people who work there and those living nearby (because they may be exposed to radiation), but it will also supply a large section of society with a reliable source of electricity.

3) Scientists try to find ways of reducing the risks involved, e.g. introducing strict safety measures at the power station.

Scientific development — a nice quiet estate of labs on the edge of town...

As you can see, science isn't just about knowing your facts — you need to think about the factors that affect the development of science, the ethical issues raised and the benefits and risks that come with scientific development.

Planning Investigations

That's all the dull stuff about the world of science over — now onto the hands-on part. The next few pages show how <u>practical investigations</u> should be carried out — by both <u>professional scientists</u> and <u>you</u>.

To Make an Investigation a Fair Test You Have to Control the Variables

An important part of planning an investigation is making sure it's a <u>fair test</u>.

1) In a lab experiment you usually <u>change one variable</u> and <u>measure</u> how it affects the <u>other variable</u>.

> **EXAMPLE:** you might change only the temperature of an enzyme-controlled reaction and measure how it affects the rate of reaction.

2) To make it a fair test <u>everything else</u> that could affect the results should <u>stay the same</u> (otherwise you can't tell if the thing that's being changed is affecting the results or not — the data won't be reliable).

> **EXAMPLE** continued: you need to keep the pH the same, otherwise you won't know if any change in the rate of reaction is caused by the change in temperature, or the change in pH.

3) The variable that you <u>change</u> is called the <u>independent</u> variable.

4) The variable that's <u>measured</u> is called the <u>dependent</u> variable.

5) The variables that you <u>keep the same</u> are called <u>control</u> variables.

> **EXAMPLE** continued:
> Independent = temperature
> Dependent = rate of reaction
> Control = pH

6) Because you can't always control all the variables, you often need to use a <u>control experiment</u> — an experiment that's kept under the <u>same conditions</u> as the rest of the investigation, but doesn't have anything done to it. This is so that you can see what happens when you don't change anything at all.

The Equipment Used has to be Right for the Job

1) When you're planning an investigation, you need to make sure you choose the <u>right equipment</u>. For example, the measuring equipment you use has to be <u>sensitive enough</u> to accurately measure the chemicals you're using, e.g. if you need to measure out 11 ml of a liquid, you'll need to use a measuring cylinder that can measure to 1 ml, not 5 or 10 ml.

2) You should also be able to <u>explain why</u> you've chosen each bit of kit.

Experiments Must be Safe

1) Part of planning an investigation is making sure that it's <u>safe</u>.

2) There are lots of <u>hazards</u> you could be faced with during an investigation, e.g. <u>radiation</u>, <u>electricity</u>, <u>gas</u>, <u>chemicals</u> and <u>fire</u>.

3) You should always make sure that you <u>identify</u> all the hazards that you might encounter.

4) You should also come up with ways of <u>reducing the risks</u> from the hazards you've identified.

5) One way of doing this is to carry out a <u>risk assessment</u>:

> For an experiment involving a <u>Bunsen burner</u>, the risk assessment might be something like this:

Hazard:
- Bunsen burner is a fire risk.

Precautions:
- Keep flammable chemicals away from the Bunsen.
- Never leave the Bunsen unattended when lit.
- Always turn on the yellow safety flame when not in use.

Hazard: revision boredom. Precaution: use CGP books

Wow, all this even before you've started the investigation — it really does make them run more smoothly though.

Getting the Data Right

There are a few things that can be done to make sure that you get the best results you possibly can.

Trial Runs Help Figure out the Range and Interval of Variable Values

1) Before you carry out an experiment, it's a good idea to do a trial run first — a quick version of your experiment.

2) Trial runs help you work out whether your plan is right or not — you might decide to make some changes after trying out your method.

3) Trial runs are used to figure out the range of variable values used (the upper and lower limit).

4) And they're used to figure out the interval (gaps) between the values too.

Enzyme-controlled reaction example from previous page continued:

- You might do trial runs at 10, 20, 30, 40 and 50 °C. If there was no reaction at 10 or 50 °C, you might narrow the range to 20-40 °C.

- If using 10 °C intervals gives you a big change in rate of reaction you might decide to use 5 °C intervals, e.g. 20, 25, 30, 35...

Data Should be as Reliable and Accurate as Possible

1) Reliable results are ones that can be consistently reproduced each time you do an experiment. If your results are reliable they're more likely to be true, so you can make valid conclusions from them.

2) When carrying out your own investigation, you can improve the reliability of your results by repeating the readings and calculating the mean (average, see next page). You should repeat readings at least twice (so that you have at least three readings to calculate an average result).

3) To make sure your results are reliable you can also take a second set of readings with another instrument, or get a different observer to cross check.

4) Checking your results match with secondary sources, e.g. studies that other people have done, also increases the reliability of your data.

5) You should also always make sure that your results are accurate. Really accurate results are those that are really close to the true answer.

6) You can get accurate results by doing things like making sure the equipment you're using is sensitive enough (see previous page), and by recording your data to a suitable level of accuracy. For example, if you're taking digital readings of something, the results will be more accurate if you include at least a couple of decimal places instead of rounding to whole numbers.

You Can Check For Mistakes Made When Collecting Data

1) When you've collected all the results for an experiment, you should have a look to see if there are any results that don't seem to fit in with the rest.

2) Most results vary a bit, but any that are totally different are called anomalous results.

3) They're caused by human errors, e.g. by a whoopsie when measuring.

4) The only way to stop them happening is by taking all your measurements as carefully as possible.

5) If you ever get any anomalous results, you should investigate them to try to work out what happened. If you can work out what happened (e.g. you measured something wrong) you can ignore them when processing your results.

Reliable data — it won't ever forget your birthday...

All this stuff is really important — without good quality data an investigation will be totally meaningless. So give this page a read through a couple of times and your data will be the envy of the whole scientific community.

Processing, Presenting and Interpreting Data

The fun doesn't stop once you've collected your data — it then needs to be **processed** and **presented**...

Data Needs to be Organised

1) Data that's been collected needs to be organised so it can be processed later on.

2) Tables are dead useful for organising data.

3) When drawing tables you should always make sure that each column has a heading and that you've included the units.

4) Annoyingly, tables are about as useful as a chocolate teapot for showing patterns or relationships in data. You need to use some kind of graph or mathematical technique for that...

Test tube	Result (ml)	Repeat 1 (ml)	Repeat 2 (ml)
A	28	37	32
B	47	51	60
C	68	72	70

Data Can be Processed Using a Bit of Maths

1) Raw data generally just ain't that useful. You usually have to process it in some way.

2) A couple of the most simple calculations you can perform are the mean (average) and the range (how spread out the data is):

- To calculate the mean **ADD TOGETHER** all the data values and **DIVIDE** by the total number of values. You usually do this to get a single value from several repeats of your experiment.

- To calculate the range find the **LARGEST** number and **SUBTRACT** the **SMALLEST** number. You usually do this to check the accuracy and reliability of the results — the greater the spread of the data, the lower the accuracy and reliability.

Test tube	Result (ml)	Repeat 1 (ml)	Repeat 2 (ml)	Mean (ml)	Range
A	28	37	32	$(28 + 37 + 32) \div 3 = 32.3$	$37 - 28 = 9$
B	47	51	60	$(47 + 51 + 60) \div 3 = 52.7$	$60 - 47 = 13$
C	68	72	70	$(68 + 72 + 70) \div 3 = 70.0$	$72 - 68 = 4$

Different Types of Data Should be Presented in Different Ways

1) Once you've carried out an investigation, you'll need to present your data so that it's easier to see patterns and relationships in the data.

2) Different types of investigations give you different types of data, so you'll always have to choose what the best way to present your data is.

Pie charts can be used to present the same sort of data as bar charts. They're mostly used when the data is in percentages or fractions though.

Bar Charts

If the independent variable is categoric (comes in distinct categories, e.g. blood types, metals) you should use a bar chart to display the data. You also use them if the independent variable is discrete (the data can be counted in chunks, where there's no in-between value, e.g. number of people is discrete because you can't have half a person).

There are some golden rules you need to follow for drawing bar charts:

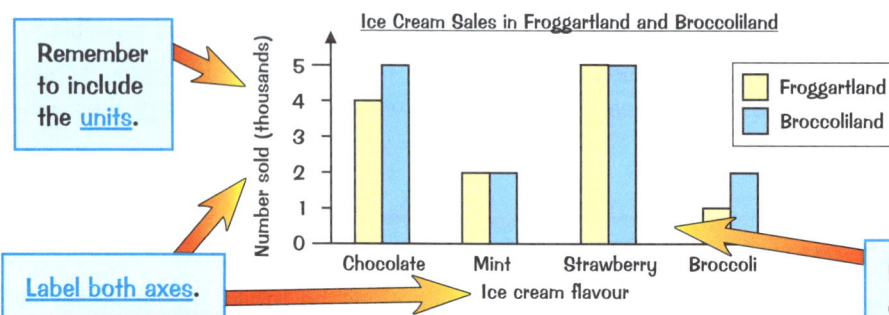

Remember to include the units.

If there's more than one set of data include a key.

Draw it nice and big.

Label both axes.

Leave a gap between different categories.

Ice Cream Sales in Froggartland and Broccoliland

Number sold (thousands) — Chocolate, Mint, Strawberry, Broccoli — Ice cream flavour

Froggartland / Broccoliland

Processing, Presenting and Interpreting Data

Line Graphs

If the independent variable is **continuous** (numerical data that can have any value within a range, e.g. length, volume, time) you should use a **line graph** to display the data.

Remember to include the **units**.

The **dependent** variable (the thing you measure) goes on the **y-axis** (the **vertical** one).

The **independent** variable (the thing you change) goes on the **x-axis** (the **horizontal** one).

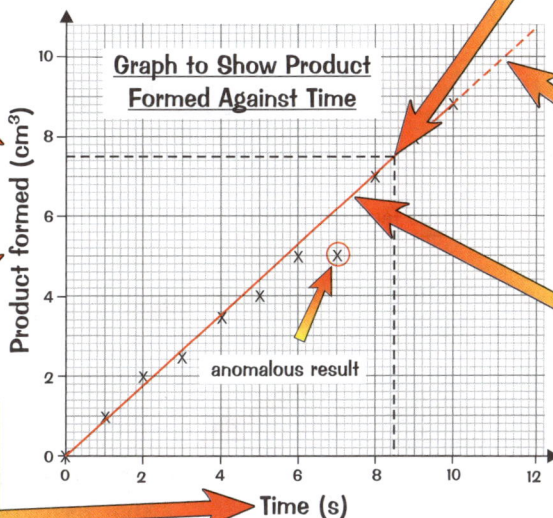

Graph to Show Product Formed Against Time

anomalous result

Product formed (cm³) — Time (s)

You can **estimate** values **within** the range of your existing data points using the **line of best fit** (see below). E.g. at 8.5 s about 7.5 cm³ of product will have been produced. This is called **interpolation**.

You can **continue** your line in the same direction so that you can **estimate** values beyond the range of your data points. This is called **extrapolation**.

Don't join the dots up. You should draw a **line of best fit** (or a **curve of best fit** if your points make a curve).

When drawing a line (or curve), try to draw the line **through** or as **near** to as **many points as possible**, ignoring anomalous results.

You can also use line graphs to **process** data a bit more. For example, if 'time' is on the x-axis, you can calculate the **gradient** (**slope**) of the line to find the **rate of reaction**:

1) Gradient = y ÷ x
2) You can calculate the gradient of the **whole line** or a **section** of it.
3) The rate for this line would be in **cm³/s**.

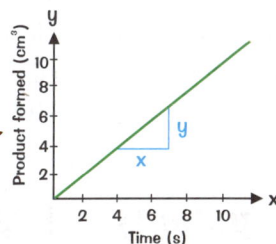

Product formed (cm³) — Time (s)

Line Graphs Can Show Relationships in Data

1) Unfortunately, when you're carrying out an investigation it's not enough to just present your data — you've got to **analyse** it to identify any patterns or relationships there might be.
2) Line graphs are great for showing relationships **between two variables**.
3) Here are the **three** different types of **correlation** (relationship) shown on line graphs:

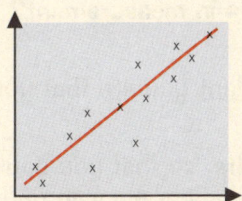

POSITIVE correlation — as one variable **increases** the other **increases**.

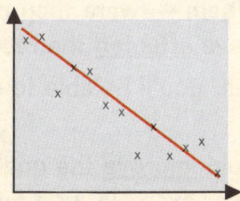

INVERSE (negative) correlation — as one variable **increases** the other **decreases**.

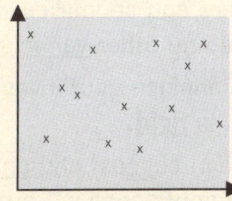

NO correlation — there's **no relationship** between the two variables.

4) You've got to be careful not to **confuse correlation** with **cause** though. A **correlation** just means that there's a **relationship** between two variables. It **doesn't mean** that the change in one variable is **causing** the change in the other (there might be **other factors** involved).

There's a positive correlation between age of man and length of nose hair...

Process, present, interpret... data's like a difficult child — it needs a lot of attention. Go on, make it happy.

Concluding and Evaluating

At the end of an investigation, the conclusion and evaluation are waiting. Don't worry, they won't bite.

A Conclusion is a Summary of What You've Learnt

1) Once all the data's been collected, presented and analysed, an investigation will always involve coming to a conclusion.

2) Drawing a conclusion can be quite straightforward — just look at your data and say what pattern you see.

EXAMPLE: The table on the right shows the heights of pea plant seedlings grown for three weeks with different fertilisers.

Fertiliser	Mean growth (mm)
A	13.5
B	19.5
No fertiliser	5.5

CONCLUSION: Fertiliser B makes pea plant seedlings grow taller over a three week period than fertiliser A.

3) However, you also need to use the data that's been collected to justify the conclusion (back it up).

EXAMPLE continued: Fertiliser B made the pea plants grow 6 mm more on average than fertiliser A.

4) There are some things to watch out for too — it's important that the conclusion matches the data it's based on and doesn't go any further.

5) Remember not to confuse correlation and cause (see previous page). You can only conclude that one variable is causing a change in another if you have controlled all the other variables (made it a fair test).

EXAMPLE continued: You can't conclude that fertiliser B makes any other type of plant grow taller than fertiliser A — the results could be totally different. Also, you can't make any conclusions beyond the three weeks — the plants could drop dead.

6) When writing a conclusion you should also explain what's been found by linking it to your own scientific knowledge (the stuff you've learnt in class).

Evaluations — Describe How it Could be Improved

An evaluation is a critical analysis of the whole investigation.

1) You should comment on the method — was the equipment suitable? Was it a fair test?

2) Comment on the quality of the results — was there enough evidence to reach a valid conclusion? Were the results reliable, accurate and precise?

3) Were there any anomalies in the results — if there were none then say so.

4) If there were any anomalies, try to explain them — were they caused by errors in measurement? Were there any other variables that could have affected the results?

5) When you analyse your investigation like this, you'll be able to say how confident you are that your conclusion is right.

6) Then you can suggest any changes that would improve the quality of the results, so that you could have more confidence in your conclusion. For example, you might suggest changing the way you controlled a variable, or changing the interval of values you measured.

7) You could also make more predictions based on your conclusion, then further experiments could be carried out to test them.

8) When suggesting improvements to the investigation, always make sure that you say why you think this would make the results better.

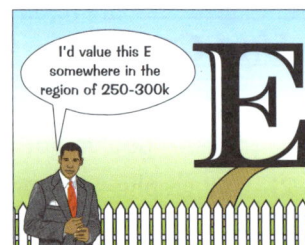

I'd value this E somewhere in the region of 250-300k

Evaluation — in my next study I will make sure I don't burn the lab down...

I know it doesn't seem very nice, but writing about where you went wrong is an important skill — it shows you've got a really good understanding of what the investigation was about. It's difficult for me — I'm always right.

Controlled Assessment

You'll probably carry out a few investigations as you go through the course, but at some point you'll have to do the one that counts... the controlled assessment. Here's a bit about it, but make sure you can recite all the stuff we've covered in this section first — it'll really help you out.

There are Three Parts to the Controlled Assessment

1) Research and Collecting Secondary Data

For Part 1 you'll be given some material to introduce the task and a research question. You'll need to read this through and then:

1) Carry out research and collect secondary data (data that other people have collected, rather than data you collect yourself).

2) Show that you considered all the different sources you could have used (e.g. books, the Internet) and chose the ones that were most suitable. You also need to explain why you chose those sources.

3) Write a full list (bibliography) of all the sources you used.

4) Present all the data you collected in an appropriate way, e.g. using tables.

2) Planning and Collecting Primary Data

For Part 2 you'll be given some more information to get your head around. Read this through and then:

1) Come up with a hypothesis based on the information you've been given.

2) Plan an experiment to test your hypothesis. You'll need to think about:
   - What equipment you're going to use (and why that equipment is right for the job).
   - What measurements you're going to take of the dependent variable.
   - How you're going to make sure your results are accurate and reliable.
   - What range of values you will use for the independent variable.
   - What interval you will use for the independent variable.
   - What variables you're going to control (and how you're going to do it).
   - How many times you're going to repeat the experiment.

3) Explain all the choices you made when planning the experiment.

4) Write a risk assessment for the experiment.

5) Carry out the experiment to collect primary data, taking any precautions from the risk assessment.

6) Present all the data you collected in an appropriate way, e.g. using tables.

3) Analysis and Evaluation

For Part 3 you'll have to complete a question paper which will ask you to do things like:

1) Process (e.g. using a bit of maths) and present (e.g. using graphs) both the primary and secondary data you collected in Part 1 and Part 2 in the most appropriate way.

2) Analyse and interpret the data to identify any patterns or relationships.

3) Write a conclusion based on all the data you collected and back it up with your own scientific knowledge.

4) Look back to your hypothesis and say whether the data support the hypothesis or not.

5) Evaluate the methods you used to collect the data and the quality of the data that was collected.

6) Say how confident you are in your conclusion and make suggestions for how the investigation could be improved. You'll also need to say why your suggestions would be an improvement.

Read this through and your assessment will be well under control...

You could use this page like a tick list for the controlled assessment — to make sure you don't forget anything.

Cells

Biology's all about living stuff. And all living stuff contains cells. So let's make a start with cells...

Learn These Animal Cell Structures...

The following cell structures are found in most animal cells:

Nucleus — contains DNA in the form of chromosomes (see next page).

Cell membrane — holds the cell together and controls what goes in and out.

Ribosome — where proteins are synthesised (see page 12).

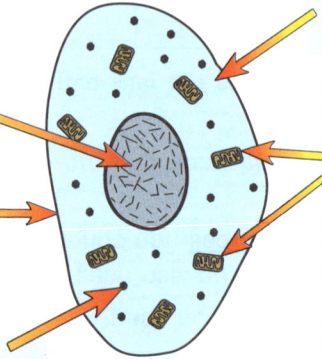

Cytoplasm — gel-like substance where most of the cell's chemical reactions happen.

Mitochondria — where most of the reactions involved in respiration take place. Respiration provides energy for cell processes (see page 20). Cells that need lots of energy contain many mitochondria, e.g.

- liver cells — which carry out lots of energy-demanding metabolic reactions,
- muscle cells — which need energy to contract (and cause movement).

Cell structures are tiny — some are even too small to be seen with a light microscope, e.g. ribosomes.

...And These Plant Cell Structures Too

Plant cells usually have all the structures that animal cells have, plus a few extra:

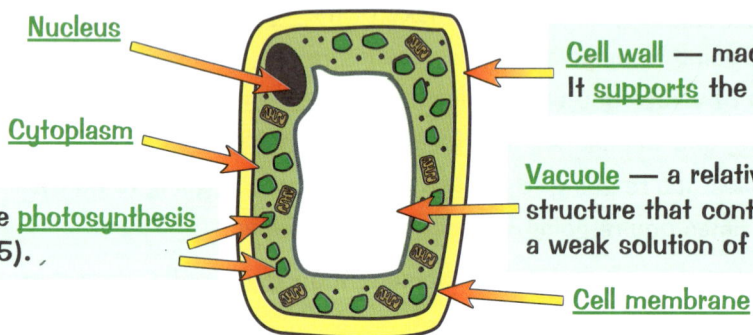

Nucleus

Cytoplasm

Chloroplasts — where photosynthesis happens (see page 65).

Cell wall — made of cellulose. It supports the cell.

Vacuole — a relatively large structure that contains cell sap, a weak solution of sugar and salts.

Cell membrane

Bacterial Cells Are A Bit Different

Bacterial cells are smaller and simpler than plant and animal cells...

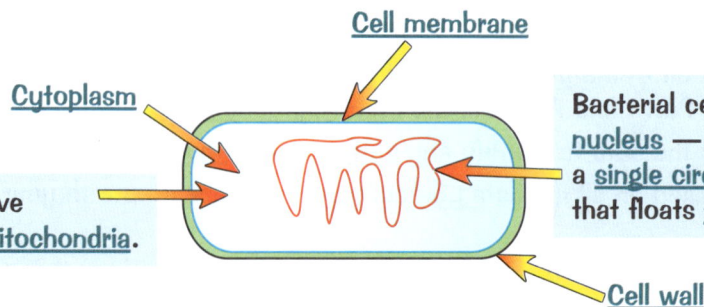

Cell membrane

Cytoplasm

Bacteria don't have chloroplasts or mitochondria.

Bacterial cells don't have a 'true' nucleus — instead they have a single circular strand of DNA that floats freely in the cytoplasm.

Cell wall

Cell structures — become a property developer...

This page needs learning from top to bottom. These cell structures crop up everywhere in biology — so make sure you know them all. You also need to know what makes bacterial cells that bit different from plant and animal cells — it's mainly the lack of anything interesting like a nucleus, chloroplasts or mitochondria.

DNA

DNA is a <u>big</u>, <u>big deal</u> in Biology, but the mystery of its <u>structure</u> was only solved relatively recently.

Chromosomes Are Made of DNA

1) <u>Chromosomes</u> are <u>long molecules</u> of <u>coiled up DNA</u>.
   The DNA is divided up into short sections called <u>genes</u> (see next page).

2) <u>DNA</u> is a <u>double helix</u> (a double-stranded spiral). Each of the two
   DNA strands is made up of lots of small groups called "<u>nucleotides</u>".

3) Each <u>nucleotide</u> contains a small molecule called a "<u>base</u>".
   DNA has just <u>four</u> different bases.

4) You only need to know the four bases by their first initials
   — A, C, G and T.

5) Each base forms <u>cross links</u> to a base <u>on the other strand</u>.
   This keeps the two DNA strands <u>tightly wound</u> together.

6) A <u>always</u> pairs up with T, and C <u>always</u> pairs up with G.
   This is called <u>complementary base-pairing</u>.

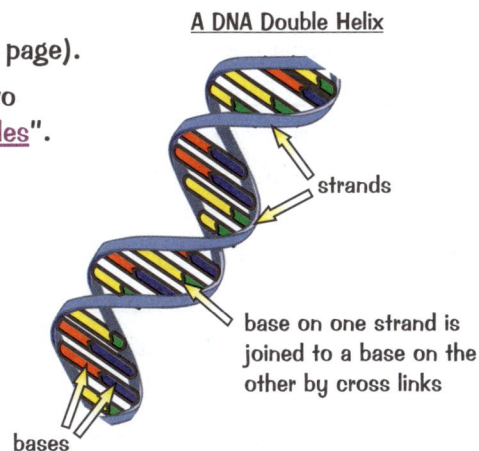

A DNA Double Helix

strands

base on one strand is
joined to a base on the
other by cross links

bases

Watson and Crick Were The First to Model DNA

1) Scientists <u>struggled</u> for <u>decades</u> to work out the <u>structure</u> of DNA.

2) <u>Francis Crick</u> and <u>James Watson</u> were the <u>first</u> scientists to build a <u>model</u> of DNA — they did it in <u>1953</u>.

3) They used <u>data</u> from <u>other scientists</u> to help them <u>understand</u> the structure of the molecule. This included:

   • <u>X-ray data</u> showing that DNA is a <u>double helix</u> formed from <u>two chains</u> wound together.

   • Other data showing that the <u>bases</u> occurred in <u>pairs</u>.

4) By putting this information <u>together</u> they were able to <u>build</u> a <u>model</u> showing what DNA looks like.

> Don't forget, <u>new discoveries</u> like Watson and Crick's aren't <u>widely accepted</u>
> <u>straight away</u>. Other scientists need to <u>repeat</u> the work first to make sure
> the results are <u>reliable</u> (see 'How Science Works' page 1 for more).

DNA Can Replicate Itself

1) DNA <u>copies itself</u> every time a cell <u>divides</u>, so that each new cell still has the full amount of DNA.

2) In order to copy itself, the DNA double helix first '<u>unzips</u>' — to form two <u>single strands</u>.

3) <u>New nucleotides</u> (floating freely in the nucleus) then join on using <u>complementary base-pairing</u>
   (A with T and C with G). This makes an <u>exact copy</u> of the DNA on the other strand.

4) The result is <u>two</u> double-stranded molecules of DNA that are <u>identical</u> to the original molecule of DNA.

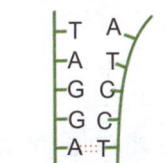

Molecule
of DNA unzips.

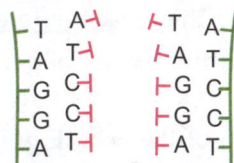

Bases on free-floating nucleotides pair up
with complementary bases on the DNA.

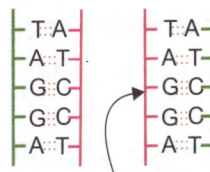

Cross links form between the bases and the
old DNA strands, and the nucleotides are
joined together to form double strands.

Q: What do DNA and a game of rounders have in common...?

Answer: <u>four bases</u>, and don't you forget it. Scientists spent <u>years and years</u> trying to work out the structure
of DNA. When Watson and Crick finally cracked it, it became the scientific discovery of the twentieth century.

Protein Synthesis

So here's how life works — <u>DNA molecules</u> contain a <u>genetic code</u> that determines which <u>proteins</u> are built. The proteins determine how all the cells in the body <u>function</u>. Simple, eh.

Proteins are Made by Reading the Code in DNA

1) <u>DNA</u> controls the production of <u>proteins</u> (<u>protein synthesis</u>) in a cell.

2) A <u>section of DNA</u> that codes for a particular <u>protein</u> is called a <u>gene</u>.

3) Proteins are made up of <u>chains</u> of molecules called <u>amino acids</u>. Each different protein has its own particular <u>number</u> and <u>order</u> of amino acids.

4) This gives each protein a different <u>shape</u>, which means each protein can have a different <u>function</u>.

5) It's the <u>order</u> of the <u>bases</u> in a <u>gene</u> that decides the order of <u>amino acids</u> in a <u>protein</u>.

6) Each amino acid is <u>coded for</u> by a sequence of <u>three bases</u> in the gene.

7) The amino acids are <u>joined together</u> to make proteins, following the order of the bases in the gene.

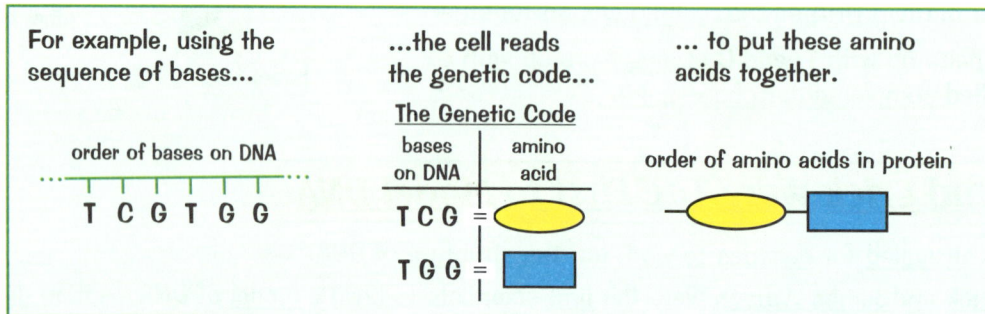

For example, using the sequence of bases... ...the cell reads the genetic code... ... to put these amino acids together.

order of bases on DNA

· · · · | | | | | · · · ·

T C G T G G

The Genetic Code

bases on DNA	amino acid
T C G	(yellow oval)
T G G	(blue rectangle)

order of amino acids in protein

(yellow oval) (blue rectangle)

8) Each gene contains a <u>different sequence</u> of <u>bases</u> — which is what allows it to code for a <u>unique protein</u>.

mRNA Carries The Code to The Ribosomes

1) Proteins are made in the cell <u>cytoplasm</u> by tiny structures called <u>ribosomes</u>.

2) To make proteins, ribosomes <u>use</u> the <u>code</u> in the <u>DNA</u>. DNA is found in the cell <u>nucleus</u> and can't move out of it because it's really big. So the cell needs to get the code <u>from</u> the DNA <u>to</u> the ribosome.

3) This is done using a molecule called <u>mRNA</u> — which is made by <u>copying</u> the code from DNA.

4) The mRNA acts as a <u>messenger</u> between the DNA and the ribosome — it carries the code between the two.

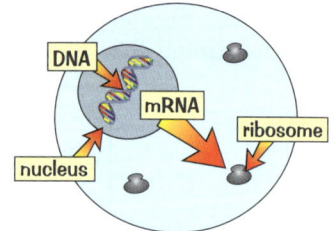

(diagram labels: DNA, mRNA, ribosome, nucleus)

DNA Controls A Cell By Controlling Protein Production

1) The <u>proteins</u> produced in a <u>cell</u> affect how it <u>functions</u>. Some of them determine <u>cell structure</u>, others (like <u>enzymes</u>) control <u>cell reactions</u> — see next page.

2) Different types of cell have <u>different functions</u> because they make <u>different proteins</u>.

3) They only make certain proteins because only <u>some</u> of the <u>full set</u> of genes is used in any one cell. Some genes are "<u>switched off</u>", which means the proteins they code for <u>aren't produced</u>.

4) The <u>genes</u> that are <u>switched on</u> determine the <u>function</u> of the <u>cell</u>. E.g. <u>in a muscle cell</u> only the genes that code for <u>muscle cell proteins</u> are <u>switched on</u>. Genes that code for proteins specific to <u>bone</u>, <u>nerve</u> or <u>skin</u> cells are all <u>switched off</u>. This allows the muscle cell to function as... well, a muscle cell.

And I thought the aliens were in control...

... but it turns out that <u>DNA</u> is really where it's at. Or maybe <u>aliens</u> are controlling my DNA that's controlling my proteins that are controlling my... Anyway. Make sure you know all the <u>details</u> on this page — it's a tricky one.

Functions of Proteins

Proteins are <u>handy</u> little things. They carry messages around the body, and even control chemical reactions.

Proteins *Have Many Different Functions*

There are <u>hundreds</u> of <u>different proteins</u> and they all have <u>different functions</u>.
Thankfully, you don't need to know about all of them — just these <u>four examples</u>:

See page 21 for more on haemoglobin.

1) ENZYMES — see below.
2) CARRIER MOLECULES — used to <u>transport</u> smaller molecules. E.g. <u>haemoglobin</u>
    (found in <u>red blood cells</u>) binds to <u>oxygen molecules</u> and transports them around the body.
3) HORMONES — used to <u>carry messages</u> around the body. E.g. <u>insulin</u> is a
    hormone released into the blood by the pancreas to <u>regulate</u> the <u>blood sugar level</u>.
4) STRUCTURAL PROTEINS — are physically <u>strong</u>. E.g. <u>collagen</u> is a structural
    protein that strengthens <u>connective tissues</u> (like ligaments and cartilage).

Enzymes *Control Cell Reactions*

1) <u>Cells</u> have thousands of different <u>chemical reactions</u> going on inside them all the time —
    like <u>respiration</u>, <u>photosynthesis</u> and <u>protein synthesis</u>.

2) These reactions need to be <u>carefully controlled</u> — to get the <u>right</u> amounts of substances
    and keep the organism working properly.

3) You can usually make a reaction happen more quickly by <u>raising the temperature</u>. This would
    speed up the useful reactions but also the unwanted ones too... not good. There's also a <u>limit</u> to
    how far you can raise the temperature inside a living creature before its <u>cells</u> start getting <u>damaged</u>.

4) So living things produce <u>ENZYMES</u>, which act as <u>BIOLOGICAL CATALYSTS</u>. A catalyst is a
    substance that <u>speeds up</u> a reaction, without being changed or used up in the reaction itself.

5) Enzymes reduce the need for high temperatures and we <u>only</u> have enzymes to speed up the
    <u>useful chemical reactions</u> in the body.

6) <u>Every</u> different biological reaction has its <u>own enzyme</u> designed especially for it.

7) Each enzyme is coded for by a <u>different gene</u>, and has a <u>unique shape</u> which it needs to do its job.

Enzymes *are Very Specific*

1) <u>Chemical reactions</u> usually involve things either being <u>split apart</u> or <u>joined together</u>.
2) The <u>substrate</u> is the molecule <u>changed</u> in the reaction.
3) <u>Every</u> enzyme has an <u>active site</u> — the part where it <u>joins on</u> to its substrate to catalyse the reaction.
4) Enzymes are really <u>picky</u> — they usually only work with <u>one substrate</u>. The posh way of saying
    this is that enzymes have a <u>high specificity for their substrate</u>.
5) This is because, for the enzyme to work, the substrate has to <u>fit</u> into the <u>active site</u>. If the substrate's
    shape doesn't <u>match</u> the active site's shape, then the reaction <u>won't</u> be catalysed. This is called the
    '<u>lock and key</u>' <u>mechanism</u>, because the substrate fits into the enzyme just like a key fits into a lock.

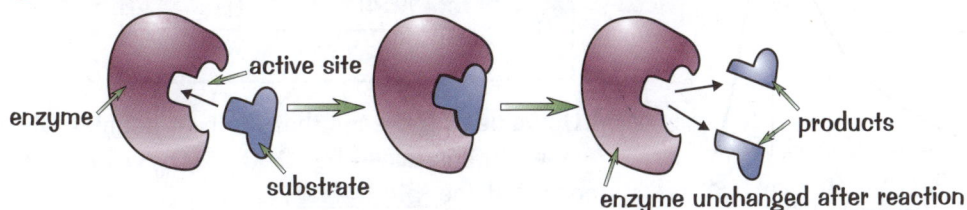

enzyme   active site   products

substrate   enzyme unchanged after reaction

If the lock & key mechanism fails, you get in through a window...

<u>Enzymes</u> aren't just useful for controlling chemical reactions in the body — we even put them in things like
<u>biological washing powders</u> to catalyse the breakdown of nasty stains (like tomato ketchup).

More On Enzymes

Enzymes are <u>fussy blighters</u> — they want the <u>right temperature</u> and the <u>right pH</u>, too...

Enzymes *Like it* Warm *but* Not Too Hot

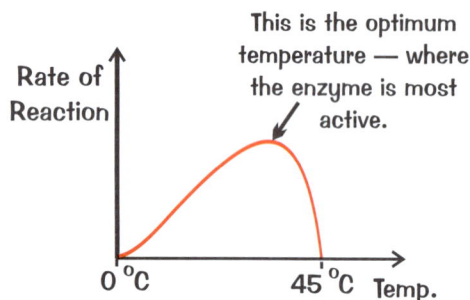

This is the optimum temperature — where the enzyme is most active.

Rate of Reaction

0 °C   45 °C   Temp.

1) Changing the <u>temperature</u> changes the <u>rate</u> of an enzyme-catalysed reaction.

2) Like with any reaction, a <u>higher temperature increases the rate</u> at first. This is because more <u>heat</u> means the enzymes and the substrate particles have more <u>energy</u>. This makes the enzymes and the substrate particles <u>move about</u> more, so they're more likely to meet up and react — they have a <u>higher collision rate</u>.

3) <u>Low temperatures</u> have the opposite effect — there's a <u>lower collision rate</u> and so a <u>slower reaction</u>.

4) If it gets <u>too hot</u>, some of the <u>bonds</u> holding the enzyme together will <u>break</u>.

5) This makes the enzyme <u>lose its shape</u> — its <u>active site</u> doesn't fit the shape of the substrate any more. This means it <u>can't</u> catalyse the reaction and the reaction <u>stops</u> — the enzyme <u>can't function</u>.

6) The enzyme is now said to be <u>denatured</u>. Its change in shape is <u>irreversible</u> (permanent).

7) Each enzyme has its own <u>optimum temperature</u> when the reaction goes <u>fastest</u>. This is the temperature just before it gets too hot and starts to denature. The optimum temperature for the most important <u>human</u> enzymes is about <u>37 °C</u> — the <u>same</u> temperature as our bodies. Lucky for us.

Enzymes *Like The Right* pH *Too*

Rate of reaction   Optimum pH

pH

1) The <u>pH</u> also has an effect on enzymes.

2) If the pH is too high or too low, it interferes with the <u>bonds</u> holding the enzyme together. This changes the shape of the <u>active site</u> and <u>denatures</u> the enzyme.

3) All enzymes have an <u>optimum pH</u> that they work best at. It's often <u>neutral</u> <u>pH 7</u>, but <u>not always</u>. For example, <u>pepsin</u> is an enzyme used to break down <u>proteins</u> in the <u>stomach</u>. It works best at <u>pH 2</u>, which means it's well-suited to the <u>acidic conditions</u> in the stomach.

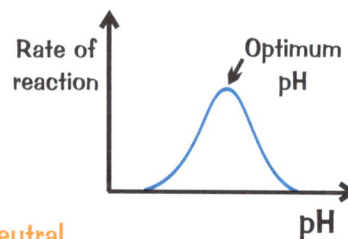

Q_{10} *Values* Show How *Rate of Reaction* Changes with *Temperature*

1) The <u>Q_{10} value</u> for a reaction shows how much the <u>rate changes</u> when the <u>temperature</u> is <u>raised</u> by <u>10 °C</u>.

2) You can <u>calculate it</u> using this <u>equation</u>:

$$Q_{10} = \frac{\text{rate at higher temperature}}{\text{rate at lower temperature}}$$

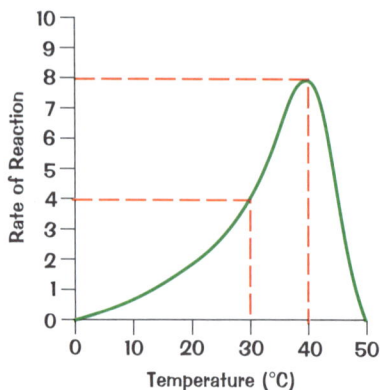

Rate of Reaction vs Temperature (°C)

3) The graph on the left shows the <u>rate of a reaction</u> between 0 °C and 50 °C. Here's how to calculate the Q_{10} value of the reaction using the rate at <u>30 °C</u> and at <u>40 °C</u>:

$$Q_{10} = \frac{\text{rate at 40 °C}}{\text{rate at 30 °C}} = \frac{8}{4} = 2$$

The reaction data you get in the exam could be in a graph like this or in a table.

4) A Q_{10} value of <u>2</u> means that the <u>rate doubles</u> when the temperature is raised by 10 °C. A Q_{10} value of <u>3</u> would mean that the <u>rate trebles</u>.

If only enzymes could speed up revision...

Make sure you understand this <u>denaturing</u> malarkey — and learn how to calculate and interpret a <u>Q_{10} value</u>.

Mutations

Mutations are really common — but sadly, they hardly ever give any of us superpowers.

Gene Mutations are Changes to Genes

1) A mutation is a change in the DNA base sequence.
2) If a mutation occurs within a gene, it could stop the production of the protein the gene normally codes for — or it might mean a different protein is produced instead.

For more on DNA base sequences see page 12.

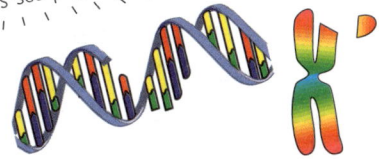

Most Mutations are Harmful

1) Producing the wrong protein or no protein at all can be a bit of a disaster — especially if the protein is an important enzyme or something.
2) If a mutation occurs in reproductive cells, then the offspring might develop abnormally or die at an early stage of their development.
3) If a mutation occurs in body cells, the mutant cells can sometimes start to multiply in an uncontrolled way and invade other parts of the body. This is cancer.

Some Mutations are Beneficial, Some Have No Effect

1) Occasionally, a different protein might be produced after a mutation that actually benefits the organism — the new protein is an improvement on the one it was supposed to be.
2) This gives the organism a survival advantage over the rest of the population. It passes on the mutated DNA to its offspring, and they survive better too, so soon the mutation becomes common in the population.
3) This is natural selection and evolution at work. A good example is a mutation in a bacterium that makes it resistant to antibiotics, so the mutant gene lives on, creating a resistant "strain" of bacteria.
4) Some mutations aren't harmful or helpful though — they don't change the protein being coded for, so they have no effect on the organism.

Radiation and Certain Chemicals Cause Mutations

Mutations can happen spontaneously — when a chromosome doesn't quite copy itself properly. However, the chance of a mutation is increased if you're exposed to:

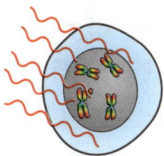

No no! not me!

1) Ionising radiation, including X-rays and ultraviolet light, together with radiation from radioactive substances. For each of these examples, the greater the dose of radiation, the greater the chance of mutation.
2) Certain chemicals which are known to cause mutations. Such chemicals are called mutagens. If the mutations produce cancer then the chemicals are often called carcinogens. Cigarette smoke contains chemical mutagens (or carcinogens).

My mutant fish army will take over the world — I call it evilution...

All living organisms have experienced mutation at some point in their evolutionary history. That's why we don't all look the same. Make sure you know what can cause a mutation — it might well turn up in the exam.

Module B3 — Living and Growing

Multiplying Cells

Cell division — pretty important if you're planning on being bigger than an amoeba. Which I am, one day.

Being Multicellular Has Some Important Advantages

There's nothing wrong with single-celled organisms — they're pretty successful. Bacteria, for example, aren't in danger of extinction any time soon. But there are some big advantages in being multicellular, and so some organisms have evolved that way. Here are some advantages you should know:

1) Being multicellular means you can be bigger. This is great because it means you can travel further, get your nutrients in a variety of different ways, fewer things can eat or squash you, etc.

2) Being multicellular allows for cell differentiation. Instead of being just one cell that has to do everything, you can have different types of cells that do different jobs. Your cells can be specially adapted for their particular jobs, e.g. carrying oxygen in the blood, reacting to light in the eyes.

3) This means multicellular organisms can be more complex — they can have specialised organs, different shapes and behaviour — and so can be adapted specifically to their particular environment.

However, being multicellular means that an organism also has to have specialised organ systems, including:

- A system to communicate between different cells, e.g. a nervous system.
- A system to supply cells with the nutrients they need, e.g. a circulatory system.
- A system that controls the exchange of substances with the environment, e.g. a respiratory system.

Mitosis Makes New Cells for Growth and Repair

"Mitosis is when a cell reproduces itself by splitting to form two identical offspring."

This happens in the body when you want identical cells — e.g. when you want to grow and you need lots of the same type of cell or when you need to replace worn-out cells and repair tissues. The important thing to understand in mitosis is what happens to the DNA.

1) Before mitosis starts, the DNA in the cell is replicated (see page 11).

2) Then at the beginning of mitosis, the DNA coils into double-armed chromosomes. These arms are exact copies of each other — they contain exactly the same DNA.

The left arm has the same DNA as the right arm of the chromosome.

3) The chromosomes line up at the centre of the cell, and then divide as cell fibres pull them apart. The two arms of each chromosome go to opposite poles (ends) of one cell. Membranes form around each of these two different sets of chromosomes.

4) The cytoplasm divides, and you get two new cells containing exactly the same genetic material.

5) And that's mitosis. You've ended up with two new cells that are genetically identical to each other. Before these can divide again, the DNA has to replicate itself to give each chromosome two arms again.

Right — now that I have your undivided attention...

There's no denying that mitosis can seem tricky at first. But don't worry — just go through it slowly, one step at a time. Even if the exam's tomorrow. Panicking and rushing through it won't help at all.

Meiosis, Gametes and Fertilisation

People can look very similar to their mum and dad, often a good mix of the two. Here's why.

Meiosis is Another Type of Cell Division — It Creates Gametes

1) Gametes are formed by meiosis in the ovaries and testes. Gametes are the sex cells — eggs and sperm.

2) The body cells of mammals are diploid. This means that each of the organism's body cells has two copies of each chromosome in its nucleus — one from the organism's mum, and one from its dad.

3) But gametes are haploid — they only have one copy of each chromosome. This is so that when the egg and the sperm combine, they'll form a cell with the diploid number of chromosomes (see below).

Meiosis Involves Two Divisions

1) Meiosis starts in exactly the same way as mitosis — the DNA replicates and curls up to form double-armed chromosomes (see previous page).

2) After replication the chromosomes arrange themselves into pairs. Humans have 23 pairs of chromosomes, that's 46 altogether. Both chromosomes in a pair contain information about the same features. One chromosome comes from your mum and one from your dad.

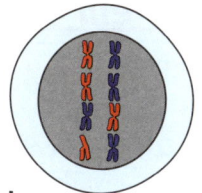

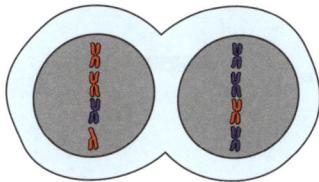

3) In the first division these pairs split up — the chromosomes in each pair move to opposite poles of the cell. In each of the two new cells, there are no pairs at all — just one of each of the 23 different types. Each new cell ends up with a mixture of your mum's and dad's chromosomes, but only half the usual number of chromosomes.

4) The second division of meiosis is like mitosis on the last page — each chromosome splits in half and one arm ends up in each new cell.

5) And that's meiosis. You've ended up with four new cells — two after the first division, and then each of those splits again. The cells are genetically different from each other because the chromosomes all get shuffled up during meiosis and each gamete only gets half of them, at random.

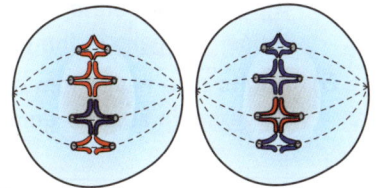

Fertilisation Creates Genetic Variation

1) At fertilisation male and female gametes combine to form a diploid cell. This cell is called a zygote.

2) The characteristics of the zygote are controlled by the combination of genes on its chromosomes.

3) Since the zygote will have inherited chromosomes from two parents, it will show features of both parents, but won't be exactly like either of them.

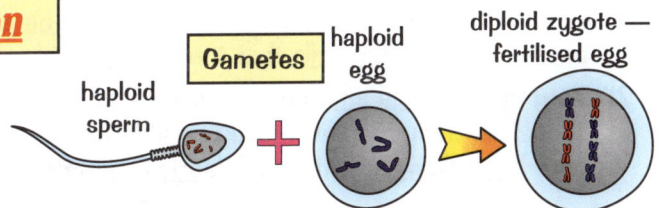

Gametes

haploid sperm + haploid egg → diploid zygote — fertilised egg

Sperm Cells are Adapted for Their Function

A sperm's function is to transport the male's DNA to the female's egg.

1) Sperm are small and have long tails so they can swim to the egg.

2) Sperm have lots of mitochondria (see page 10) to provide the energy needed to swim this distance.

3) Sperm also have an acrosome at the front of the 'head', which can release the enzymes they need to digest their way through the membrane of the egg cell.

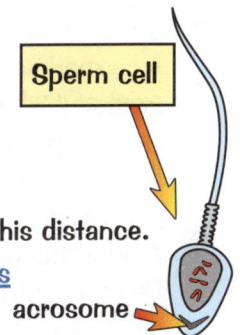

Sperm cell

acrosome

No sniggering in the back, please...

For many kids in year seven, the mere sight of a sperm is enough to convulse them in giggles. Those of them that don't think it's an innocent tadpole, anyway. But that's not the case for you lot. We hope.

Module B3 — Living and Growing

Stem Cells, Differentiation and Growth

Plants and animals have different tactics for growth, but they both have stem cells.

Animals Stop Growing, Plants Can Grow Continuously

Plants and animals grow differently:

1) Animals tend to grow until they reach a finite size (full growth) and then stop growing. Plants often grow continuously — even really old trees will keep putting out new branches.

2) In animals, growth happens by cell division. In plants, growth in height is mainly due to cell enlargement (elongation). Growth by cell division usually just happens in areas of the plant called meristems (at the tips of the roots and shoots).

Stem Cells Can Turn into Different Types of Cells

1) Differentiation is the process by which a cell changes to become specialised for its job. In most animal cells, the ability to differentiate is lost at an early stage, but lots of plant cells don't ever lose this ability.

2) Most cells in your body are specialised for a particular job. E.g. white blood cells are brilliant at fighting invaders but can't carry oxygen, like red blood cells.

3) Some cells are undifferentiated. They can develop into different types of cells, tissues and organs depending on what instructions they're given. These cells are called STEM CELLS.

4) Stem cells are found in early human embryos. They have the potential to turn into any kind of cell at all. This makes sense if you think about it — all the different types of cell found in a human being have to come from those few cells in the early embryo.

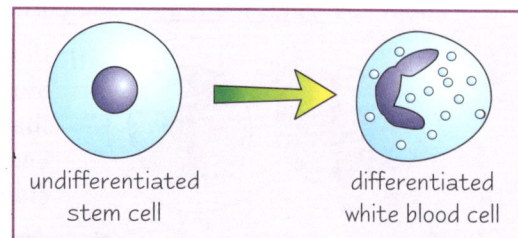

undifferentiated stem cell → differentiated white blood cell

5) Adults also have stem cells, but they're only found in certain places, like bone marrow. These aren't as versatile as embryonic stem cells — they can't turn into any cell type at all, only certain ones.

Stem Cells May be Able to Cure Many Disorders

1) Medicine already uses stem cells to cure disease. For example, people with blood disorders (e.g. leukaemia and sickle cell anaemia) can be cured by bone marrow transplants. Bone marrow contains adult stem cells that turn into new blood cells (but nothing else) to replace faulty old ones.

2) Very early human embryos contain a lot of stem cells. Scientists can extract these cells and grow them. They think they may eventually be able to grow tissues to treat medical conditions, e.g. nerve cells to cure brain damage and spinal injuries, skin cells for skin grafts, etc. This is known as stem cell therapy.

Some People Are Against Stem Cell Research

1) Some people are against stem cell research because they feel that human embryos shouldn't be used for experiments since each one is a potential human life. Others think that curing patients who already exist and who are suffering is more important than the rights of embryos.

2) One fairly convincing argument in favour of this point of view is that the embryos used in the research are usually unwanted ones from fertility clinics which, if they weren't used for research, would probably just be destroyed. But of course, campaigners for the rights of embryos usually want this banned too.

3) Around the world, there are now 'stocks' of stem cells that scientists can use for their research. Some countries (e.g. the USA) won't fund research to make new stem cell stocks, but in the UK it's allowed as long as it follows strict guidelines.

But florists cell stems — and nobody complains about that...

Research has recently been done into getting stem cells from alternative sources. E.g. some researchers think it might be possible to get cells from umbilical cords to behave like embryonic stem cells.

Growth

Growth is an increase in size or mass. But you need to know a lot more than that...

There are Different Methods for Measuring Growth

Growth of plants and animals can be quite tricky to measure — there are different methods, but they all have pros and cons.

To work out if something's grown (i.e. increased in size), you need to take more than one measurement.

Method	What it involves	Advantages	Disadvantages
LENGTH	Just measure the length (or height) of a plant or animal.	Easy to measure.	It doesn't tell you about changes in width, diameter, number of branches, etc.
WET MASS	Weigh the plant or animal and bingo — you have the wet mass.	Easy to measure.	Wet mass is very changeable. For example, a plant will be heavier if it's recently rained because it will have absorbed lots of water. Animals will be heavier if they've just eaten or if they've got a full bladder.
DRY MASS	Dry out the organism before weighing it.	It's not affected by the amount of water in a plant or animal or how much an organism has eaten.	You have to kill the organism to work it out. This might be okay for an area of grass, but it's not so good if you want to know the dry mass of a person.

Dry mass is actually the best measure of growth in plants and animals — it's not affected by changes in water content and it tells you the size of the whole organism.

Human Growth has Different Phases

1) Humans go through five main phases of growth:

PHASE	DESCRIPTION
Infancy	Roughly the first two years of life. Rapid growth.
Childhood	Period between infancy and puberty. Steady growth.
Adolescence	Begins with puberty and continues until body development and growth are complete. Rapid growth.
Maturity/adulthood	Period between adolescence and old age. Growth stops.
Old age	Usually considered to be between age 65 and death.

2) The two main phases of rapid growth take place just after birth and during adolescence. Growth stops when a person reaches adulthood.

3) The graph on the right is an example of a typical human growth curve. It shows how weight increases for boys between the ages of 2 and 20. When the line is steeper, growth is more rapid (e.g. during adolescence).

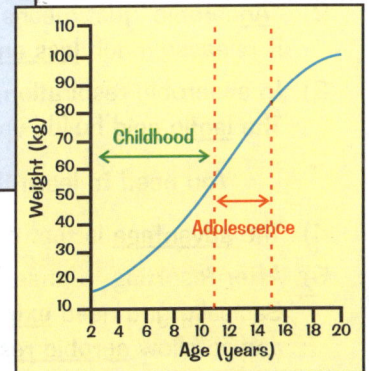

Certain Parts of the Body Grow Faster or Slower than Others

1) Organisms don't grow evenly. At different times, different parts of the body will grow at different rates.

2) For example, when a baby is developing in the womb, the brain grows at a greater rate than the rest of the body. This is because a large and well-developed brain gives humans a big survival advantage — it's our best tool for finding food, avoiding predators, etc.

I'm growing rather sick of this topic...

Listen, you think you're sick of reading these lame jokes? Just think how I feel, having to make them up.

Respiration

You need energy to keep your body going. Energy comes from food, and it's released by respiration.

Respiration is NOT "Breathing In and Out"

1) Respiration goes on in every cell in your body. It's the process of releasing energy from glucose.

2) The energy from respiration can't be used directly by cells — so it's used to make a substance called ATP.

3) ATP acts as the energy source for many cell processes and transports energy to where it's needed in a cell.

4) Respiration is controlled by enzymes. This means that the rate of respiration is affected by both temperature and pH (see page 14).

5) There are two types of respiration, aerobic and anaerobic.

Aerobic Respiration Needs Plenty of Oxygen

1) Aerobic respiration is what happens when there's plenty of oxygen available.

2) "Aerobic" just means "with oxygen" and it's the most efficient way to release energy from glucose.

3) This is the type of respiration that you're using most of the time.

4) You need to learn the word and chemical equations:

$$\text{glucose } + \text{ oxygen} \longrightarrow \text{carbon dioxide} + \text{water} \text{ (+ ENERGY)}$$
$$C_6H_{12}O_6 + 6O_2 \longrightarrow 6CO_2 + 6H_2O \text{ (+ ENERGY)}$$

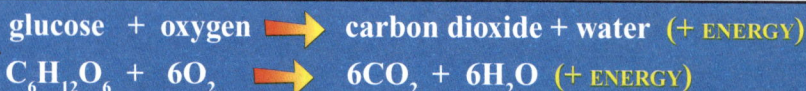

5) So, when respiration rate increases, both oxygen consumption and carbon dioxide production increase.

6) This means that the rate of oxygen consumption can be used to estimate metabolic rate (the amount of energy being used).

Anaerobic Respiration Doesn't Use Oxygen At All

1) When you do really vigorous exercise your body can't supply enough oxygen to your muscles for aerobic respiration — even though your heart rate and breathing rate increase as much as they can. Your muscles have to start respiring anaerobically as well.

2) "Anaerobic" just means "without oxygen". It's not the best way to convert glucose to energy because it releases much less energy per glucose molecule than aerobic respiration.

3) In anaerobic respiration, the glucose is only partially broken down, and lactic acid is also produced. The lactic acid builds up in the muscles, which gets painful and makes your muscles fatigued.

You need to learn the word equation:

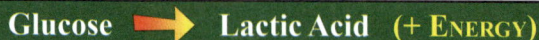

$$\text{Glucose} \longrightarrow \text{Lactic Acid} \text{ (+ ENERGY)}$$

4) The advantage is that at least you can keep on using your muscles.

5) After resorting to anaerobic respiration, when you stop exercising you'll have an oxygen debt. Basically you need extra oxygen to break down all the lactic acid that's built up in your muscles and to allow aerobic respiration to begin again.

6) This means you have to keep breathing hard for a while after you stop exercising — to repay the debt.

7) The lactic acid has to be carried to the liver to be broken down, so your heart rate has to stay high too.

The Respiratory Quotient

1) The respiratory quotient (RQ) can tell you whether someone is respiring aerobically or anaerobically. You can calculate it using this equation:

$$RQ = \frac{\text{Amount of } CO_2 \text{ produced}}{\text{Amount of } O_2 \text{ used}}$$

2) The RQ is usually between 0.7 and 1 — this means that the person is respiring aerobically. If the RQ value is greater than 1 then the person is short of oxygen and is respiring anaerobically, too.

I reckon aerobics classes should be called anaerobics instead...

You might get a question in the exam asking you to use data from experiments to compare respiration rates — just remember, increased oxygen consumption (or carbon dioxide production) means an increased respiration rate.

Functions of the Blood

Blood is very useful stuff. It's a big transport system for moving things around the body. The blood cells do good work too. Red blood cells, for example, are responsible for transporting oxygen about, and they carry 100 times more than could be moved just dissolved in the blood. Amazing.

Plasma is the Liquid Bit of Blood

It's basically blood minus the blood cells. Plasma is a pale yellow liquid which carries just about everything that needs transporting around your body:

1) Red blood cells (see below), white blood cells, and platelets (used in blood clotting).

2) Water.

3) Digested food products like glucose and amino acids from the gut to all the body cells.

4) Carbon dioxide from the body cells to the lungs.

5) Urea from the liver to the kidneys (where it's removed in the urine).

6) Hormones — these act like chemical messengers.

7) Antibodies — these are proteins involved in the body's immune response.

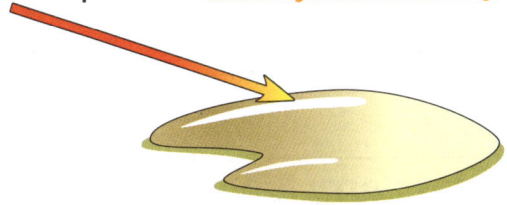

Carbon dioxide and urea are both waste products, which need to be removed.

Red Blood Cells Have the Job of Carrying Oxygen

Red blood cells transport oxygen from the lungs to all the cells in the body. The structure of a red blood cell is adapted to its function:

1) Red blood cells are small and have a biconcave shape to give a large surface area to volume ratio for absorbing and releasing oxygen.

Biconcave is just a posh way to say they look a bit like doughnuts (see diagram below).

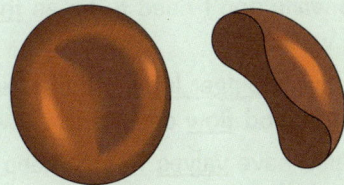

2) They contain haemoglobin, which is what gives blood its colour — it contains a lot of iron. In the lungs, haemoglobin combines with oxygen to become oxyhaemoglobin. In body tissues the reverse happens to release oxygen to the cells.

3) Red blood cells don't have a nucleus — this frees up space for more haemoglobin, so they can carry more oxygen.

4) Red blood cells are very flexible. This means they can easily pass through the tiny capillaries (see next page).

It's all blood, sweat and tears — kind of...

...without the sweat... or the tears... just the blood then... yep... anyway...

The average human body contains about six and a half pints of blood altogether, and every single drop contains millions of red blood cells — all of them perfectly designed for carrying plenty of oxygen to where its needed.

Blood Vessels

The blood has to get around the body somehow — which is what the blood vessels are for.

Blood Vessels are Designed for Their Function

There are three different types of blood vessel:

1) ARTERIES — these carry the blood away from the heart.
2) CAPILLARIES — these are involved in the exchange of materials at the tissues.
3) VEINS — these carry the blood to the heart.

Arteries Carry Blood Under Pressure

1) The heart pumps the blood out at high pressure so the artery walls are strong and elastic.

2) The walls are thick compared to the size of the hole down the middle (the "lumen" — silly name!). They contain thick layers of muscle to make them strong.

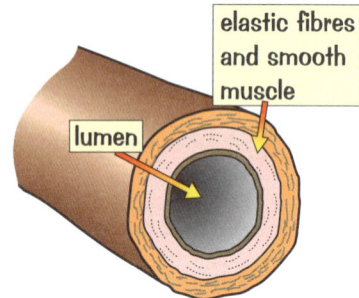

elastic fibres and smooth muscle

lumen

Capillaries are Really Small

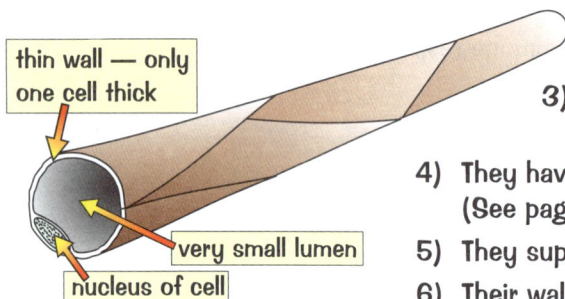

thin wall — only one cell thick

very small lumen

nucleus of cell

1) Arteries branch into capillaries.
2) Capillaries are really tiny — too small to see.
3) They carry the blood really close to every cell in the body to exchange substances with them.
4) They have permeable walls, so substances can diffuse in and out. (See page 68 for more on diffusion.)
5) They supply food and oxygen, and take away wastes like CO_2.
6) Their walls are usually only one cell thick. This increases the rate of diffusion by decreasing the distance over which it occurs.

Veins Take Blood Back to the Heart

1) Capillaries eventually join up to form veins.
2) The blood is at lower pressure in the veins so the walls don't need to be as thick as artery walls.
3) They have a bigger lumen than arteries to help the blood flow despite the lower pressure.
4) They also have valves to help keep the blood flowing in the right direction.

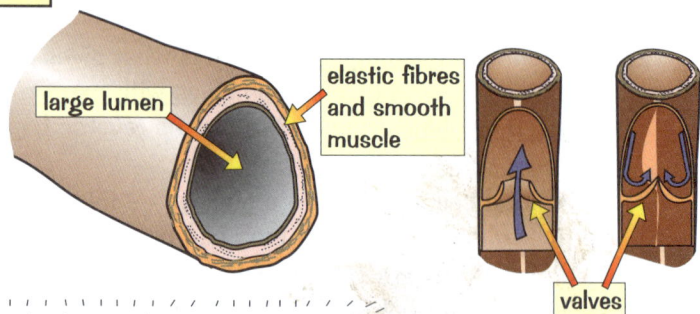

large lumen

elastic fibres and smooth muscle

valves

Arteries don't need valves — the pressure in them is high enough to keep the blood flowing the right way.

Learn this page — don't struggle in vein...

Here's an interesting fact for you — your body contains about 60 000 miles of blood vessels. That's about six times the distance from London to Sydney in Australia. Of course, capillaries are really tiny, which is how there can be such a big length — they can only be seen with a microscope.

The Heart

Blood doesn't just move around the body <u>on its own</u>, of course. It needs a <u>pump</u>.

Mammals *Have a* Double Circulatory System

1) The first system connects the <u>heart</u> to the <u>lungs</u>.
   <u>Deoxygenated</u> blood is pumped to the <u>lungs</u> to take in <u>oxygen</u>.
   The blood then <u>returns</u> to the heart.

2) The second system connects the <u>heart</u> to the <u>rest of the body</u>.
   The <u>oxygenated</u> blood in the heart is pumped out to the <u>body</u>.
   It <u>gives up</u> its oxygen, and then the <u>deoxygenated</u> blood
   <u>returns</u> to the heart to be pumped out to the <u>lungs</u> again.

3) Not all animals have a double circulatory system
   — <u>fish don't</u>, for example.

4) There are <u>advantages</u> to mammals having a double circulatory system though.
   Returning the blood to the <u>heart</u> after it's picked up oxygen at the <u>lungs</u> means it can be pumped out
   around the body at a much <u>higher pressure</u>. This <u>increases</u> the <u>rate of blood flow</u> to the tissues
   (i.e. blood can be pumped around the body much <u>faster</u>), so <u>more oxygen</u> can be delivered to the cells.
   This is important for mammals because they use up a lot of oxygen <u>maintaining their body temperature</u>.

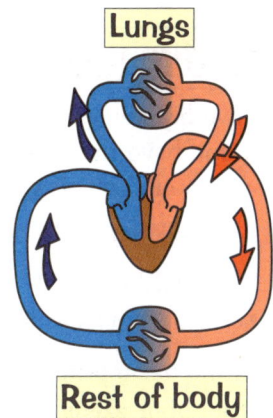

Lungs

Rest of body

Learn *This* Diagram *of the Heart* with All Its Labels

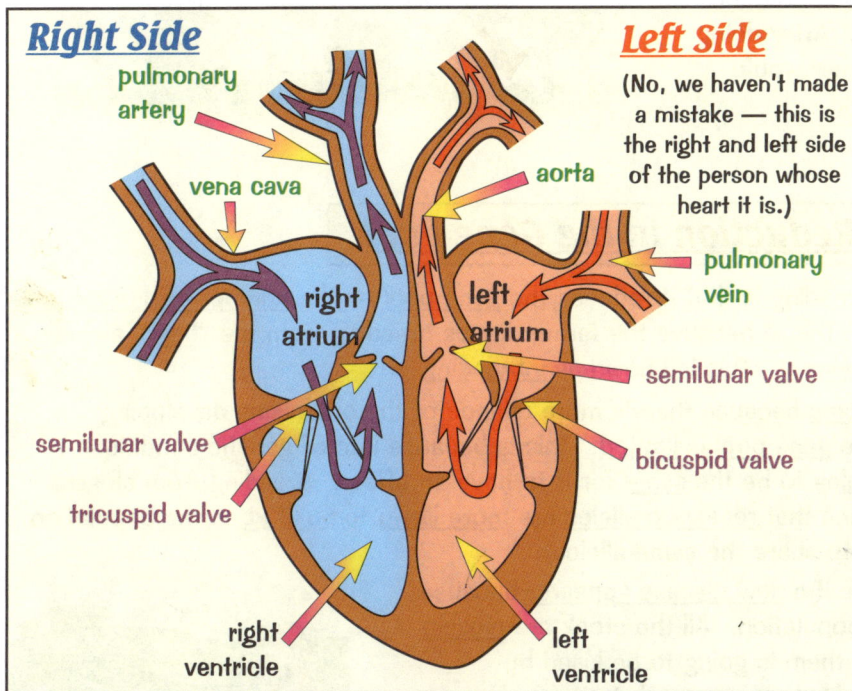

Right Side

- pulmonary artery
- vena cava
- semilunar valve
- tricuspid valve
- right atrium
- right ventricle

Left Side

(No, we haven't made a mistake — this is the right and left side of the person whose heart it is.)

- aorta
- left atrium
- pulmonary vein
- semilunar valve
- bicuspid valve
- left ventricle

1) The <u>right atrium</u> of the heart receives <u>deoxygenated</u> blood from the <u>body</u> (through the <u>vena cava</u>).
   (The plural of atrium is atria.)

2) The deoxygenated blood moves through to the <u>right ventricle</u>, which pumps it to the <u>lungs</u> (via the <u>pulmonary artery</u>).

3) The <u>left atrium</u> receives <u>oxygenated</u> blood from the <u>lungs</u> (through the <u>pulmonary vein</u>).

4) The oxygenated blood then moves through to the <u>left ventricle</u>, which pumps it out round the <u>whole body</u> (via the <u>aorta</u>).

5) The <u>left</u> ventricle has a much <u>thicker wall</u> than the <u>right</u> ventricle. It needs more <u>muscle</u> because it has
   to pump blood around the <u>whole body</u>, whereas the right ventricle only has to pump it to the <u>lungs</u>.

6) The <u>semilunar</u>, <u>tricuspid</u> and <u>bicuspid valves</u> prevent the <u>backflow</u> of blood.

Okay — let's get to the heart of the matter...

The human heart beats <u>100 000 times a day</u> on average — it's exhausting just thinking about it. You can feel a
pulse in your wrist or neck (where the vessels are close to the surface). This is the <u>blood</u> being pushed along by
another beat. Doctors use a <u>stethoscope</u> to listen to your heart — it's actually the <u>valves closing</u> that they hear.

Selective Breeding

'Selective breeding' sounds like it has the potential to be a tricky topic, but it's actually dead simple. You take the best plants or animals and breed them together to get the best possible offspring. That's it.

Selective Breeding is Very Simple

Selective breeding is when humans artificially select the plants or animals that are going to breed and have their genes remain in the population, according to what we want from them. Organisms are selectively bred to develop the best features, which are things like:

- Maximum yield of meat, milk, grain etc.
- Good health and disease resistance.
- Other qualities like temperament, speed, attractiveness, etc.

This is the basic process involved in selective breeding:

1) From your existing stock select the ones which have the best characteristics.
2) Breed them with each other.
3) Select the best of the offspring, and breed them together.
4) Continue this process over several generations, and the desirable trait gets stronger and stronger.

> **EXAMPLE:**
>
> In agriculture (farming), selective breeding can be used to improve yields. E.g. to improve meat yields, a farmer could breed together the cows and bulls with the best characteristics for producing meat, e.g. large size. After doing this for several generations the farmer would get cows with a very high meat yield.

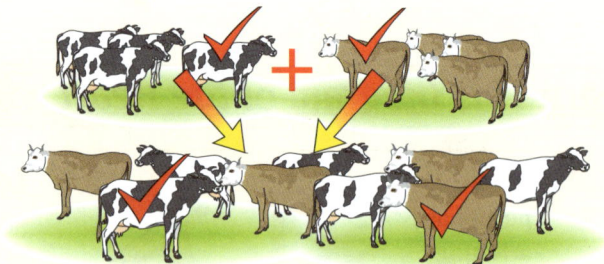

The Main Drawback is a Reduction in the Gene Pool

1) The main problem with selective breeding is that it reduces the gene pool — the number of different alleles (forms of a gene) in a population. This is because the farmer keeps breeding from the "best" animals or plants — which are all closely related. This is known as inbreeding.

2) Inbreeding can cause health problems because there's more chance of the organisms developing harmful genetic disorders when the gene pool is limited. This is because lots of genetic conditions are recessive — you need two alleles to be the same for it to have an effect. Breeding from closely related organisms all the time means that recessive alleles are more likely to build up in the population (because the organisms are likely to share the same alleles).

3) There can also be serious problems if a new disease appears, because there's not much variation in the population. All the stock are closely related to each other, so if one of them is going to be killed by a new disease, the others are also likely to succumb to it.

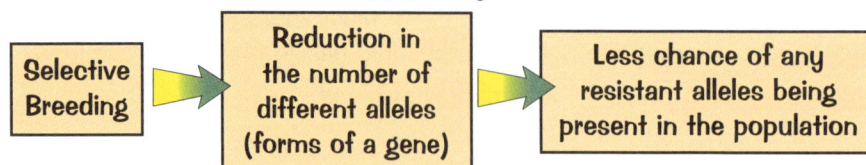

Oh Eck!

| Selective Breeding | → | Reduction in the number of different alleles (forms of a gene) | → | Less chance of any resistant alleles being present in the population |

I use the same genes all the time too — they flatter my hips...

Selective breeding's not a new thing. People have been doing it for absolutely yonks. That's how we ended up with something like a poodle from a wolf. Somebody thought 'I really like this small, woolly, yappy, wolf — I'll breed it with this other one'. And after thousands of generations, we got poodles. Hurrah.

Genetic Engineering

Genetic engineering — playing around with genes. Cool.

Genetic Engineering is Great — Hopefully

The basic idea behind genetic engineering is to move genes (sections of DNA) from one organism
to another so that it produces useful biological products. You need to be able to explain some
of the advantages and risks involved in genetic engineering.

1) The main advantage is that you can produce organisms with new and useful features very quickly.
    There are some examples of this below — make sure you learn them.

2) The main risk is that the inserted gene might have unexpected harmful effects. For example, genes are
    often inserted into bacteria so they produce useful products. If these bacteria mutated and became
    pathogenic (disease-causing), the foreign genes might make them more harmful and unpredictable.
    People also worry about the engineered DNA 'escaping' — e.g. weeds could gain rogue genes from
    a crop that's had genes for herbicide resistance inserted into it. Then they'd be unstoppable. Eeek.

Genetic Engineering Involves These Important Stages:

1) First the gene that's responsible for producing the desirable characteristic
    is selected (say the gene for human insulin).

2) It's then 'cut' from the DNA using enzymes, and isolated.

3) The useful gene is inserted into the DNA of another organism (e.g. a bacterium).

4) The organism then replicates and soon there are loads of similar organisms all
    producing the same thing (e.g. loads of bacteria producing human insulin).

Learn These Three Examples of Genetic Engineering:

1) In some parts of the world, the population relies heavily on rice for food. In these areas,
    vitamin A deficiency can be a problem, because rice doesn't contain much of this vitamin,
    and other sources are scarce. Genetic engineering has allowed scientists to take a gene
    that controls beta-carotene production from carrot plants, and put it into rice plants.
    Humans can then change the beta-carotene into vitamin A. Problem solved.

2) The gene for human insulin production has been put into bacteria. These are cultured in a fermenter,
    and the human insulin is simply extracted from the medium as they produce it. Great.

3) Some plants have resistance to things like herbicides, frost damage and disease. Unfortunately, it's not
    always the plants we want to grow that have these features. But now, thanks to genetic engineering,
    we can cut out the gene responsible and stick it into useful plants such as crops. Splendid.

There Are Moral and Ethical Issues Involved

All this is nice, but you need to be able to discuss the ethical issues surrounding genetic modification:

1) Some people think it's wrong to genetically engineer other organisms purely for human benefit. This is
    a particular problem in the genetic engineering of animals, especially if the animal suffers as a result.

2) People worry that we won't stop at engineering plants and animals. In the future, those who can afford
    genetic engineering might be able to decide the characteristics they want their children to have —
    and those who can't afford it may become a 'genetic underclass'.

3) The evolutionary consequences of genetic engineering are unknown, so some people think it's
    irresponsible to carry on when we're not sure what the impact on future generations might be.

If only they could genetically engineer you to be better at exams...

You can do great things with genetic engineering. But some people worry that we don't know enough about it,
or that some maniac is going to come along and combine David Cameron with a grapefruit. Possibly.

Gene Therapy and Cloning Animals

If you thought that was it for genetic engineering, you'd be wrong. Next up is gene therapy...

Gene Therapy Could Be Used to Cure Genetic Disorders...

1) Gene therapy involves altering a person's genes in an attempt to cure genetic disorders.
    Scientists haven't got it to work properly yet, but they're working on it for the future.

2) There are two types of gene therapy:

    • The first would involve changing the genes in body cells, particularly the cells that are most affected
      by the disorder. For example, cystic fibrosis affects the lungs, so therapy for it would target the
      cells lining the lungs. This wouldn't affect the individual's gametes (sperm or eggs) though, so any
      offspring could still inherit the disease.

    • The second type of gene therapy would involve changing the genes in the gametes. This means that
      every cell of any offspring produced from these gametes will be affected by the gene therapy — and
      the offspring won't suffer from the disease. This type of therapy in humans is currently illegal though.

3) Gene therapy involving gametes is controversial.

    • For example, it might have unexpected consequences, which cause a whole new set of problems.
      These problems would then be inherited by all future generations.

    • There are fears that this kind of gene therapy could lead to the creation of 'designer babies' —
      where parents are able to choose the genes they want their children to have.

Now for something completely different — cloning...

Cloning is Making an Exact Copy of Another Organism

Learn what clones are:

Clones are genetically identical organisms.

Clones occur naturally in both plants and animals. Identical twins are clones of each other.

Cloning an Adult Animal is Done by Transferring a Cell Nucleus

The first mammal to be successfully cloned from an adult cell was a sheep called "Dolly".
Dolly was produced using a method called nuclear transfer. This involves placing the nucleus of a body cell
into an egg cell. Here's how it works:

1) The nucleus of a sheep's egg cell was removed — this left the egg cell without any genetic information.

2) Another nucleus was inserted in its place.
    This was a diploid nucleus from an udder cell
    of a different sheep (the one being cloned)
    and had all its genetic information.

3) The cell was given an electric shock so that it started
    dividing by mitosis (as if it was a normal fertilised egg).

4) The dividing cell (now an embryo) was implanted into
    the uterus of a surrogate mother sheep, to develop
    until it was ready to be born.

5) The result was Dolly, a clone of the sheep
    from which the udder cell came.

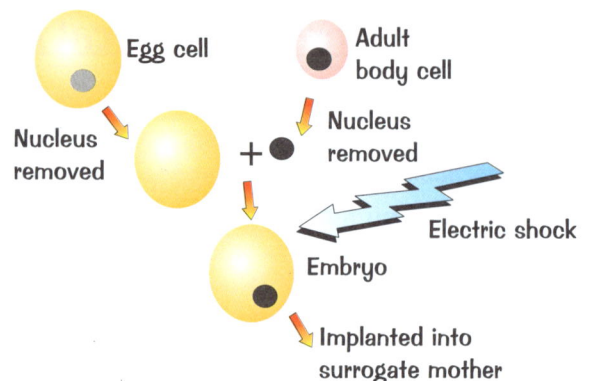

Egg cell · Adult body cell · Nucleus removed · Nucleus removed · Electric shock · Embryo · Implanted into surrogate mother

A whole lamb from a single cell? Pull the udder one...

Gene therapy is a bit of an ethical minefield. Most people would agree that treating diseases is a good thing, but
there are concerns that it could lead to designer babies. The ethical issues of cloning are covered on the next page.

Uses and Risks of Cloning Animals

Cloning animals can lead to lots of potential benefits, for example, in medicine. But it can raise a lot of tricky issues, too — especially when the animals being cloned are humans.

There are Both Benefits and Risks Involved in Cloning

There are many possible BENEFITS of cloning:

1) Cloning allows you to mass produce animals with desirable characteristics, e.g.
   - Animals that can produce medicines in their milk could be developed by genetic engineering and then cloned. Researchers have managed to transfer human genes that produce useful proteins into sheep and cows. This means these animals can produce things like the blood clotting agent factor VIII (used for treating haemophilia).
   - Animals (like pigs) that have organs suitable for transplantation into humans could be developed by genetic engineering and then cloned. This would ensure a constant supply of organs for transplant — organs from human donors are currently in short supply. There are issues to consider with this type of transplant though — including concerns that viruses could be passed from the animals to humans.

2) Human embryos could be produced by cloning adult body cells. The embryos could then be used to supply stem cells for stem cell therapy (see page 18). These cells would have exactly the same genetic information as the patient, reducing the risk of rejection (a common problem with transplants).

But there are RISKS too:

1) There is some evidence that cloned animals might not be as healthy as normal ones.
2) Cloning is a new science and it might have consequences that we're not yet aware of.

Cloning Humans is a Possibility — with a Lot of Ethical Issues

Some people are worried that cloning animals is a short step away from using adult DNA to produce embryos which are allowed to grow into human clones.
There are ethical issues to consider with this...

1) There would have to be lots of surrogate pregnancies, probably with high rates of miscarriage and stillbirth.
2) Clones of other mammals have been unhealthy and often die prematurely — which means human clones might too.
3) Even if a healthy clone were produced, it might be psychologically damaged by the knowledge that it's just a clone of another human being.

An evil dictator might make an army of clones to rule the Galaxy...

That might be a good idea for a film, come to think of it. Cloning is exciting stuff — it's got loads of potential for helping to save lives, for one thing. But there are risks involved, as well as ethical issues, which shouldn't be ignored. You need to learn both the positives and the negatives of cloning for the exam.

Cloning Plants

More cloning here, I'm afraid, and this time it's all about plants. But this is the last page on it, I promise.

It's Fairly Easy to Clone Plants

1) Gardeners are familiar with taking cuttings from good parent plants, and then planting them to produce genetically identical copies — clones — of the parent plant.

2) Cloning plants is easier than cloning animals because many plant cells keep their ability to differentiate (see page 18) — animal cells lose this at an early stage.

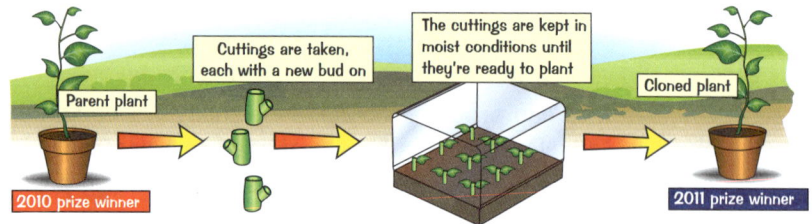

Parent plant | 2010 prize winner

Cuttings are taken, each with a new bud on

The cuttings are kept in moist conditions until they're ready to plant

Cloned plant | 2011 prize winner

Commercial Cloning Often Involves Tissue Culture

1) First you choose the plant you want to clone based on its characteristics — e.g. a beautiful flower, a good fruit crop.

2) You remove several small pieces of tissue from the parent plant. You get the best results if you take tissue from fast-growing root and shoot tips.

3) You grow the tissue in a growth medium containing nutrients and growth hormones. This is done under aseptic (sterile) conditions to prevent growth of microbes that could harm the plants.

4) As the tissues produce shoots and roots they can be moved to potting compost to carry on growing.

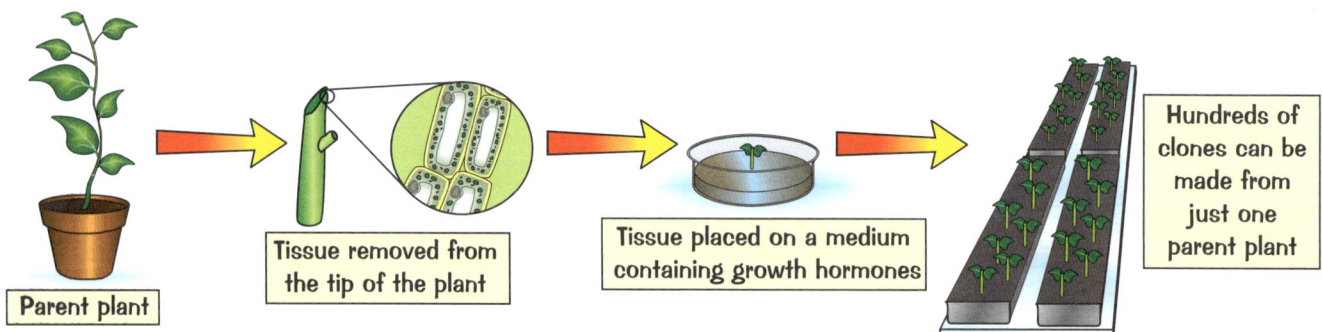

Parent plant

Tissue removed from the tip of the plant

Tissue placed on a medium containing growth hormones

Hundreds of clones can be made from just one parent plant

Commercial Use of Cloned Plants Has Pros and Cons

1) You can be fairly sure of the characteristics of the plant because it'll be genetically identical to the parent — so you'll only get good ones, and won't waste time and money growing duds.

2) It's possible to mass-produce plants that are hard to grow from seeds.

3) But, if the plants suffer from a disease or start doing badly because of a change in environment, they'll all have the same problems because they all have the same genes.

4) And there are the usual problems with lack of genetic variation (see page 24).

Stop cloning around — just learn it...

Plants are much better at being cloned than mammals are. They don't start dropping dead or having health problems, they just get on with it. And nobody seems that bothered about ethics when it's a tulip.

Revision Summary for Module B3

Here goes, folks — a beautiful page of revision questions to keep you at your desk studying hard until your parents have gone out and you can finally nip downstairs to watch TV. Think twice though before you reach for that remote control. These questions are actually pretty good — certainly more entertaining than 'Train Your Husband Like He's a Dog'. Question 14 is almost as good as an episode of 'Supernanny'. Question 4 is the corker though — like a reunion episode of 'Friends' but a lot funnier. Give the questions a go. Oh go on.

1) Why do liver and muscle cells have large numbers of mitochondria?
2) Give two ways in which bacterial cells differ from animal and plant cells.
3) What are the four bases in DNA?
4) What evidence did Watson and Crick use to build a model of DNA?
5) Explain how DNA replicates itself.
6) Briefly describe how DNA codes for a protein.
7) Name the molecule used to carry the code from DNA to the ribosomes.
8) Other than enzymes, give three different functions of proteins.
9) What are enzymes?
10) An enzyme with an optimum temperature of 37 °C is heated to 60 °C. Suggest what will happen to the enzyme.
11) What does the Q_{10} value of an enzyme-controlled reaction show?
12) Why are mutations in an organism's DNA often harmful to that organism?
13) Give two things that increase the chance of mutation if you are exposed to them.
14) Give three advantages of being multicellular.
15) How many cells are produced after a mitotic division? Are they genetically identical?
16) How many cells are produced after a meiotic division? Are they genetically identical?
17) Give three ways that sperm cells are adapted for their function.
18) Describe two differences in the way plant cells and animal cells grow and develop.
19) Suggest why some people are against stem cell research.
20) Give one advantage and one disadvantage for each of the following ways of measuring growth:
    a) length   b) wet mass   c) dry mass
21) Humans go through two main phases of rapid growth. When do these take place?
22) Give the chemical equation for aerobic respiration.
23) What is the formula for calculating the respiratory quotient?
24) Name seven things that blood plasma transports around the body.
25) Name the substance formed in red blood cells when haemoglobin reacts with oxygen.
26) Why do arteries need very muscular, elastic walls?
27) Explain how capillaries are adapted to their function.
28) Name the blood vessel that joins to the right ventricle of the heart. Where does it take the blood?
29) Why does the left ventricle have a thicker wall than the right ventricle?
30) What is selective breeding?
31) Give two disadvantages of selective breeding.
32) Give one advantage and one risk of genetic engineering.
33) Describe three examples of genetic engineering.
34) Describe the two types of gene therapy.
35) Why is gene therapy involving gametes controversial?
36) Describe the method of cloning that was used to produce Dolly the sheep.
37) Give two potential benefits and two potential risks of cloning animals.
38) Suggest three reasons why some people are concerned about cloning humans.
39) Describe how plants can be cloned using tissue culture.
40) Suggest two advantages and two disadvantages of the commercial use of cloned plants.

Atoms, Molecules and Compounds

You should already know these basics, but just in case your memory is a bit hazy here's a refresher...

Atoms Have a Positive Nucleus with Orbiting Electrons

Atoms are really tiny. They're too small to see, even with a microscope. They have a nucleus which is positively charged, and electrons which are negatively charged. The electrons move around the nucleus in layers known as shells.

Atoms can form bonds to make molecules or compounds. It's the electrons that are involved in making bonds. Sometimes an atom loses or gains one or more electrons and this gives it a charge (positive if it loses an electron, and negative if it gains one).

Charged atoms are known as ions. If a positive ion meets a negative ion they'll be attracted to one another and join together. This is called an ionic bond.

The other main type of bond is called a covalent bond. When non-metal atoms combine together they form covalent bonds by sharing pairs of electrons. Because the bond is a shared pair, no atom loses electrons.

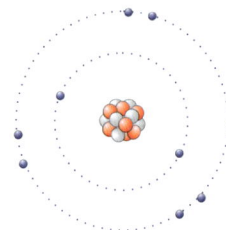

See page 86-88 for more about bonding.

You Need to Know About Displayed and Molecular Formulas

You need to be able to say how many atoms of each type there are in a substance when you're given its formula. Here are some examples:

This is called a molecular formula. It shows the number and type of atoms in a molecule.

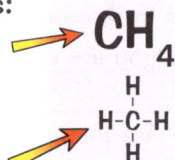

CH_4

H
H–C–H
H

Methane contains 1 carbon atom and 4 hydrogen atoms.

H_2O

H   H
 O

Water contains 2 hydrogen atoms and 1 oxygen atom.

This is called a displayed formula. It shows the atoms and the covalent bonds in a molecule as a picture.

Don't panic if the molecular formula has brackets in it. They're easy too.

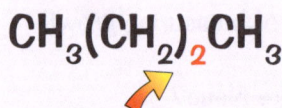

$CH_3(CH_2)_2CH_3$

The **2** after the bracket means that there are **2** lots of CH_2. So altogether there are 4 carbon atoms and 10 hydrogen atoms.

Drawing the displayed formula of the compound is a good way to count up the number of atoms.

Do it a bit at a time.

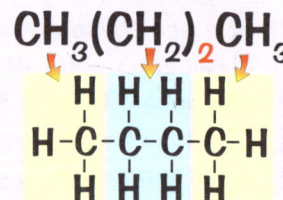

$CH_3(CH_2)_2CH_3$

H H H H
H–C–C–C–C–H
H H H H

In the exam they might give you a displayed formula and ask you to write down the molecular formula. Easy — just count up the number of each type of atom and write it as above, e.g. CH_4, H_2O, etc. Even better... you can write $CH_3(CH_2)_2CH_3$ as C_4H_{10}. It just doesn't get any easier. Not in Chemistry.

You Need to Remember Some Formulas

One formula, two formulas, or even two formula*e*.

Here are some formulas. Learn them now. There are only ten, and you'll have come across most of them already. You'll need to learn others later, but these'll be a good start.

1) Carbon dioxide — CO_2
2) Hydrogen — H_2
3) Water — H_2O
4) Hydrochloric acid — HCl
5) Calcium chloride — $CaCl_2$
6) Carbon monoxide — CO
7) Magnesium chloride — $MgCl_2$
8) Calcium carbonate — $CaCO_3$
9) Sulfuric acid — H_2SO_4
10) Magnesium sulfate — $MgSO_4$

Some chemicals have slightly more interesting names...

With so many chemicals around, some must have interesting names... Well some do. Like windowpane (C_9H_{12}). And angelic acid ($CH_3CHC(CH_3)COOH$). There's the mineral that's named after the mineralogist Wilfred Welsh, which goes by the name of welshite ($Ca_2SbMg_4FeBe_2Si_4O_{20}$). Better than boring names like 'ethene'.

Chemical Equations

If you're going to get anywhere in chemistry you need to know about <u>chemical equations</u>...

Chemical Changes <u>are Shown</u> Using Chemical Equations

One way to show a chemical reaction is to write a <u>word equation</u>. It's not as <u>quick</u> as using chemical symbols and you can't tell straight away <u>what's happened</u> to each of the <u>atoms</u>, but it's <u>dead easy</u>. Here's an example — you're told that <u>methane</u> burns in <u>oxygen</u> giving <u>carbon dioxide</u> and <u>water</u>. So here's the word equation:

The molecules on the left-hand side of the equation are called the <u>reactants</u> (because they react with each other).

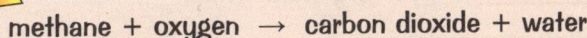

methane + oxygen → carbon dioxide + water

The molecules on the right-hand side are called the <u>products</u> (because they've been produced from the reactants).

Symbol Equations Show the Atoms on Both Sides

Chemical <u>changes</u> can be shown in a kind of <u>shorthand</u> using symbol equations. Symbol equations just show the <u>formulas</u> of the <u>reactants</u> and <u>products</u>...

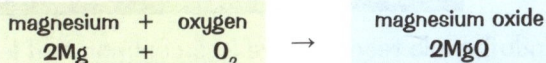

magnesium	+	oxygen		magnesium oxide
$2Mg$	+	O_2	→	$2MgO$

You'll have spotted that there's a '2' in front of the Mg and the MgO. The reason for this is explained below...

Symbol Equations Need to be Balanced

1) There must always be the <u>same</u> number of atoms on <u>both sides</u> — they can't just <u>disappear</u>.

2) You <u>balance</u> the equation by putting numbers <u>in front</u> of the formulas where needed. Take this equation for reacting sulfuric acid with sodium hydroxide:

$$H_2SO_4 + NaOH \rightarrow Na_2SO_4 + H_2O$$

The <u>formulas</u> are all correct but the numbers of some atoms <u>don't match up</u> on both sides. You <u>can't change formulas</u> like H_2SO_4 to H_2SO_5. You can only put numbers <u>in front of them</u>:

Method: Balance Just <u>One Type of Atom</u> at a Time

The more you <u>practise</u>, the <u>quicker</u> you get, but all you do is this:

1) Find an element that <u>doesn't balance</u> and <u>pencil in a number</u> to try and sort it out.

2) <u>See where it gets you</u>. It may create <u>another imbalance</u>, but if so, pencil in <u>another number</u> and see where that gets you.

3) Carry on chasing <u>unbalanced</u> elements and it'll <u>sort itself out</u> pretty quickly.

<u>I'll show you</u>: In the equation above you'll notice we're short of <u>H atoms</u> on the RHS (Right-Hand Side).

1) The only thing you can do about that is make it <u>2H₂O</u> instead of just H_2O:

$$H_2SO_4 + NaOH \rightarrow Na_2SO_4 + 2H_2O$$

2) But that now gives <u>too many</u> H atoms and O atoms on the RHS, so to balance that up you could try putting <u>2NaOH</u> on the LHS (Left-Hand Side):

$$H_2SO_4 + 2NaOH \rightarrow Na_2SO_4 + 2H_2O$$

3) And suddenly there it is! <u>Everything balances</u>. And you'll notice the Na just sorted itself out.

They can ask you in the exam to balance symbol equations using formulas that have bits in <u>brackets</u> — like $CH_3(CH_2)_2CH_3$ on the last page. Don't worry about that, just make sure you're clear before you start <u>how many</u> of <u>each type</u> of atom there are — in this case it's <u>4 carbons</u> and <u>10 hydrogens</u>.

It's all about getting the balance right...

Balancing equations isn't as scary as it looks — you just plug numbers in until it works itself out. Get some practice in — you'll see. You can balance equations with <u>displayed formulas</u> in exactly the same way. Just make sure there are the same number of each type of atom on both sides — dead easy.

Energy Transfer in Reactions

Chemical reactions can either <u>release</u> heat energy, or <u>take in</u> heat energy.

Combustion is an Exothermic Reaction — Heat's Given Out

An <u>EXOTHERMIC REACTION</u> is one which <u>GIVES OUT ENERGY</u> to the surroundings, usually in the form of <u>HEAT</u>, which is shown by a <u>RISE IN TEMPERATURE</u>.

The best example of an <u>exothermic</u> reaction is <u>burning fuels</u>. This obviously <u>gives out a lot of heat</u> — it's very exothermic.

In an Endothermic Reaction, Heat is Taken In

An <u>ENDOTHERMIC REACTION</u> is one which <u>TAKES IN ENERGY</u> from the surroundings, usually in the form of <u>HEAT</u>, which is shown by a <u>FALL IN TEMPERATURE</u>.

Endothermic reactions are <u>less common</u> and less easy to spot. One example is <u>thermal decomposition</u>. Heat must be supplied to cause the compound to <u>decompose</u>, e.g. decomposition of $CuCO_3$ see p.93).

Temperature Changes Help Decide If a Reaction's Exo or Endo

1) You can measure the amount of <u>energy produced</u> by a <u>chemical reaction</u> (in solution) by taking the <u>temperature of the reactants</u>, <u>mixing</u> them in a <u>polystyrene cup</u> and measuring the <u>temperature of the solution</u> at the <u>end</u> of the reaction. Easy.

2) Adding an <u>acid to an alkali</u> is an <u>exothermic</u> reaction. Measure the temperature of the alkali before you add the acid, then measure the temperature again after adding the acid and mixing — you'll see an <u>increase in temperature</u>.

3) Dissolving <u>ammonium nitrate</u> in water is an endothermic reaction. Adding a couple of spatulas of ammonium nitrate to a polystyrene cup of water results in a <u>drop in temperature</u>.

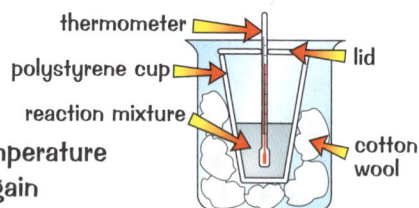

thermometer
polystyrene cup
reaction mixture
lid
cotton wool

Energy Must Always be Supplied to Break Bonds...
...and Energy is Always Released When Bonds Form

1) During a chemical reaction, <u>old bonds are broken</u> and <u>new bonds are formed</u>.

2) Energy must be <u>supplied</u> to break <u>existing bonds</u> — so bond breaking is an <u>endothermic</u> process.

3) Energy is <u>released</u> when new bonds are <u>formed</u> — so bond formation is an <u>exothermic</u> process.

BOND BREAKING - ENDOTHERMIC

Na Cl → Energy Supplied → Na + Cl
Strong Bond — Bond Broken

BOND FORMING - EXOTHERMIC

Mg + O → Mg O + Energy Released
Strong Bond Formed

4) In an <u>exothermic</u> reaction, the energy <u>released</u> in bond formation is <u>greater</u> than the energy used in <u>breaking</u> old bonds.

5) In an <u>endothermic</u> reaction, the energy <u>required</u> to break old bonds is <u>greater</u> than the energy <u>released</u> when <u>new bonds</u> are formed.

Chemistry in "real-world application" shocker...

When you see <u>Stevie Gerrard</u> hobble off the pitch and press a bag to his leg, he's using an <u>endothermic reaction</u>. The cold pack contains an inner bag full of water and an outer one full of ammonium nitrate. When he presses the pack the inner bag <u>breaks</u> and they <u>mix together</u>. The ammonium nitrate dissolves in the water and, as this is an endothermic reaction, it <u>draws in heat</u> from Stevie's injured leg.

Measuring the Energy Content of Fuels

Different fuels give out different amounts of energy when they burn. Here's how you measure that energy...

Use Specific Heat Capacity to Calculate Energy Transferred

1) This "calorimetric" experiment involves heating water by burning a liquid fuel.

2) If you measure (i) how much fuel you've burned and (ii) the temperature change of the water, you can work out how much energy is supplied by each gram of fuel.

3) You also need to know water's specific heat capacity — this is the amount of energy needed to raise the temperature of 1 gram of water by 1 °C. The specific heat capacity of water is 4.2 J/g/°C — so it takes 4.2 joules of energy to raise the temperature of 1 g of water by 1 °C.

4) If you do the same experiment with different fuels, you can compare their energy transferred per gram. If a fuel has a higher energy content per gram, you need less fuel to cause the same temperature rise.

Calorimetric Method — Reduce Heat Loss as Much as Possible

1) It's dead important to make as much heat as possible go into heating up the water. Reducing draughts is the key here — use a screen to act as a draught excluder (and don't do it next to an open window).

2) Put some fuel into a spirit burner (or use a bottled gas burner if the fuel is a gas) and weigh the burner full of fuel.

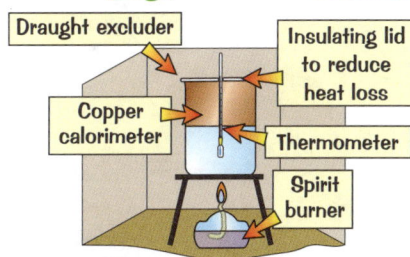

Labels: Draught excluder; Insulating lid to reduce heat loss; Copper calorimeter; Thermometer; Spirit burner

3) Measure out, say, 200 cm³ of water (this is the same as 200 g of water) into a copper calorimeter.

4) Take the initial temperature of the water — then put the burner under the calorimeter and light the wick.

5) When the heat from the burner has made the water temperature rise by 20-30 °C, blow out the spirit burner and make a note of the highest temperature the water reaches.

6) Reweigh the burner and fuel.

7) If you're comparing two fuels, repeat the procedure with the second fuel.

Three Calculations to Find the Energy Output Per Gram of Fuel

1) You find the mass of fuel burned by subtracting the final mass of fuel and burner from the initial mass of fuel and burner. Simple.

2) The amount of energy transferred to the water is given by:

$$\text{ENERGY TRANSFERRED (in J)} = \text{MASS OF WATER (in g)} \times \text{SPECIFIC HEAT CAPACITY OF WATER (= 4.2 J/g °C)} \times \text{TEMPERATURE CHANGE (in °C)}$$

Which can also be written like this:

$$\text{Energy transferred} = m \times c \times \Delta T$$

ΔT just means the change in the temperature.

3) Then the energy given out per gram of fuel is given by:

$$\text{ENERGY GIVEN OUT PER GRAM (in J/g)} = \frac{\text{ENERGY RELEASED (in J)}}{\text{MASS OF FUEL BURNED (in g)}}$$

Make It a Fair Test by Keeping Conditions the Same

1) To compare the energy content of different fuels you need to do the same experiment several times, but using a different fuel in the burner each time.

2) For the comparison to be fair, everything (except the fuel used) should be the same.

3) This means that: (i) you should use the same apparatus, (ii) you should use the same amount of water each time, (iii) the water should start and finish at the same temperature each time.

4) In order for the results to be reliable you would have to repeat the experiment several times and discount any anomalous results.

Hope you've got the energy to revise all this...

In the exam they might give you data from simple calorimetric experiments involving the combustion of fuel to compare, and you'll have to use it to say which fuel releases the most energy. Pretty easy.

Chemical Reaction Rates

The rate of a chemical reaction is how fast the reactants are changed into products (the reaction is over when one of the reactants is completely used up). People working in the chemical industry like to know what affects the rate of a reaction — because the faster you make chemicals, the faster you make money.

Reactions Can Go at All Sorts of *Different Rates*

1) One of the slowest is the rusting of iron (it's not slow enough though — what about my little MGB).

2) Other slow reactions include chemical weathering — like acid rain damage to limestone buildings.

3) An example of a moderate speed reaction is a metal (e.g. magnesium) reacting with dilute acid to produce a gentle stream of bubbles.

4) Burning is a fast reaction, but an explosion is really fast and releases a lot of gas. Explosive reactions are all over in a fraction of a second.

You Can Do an *Experiment* to Follow a *Reaction*

The rate of a reaction that produces a gas can be observed by measuring how quickly the gas is produced. There are two ways of doing this:

MEASURE THE CHANGE IN MASS

If you carry out the reaction on a balance, the mass will fall as the gas is released. You need to take readings of the mass at regular time intervals.

MEASURE THE VOLUME OF GAS GIVEN OFF

This method is pretty similar, except you use a gas syringe to measure the volume of gas given off after regular time intervals.

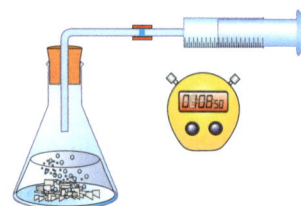

Whichever of these methods you use, you can plot your results on a graph. Page 36 shows you the type of graph you'll get and what it shows.

Particles *Must Collide* with *Enough Energy* in Order to React

Reaction rates are explained perfectly by collision theory. It's simple really. The rate of a chemical reaction depends on:

- The collision frequency of reacting particles (how often they collide). The more collisions there are the faster the reaction is.

- The energy transferred during a collision. Particles have to collide with enough energy for the collision to be successful.

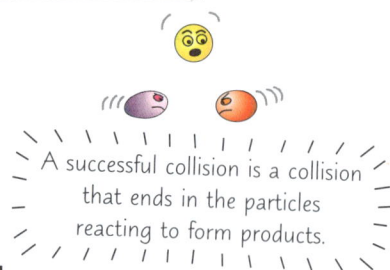

A successful collision is a collision that ends in the particles reacting to form products.

More Reactant Used Means More Product Formed

1) The amount of product you get from a reaction (the yield) depends on the amount of reactant you start with.

2) More reactant means more particles. These particles go on to have more reactions so create more product.

3) The amount of product you get is directly proportional to the amount of limiting reactant (the reactant that's totally used up). For example, if you half the particles of limiting reactant, you get half the yield.

4) Once all of the limiting reactant is used up, the reaction can't continue and you can't get any more product.

5) There might still be some of the other reactant left at the end — we say this reactant is in excess.

Get a fast, furious reaction — tickle your teacher...

First off... remember that the amount of product you get is proportional to the amount of limiting reactant you start with. So all the stuff about the rate of a reaction is only talking about how quickly your products form — not how much of them you get. It's an important difference — so get your head round it asap.

Collision Theory

The rate of a reaction depends on <u>four</u> things — <u>temperature</u>, <u>concentration</u> (or <u>pressure</u> for gases), the presence of a <u>catalyst</u> and the <u>size of the particles</u>. This page explains <u>why</u> these things affect the reaction rate.

More Collisions Increases the Rate of Reaction

Reactions happen if <u>particles collide</u>. So if you <u>increase</u> the <u>number</u> of collisions, the reaction happens <u>more quickly</u>. The four factors below all lead to more collisions... (Well, a catalyst's a bit different, I guess — there are the same number of collisions, it's just that more of them lead to a reaction.)

1) Increasing the Temperature Means the Particles are Going Faster and have More Energy

When the <u>temperature is increased</u> the particles all <u>move quicker</u>. If they're moving quicker, they're going to have <u>more collisions</u>.

Higher temperatures also increase the <u>energy of the collisions</u>, since the particles are moving <u>faster</u>. Reactions <u>only happen</u> if the particles collide with <u>enough energy</u>. At a <u>higher temperature</u> there'll be <u>more particles</u> colliding with <u>enough energy</u> to make the reaction happen.

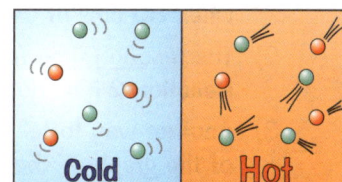

Cold   Hot

2) Increasing the Concentration (or Pressure) Means the Particles are More Crowded Together

If a solution is made more <u>concentrated</u> it means there are more particles of <u>reactant</u> in the same volume, which makes collisions <u>more likely</u>. In a <u>gas</u>, increasing the <u>pressure</u> means the molecules are <u>more crowded</u>, so the frequency of the collisions <u>increases</u>.

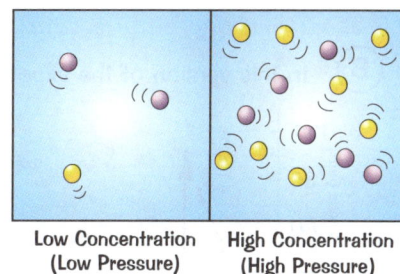

Low Concentration (Low Pressure)   High Concentration (High Pressure)

3) Smaller Solid Particles (or More Surface Area) Means Other Particles Can Get to It More Easily

If one of the reactants is a <u>solid</u> then <u>breaking it up</u> into <u>smaller</u> pieces will <u>increase its surface area</u>. This means the particles around it will have <u>more area to work on</u> so the frequency of collisions will <u>increase</u>. For example, soluble pain killers dissolve faster when they're broken into bits.

<u>Fine powders</u> of <u>combustible materials</u> dispersed in the air burn very very fast because they have such a <u>big surface area</u>. In fact, if there's a spark, they'll <u>EXPLODE</u> (an explosion is basically a very fast reaction that releases a lot of gaseous products very quickly). That's why factories that make <u>custard powder</u>, <u>flour</u> and powdered <u>sulfur</u> have to be careful.

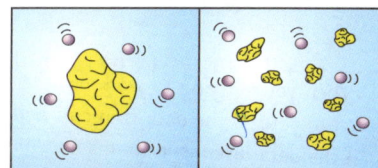

4) A Catalyst Increases the Number of Successful Collisions

A <u>catalyst</u> is a substance which increases the <u>speed of a reaction</u>, <u>without</u> being chemically changed or used up in the reaction — and because it isn't used up, you only need a <u>tiny bit</u> of it to catalyse large amounts of reactants. Catalysts tend to be very <u>fussy</u> about which reactions they catalyse though — you can't just stick any old catalyst in a reaction and expect it to work.

A catalyst works by giving the reacting particles a <u>surface</u> to stick to where they can bump into each other — and <u>reduces the energy needed</u> by the particles before they react. So the <u>overall number</u> of collisions isn't increased, but the number of <u>successful collisions</u> is.

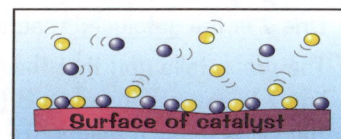

Surface of catalyst

Collision theory — it's always the other driver...

Industries that use chemical reactions to make their products have to think <u>carefully</u> about reaction rates. <u>Ideally</u>, they want to <u>speed up</u> the reaction to get the products quickly, but high temperatures and pressures are <u>expensive</u>. So they <u>compromise</u> — they use a <u>slower</u> reaction but a <u>cheaper</u> one.

Rate of Reaction Data

In the exam they might ask you to interpret <u>rate of reaction data</u>. Read on...

Reaction Rate Graphs <u>Show</u> Rate of Reaction Data

A When marble chips are added to hydrochloric acid, CO_2 is given off. In this experiment, 5 g of marble chips were added to hydrochloric acid, and the volume of CO_2 measured every 10 seconds. The results are plotted below. Line 1 is for <u>small chips</u> and line 2 is for <u>large chips</u>.

1) Both reactions finish (the line goes flat) when 80 cm³ of CO_2 are produced.

2) The <u>reaction time</u> for Reaction 1 is about 60 s, and for Reaction 2 it's about 90 s — <u>Reaction 1 is faster</u>.

3) Another way to tell the rate of reaction is to look at the <u>slope</u> of the graph — the <u>steeper</u> the graph, the <u>faster</u> the reaction. Reaction 1 is <u>faster</u> than Reaction 2 — the <u>slope of its graph is steeper</u>.

4) <u>Reaction 1</u> is <u>faster</u> because small chips have a <u>larger surface area</u> than the same mass of large chips.

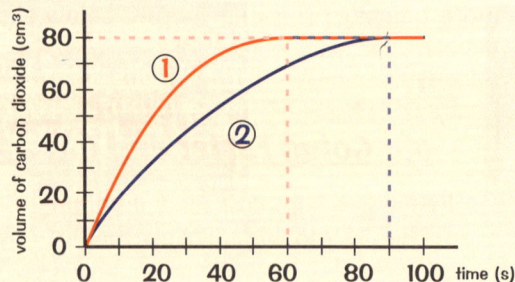

You might have to draw sketch graphs like these ones in the exam.

B In this version of the experiment the size of the chips is the same but two <u>different temperatures</u> are used.

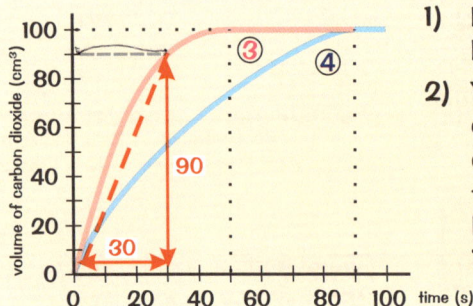

1) Both reactions finish when 100 cm³ of CO_2 have been produced. Reaction 3 is faster (about 50 s, compared to Reaction 4's 90 s or so).

2) You can calculate the <u>rate of reaction</u> by calculating the slope of the line. To find the <u>average rate</u> during the first 30 s, draw a line from the volume of CO_2 produced at the start to the volume produced at 30 s then find the slope of this line. For Reaction 3, the slope is $90 \div 30 = 3$. This means that you're getting <u>3 cm³ of CO_2 per second (3 cm³/s)</u>.

When you're trying to work out the units of a reaction rate, take a look at the data given to you. If the data is in cm³ and seconds then the units will be cm³ per s (cm³/s). If the data given is in grams and minutes then the units will be g per min (g/min).

C This time, a piece of magnesium has been added to hydrochloric acid. The graphs show the volume of hydrogen produced when two <u>different concentrations</u> of acid are used.

1) <u>Reaction 5</u> is <u>faster</u> than Reaction 6 — its <u>slope is steeper</u> (or use the fact that Reaction 5 takes about 30 s, and Reaction 6 about 50 s).

2) Since Reaction 5 is <u>faster</u>, it must use the <u>more concentrated</u> acid.

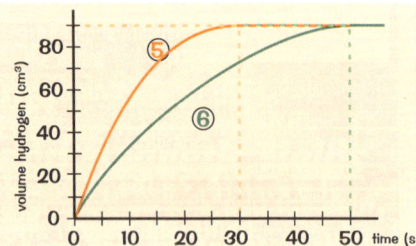

D This graph shows the effect of adding a catalyst. Line 7 is the <u>catalysed</u> reaction, line 8 is the <u>uncatalysed</u> reaction.

The graph tells you that the <u>catalyst speeds up the reaction</u> because line 7 is <u>steeper</u> than line 8 (but the <u>total volume of gas</u> produced is the <u>same</u> in each reaction).

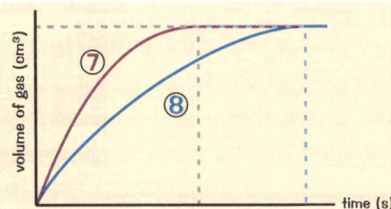

My reactions slow down when it gets hot — I get sleepy...

You can easily compare the <u>rate</u> of two reactions by comparing the <u>slopes</u> of their graphs. The <u>steeper</u> the slope, the <u>faster</u> the reaction. It's as simple as falling down a hill — the steeper the hill, the faster you'll fall.

Reacting Masses

The biggest trouble with <u>relative atomic mass</u> and <u>relative formula mass</u> is that they <u>sound</u> so blood-curdling. They're very important though, so take a few deep breaths, and just enjoy, as the mists slowly clear...

Relative Atomic Mass, A_r — Easy Peasy

In the periodic table, the elements all have <u>two</u> numbers. The <u>bigger one</u> is the <u>relative atomic mass</u>.

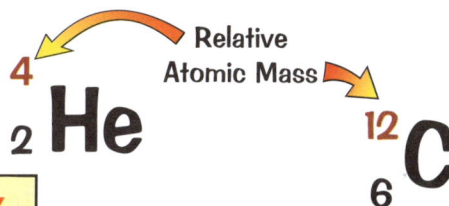

$_2^4$He $_6^{12}$C   Relative Atomic Mass

Relative Formula Mass, M_r — Also Easy Peasy

If you have a compound like $MgCl_2$ then it has a <u>relative formula mass</u>, M_r, which is just all the relative atomic masses <u>added together</u>.

For $MgCl_2$ it would be: $Mg + (2 \times Cl) = 24 + (2 \times 35.5) = \underline{95}$

So M_r for $MgCl_2$ is simply <u>95</u>.

Compounds with Brackets in...

<u>Example</u>: Find the relative formula mass for calcium hydroxide, $Ca(OH)_2$

<u>Method</u>: The <u>small number 2</u> after the bracket in the formula $Ca(OH)_2$ means that <u>there's two of everything inside the brackets</u>.
So... $Ca + (O + H) \times 2 = 40 + (16 + 1) \times 2 = 40 + 34 = \underline{74}$

So the Relative Formula Mass for $Ca(OH)_2$ is <u>74</u>.

In a Chemical Reaction, Mass is Always Conserved

1) During a chemical reaction <u>no atoms are destroyed</u> and <u>no atoms are created</u>.

2) This means there are the <u>same number and types of atoms</u> on each side of a reaction equation.

3) Because of this no mass is lost or gained — we say that mass is <u>conserved</u> during a reaction.

<u>Example</u>: $2Li + F_2 \rightarrow 2LiF$

<u>Method</u>: There are <u>2</u> lithium atoms and <u>2</u> fluorine atoms on <u>each side</u> of the equation.

4) By adding up the relative formula masses on each side of the equation you can see that mass is conserved.

<u>Example</u>: $2Li$ + F_2 $\rightarrow$ $2LiF$
<u>Method</u>: $(2 \times 7) + (2 \times 19) \rightarrow 2 \times 26$
            $14 + 38 \rightarrow 52$
            $52 \rightarrow 52$ So, <u>mass is conserved</u> in this equation.

5) You can use simple <u>ratios</u> to calculate the reacting masses in a reaction.

<u>Example</u>: In the reaction, $2Li + F_2 \rightarrow 2LiF$, 14 g of lithium will react with 38 g of fluorine.

<u>Method</u>: The only product that's formed is lithium fluoride, so $14 + 38 = 52$ g will be produced.

The masses for this reaction will always be in the same proportions as this.

Multiplying or dividing these masses by the same number gives you other sets of reacting masses.

Element / compound in reaction	Lithium	Fluorine	Lithium fluoride
Original reacting masses	14 g	38 g	52 g
Reacting masses set 2	$14 \div 2 = 7$ g	$38 \div 2 = 19$ g	$52 \div 2 = 26$ g
Reacting masses set 3	$14 \times 1.5 = 21$ g	$38 \times 1.5 = 57$ g	$52 \times 1.5 = 78$ g

Phew, Chemistry — scary stuff sometimes, innit...

This page is <u>really important</u>... You've gotta remember that in a reaction <u>no mass is lost</u> and <u>no mass is gained</u>. Otherwise you'll be messing with the first law of thermodynamics — and you wouldn't want that, would you..

Calculating Masses in Reactions

These can be kinda scary too, but chill out, little trembling one — just relax and enjoy.

The Three Important Steps — Not to Be Missed...

(Miss one out and it'll all go horribly wrong, believe me.)

1) **Write out** the balanced **equation**

2) **Work out M_r** — just for the **two bits you want**

3) Apply the rule: **Divide to get one, then multiply to get all**
   (But you have to apply this first to the substance they give information about, and then the other one!)

Don't worry — these steps should all make sense when you look at the example below.

Example: What mass of magnesium oxide is produced when 60 g of magnesium is burned in air?

Method:

1) Write out the balanced equation:

$$2Mg + O_2 \rightarrow 2MgO$$

2) Work out the relative formula masses: (don't do the oxygen — we don't need it)

$$2 \times 24 \quad\quad \rightarrow 2 \times (24 + 16)$$
$$48 \quad\quad\quad \rightarrow \quad\quad 80$$

3) Apply the rule: Divide to get one, then multiply to get all
   The two numbers, 48 and 80, tell us that 48 g of Mg react to give 80 g of MgO.
   Here's the tricky bit. You've now got to be able to write this down:

> 48 g of Mg ...... reacts to give ..... 80 g of MgO
> 1 g of Mg ...... reacts to give .....   ?
> 60 g of Mg ...... reacts to give .....   ?

The big clue is that in the question they've said we want to burn '60 g of magnesium', i.e. they've told us how much magnesium to have (it's the limiting reactant — there's almost unlimited O_2 in the air), and that's how you know to write down the left-hand side of it first, because:

> We'll first need to divide by 48 to get 1 g of Mg
> and then need to multiply by 60 to get 60 g of Mg.

Then you can work out the numbers on the other side (shown in blue below) by realising that you must divide both sides by 48 and then multiply both sides by 60. It's tricky.

$\div 48$ 48 g of Mg .... 80 g of MgO $\div 48$

1 g of Mg .... 1.67 g of MgO

$\times 60$ 60 g of Mg .... 100 g of MgO $\times 60$

The mass of product is called the yield of a reaction. In practice you never get 100% of the yield, so the amount of product will be slightly less than calculated (see p.40).

This finally tells us that 60 g of magnesium will produce 100 g of magnesium oxide.

If the question had said 'Find how much magnesium gives 500 g of magnesium oxide', you'd fill in the MgO side first, because that's the one you'd have the information about. Got it? Good-O!

Reaction mass calculations? — no worries, matey...

Calculating masses is a very useful skill to have. If you're trying to get 10 g of magnesium oxide, say, for use in a medicine or fertiliser, you're going to need to be able to work out how much magnesium to use, or you could get too much or too little. A wrong calculation could be an expensive mistake...

Atom Economy

It's important in industrial reactions that as much of the reactants as possible get turned into useful products. This depends on the atom economy and the percentage yield (see next page) of the reaction.

"Atom Economy" — % of Reactants Changed to Useful Products

1) A lot of reactions make more than one product. Some of them will be useful, but others will just be waste, e.g. when you make quicklime from limestone, you also get CO_2 as a waste product.

2) The atom economy of a reaction tells you how much of the mass of the reactants is wasted when manufacturing a chemical. Learn the equation:

$$\text{atom economy} = \frac{\text{total } M_r \text{ of desired products}}{\text{total } M_r \text{ of all products}} \times 100$$

3) 100% atom economy means that all the atoms in the reactants have been turned into useful (desired) products. The higher the atom economy the 'greener' the process.

> **Example:** Hydrogen gas is made on a large scale by reacting natural gas (methane) with steam.
> $$CH_4(g) + H_2O(g) \rightarrow CO(g) + 3H_2(g)$$
> Calculate the atom economy of this reaction.

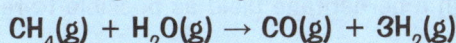

Method:
1) Identify the useful product — that's the hydrogen gas.
2) Work out the M_r of all the products and the useful product:

CO	$3H_2$	$3H_2$
12 + 16	3 × (2 × 1)	3 × (2 × 1)
34		**6**

3) Use the formula to calculate the atom economy: atom economy $= \frac{6}{34} \times 100 = \underline{17.6\%}$

So in this reaction, over 80% of the starting materials are wasted.

High Atom Economy is Better for Profits and the Environment

1) Pretty obviously, if you're making lots of waste, that's a problem.

2) Reactions with low atom economy use up resources very quickly. At the same time, they make lots of waste materials that have to be disposed of somehow. That tends to make these reactions unsustainable — the raw materials will run out and the waste has to go somewhere.

3) For the same reasons, low atom economy reactions aren't usually profitable. Raw materials are expensive to buy, and waste products can be expensive to remove and dispose of responsibly.

4) The best way around the problem is to find a use for the waste products rather than just throwing them away. There's often more than one way to make the product you want, so the trick is to come up with a reaction that gives useful "by-products" rather than useless ones.

5) The reactions with the highest atom economy are the ones that only have one product. Those reactions have an atom economy of 100%.

Atom economy — important but not the whole story...

You could get asked about any industrial reaction in the exam. Don't panic — whatever example they give you, the same stuff applies. In the real world, high atom economy isn't enough, though. You need to think about the percentage yield of the reaction (next page) and the energy cost as well.

Percentage Yield

Percentage yield tells you about the <u>overall success</u> of an experiment. It compares what you think you should get (<u>predicted yield</u>) with what you get in practice (<u>actual yield</u>).

Percentage Yield Compares Actual and Predicted Yield

The more reactants you start with, the higher the <u>actual yield</u> will be — that's pretty obvious. But the <u>percentage yield doesn't</u> depend on the amount of reactants you started with — it's a <u>percentage</u>.

1) The <u>predicted yield</u> of a reaction can be calculated from the <u>balanced reaction equation</u> (see page 38).

2) Percentage yield is given by the formula:

$$\text{percentage yield} = \frac{\text{actual yield (grams)}}{\text{predicted yield (grams)}} \times 100$$

3) Percentage yield is <u>always</u> somewhere between 0 and 100%.

4) 100% yield means that you got <u>all</u> the product you expected to get.

5) 0% yield means that <u>no</u> reactants were converted into product, i.e. no product at all was <u>made</u>.

6) Industrial processes want as <u>high</u> a percentage yield as possible to <u>reduce waste</u> and <u>reduce costs</u>.

Yields are Always Less Than 100%

In real life, you <u>never</u> get a 100% yield. Some product or reactant <u>always</u> gets lost along the way — and that goes for big <u>industrial processes</u> as well as school lab experiments.

How this happens depends on <u>what sort of reaction</u> it is and what <u>apparatus</u> is being used.

Lots of things can go wrong, but the four you need to <u>know about</u> are:

1) Evaporation

Liquids evaporate <u>all the time</u> — and even more so while they're being heated.

Liquid evaporating...

2) Not All Reactants React to Make a Product

In <u>reversible reactions</u>, the products can <u>turn back</u> into reactants, so the yield will <u>never</u> be <u>100%</u>.

BOTH WAYS

For example, in the Haber process, at the same time as the reaction $N_2 + 3H_2 \rightarrow 2NH_3$ is taking place, the <u>reverse</u> reaction $2NH_3 \rightarrow N_2 + 3H_2$ is <u>also</u> happening.

3) Filtration

When you <u>filter a liquid</u> to remove <u>solid particles</u>, you nearly always lose a bit of liquid or a bit of solid.

- If you want to <u>keep the liquid</u>, you lose the bit that remains with the solid and filter paper (as they always stay a bit wet).

- If you want to <u>keep the solid</u>, some of it usually gets left behind when you scrape it off the filter paper — even if you're really careful.

4) Transferring Liquids

You always lose a bit of liquid when you <u>transfer</u> it from one container to another — even if you manage not to spill it.

Some of it always gets left behind on the <u>inside surface</u> of the old container. Think about it — it's always wet when you finish.

LIQUID NITROGEN

You can't always get what you want...

Unfortunately, no matter how careful you are, you're not going to get a 100% yield in any reaction. So you'll <u>always</u> get a little loss of product. In industry, people work very hard to keep wastage as <u>low</u> as possible — so <u>reactants</u> that don't react first time are <u>collected</u> and <u>recycled</u> whenever possible.

Chemical Production

There are lots of ways you could manufacture drugs — it all depends on how much you want to make.

The Type of Manufacturing Process Depends on the Product

Batch Production Only Operates at Certain Times

Pharmaceutical drugs are complicated to make and there's fairly low demand for them. Batch production is often the most cost-effective way to produce small quantities of different drugs to order, because:

1) It's flexible — several different products can be made using the same equipment.

2) Start-up costs are relatively low — small-scale, multi-purpose equipment can be bought off the shelf.

But batch production does have disadvantages:

1) It's labour-intensive — the equipment needs to be set up and manually controlled for each batch and then cleaned out at the end.

2) It can be tricky to keep the same quality from batch to batch.

Continuous Production Runs All the Time

Large-scale industrial manufacture of popular chemicals, e.g. the Haber process for making ammonia uses continuous production because:

1) Production never stops, so you don't waste time emptying the reactor and setting it up again.

2) It runs automatically — you only need to interfere if something goes wrong.

3) The quality of the product is very consistent.

But, start-up costs to build the plant are huge, and it isn't cost-effective to run at less than full capacity.

Pharmaceutical Drugs Often Cost A Lot — For Several Reasons

1) Research and Development — finding a suitable compound, testing it, modifying it, testing again, until it's ready. This involves the work of lots of highly paid scientists.

2) Trialling — no drug can be sold until it's gone through loads of time-consuming tests including animal trials and human trials. The manufacturer has to prove that the drug meets legal requirements so it works and it's safe.

3) Manufacture — multi-step batch production is labour-intensive and can't be automated. Other costs include energy and raw materials. The raw materials for pharmaceuticals are often rare and sometimes need to be extracted from plants (an expensive process).

> It takes about 12 years and £900 million to develop a new drug and get it onto the market. Ouch.

To extract a substance from a plant, it has to be crushed then boiled and dissolved in a suitable solvent. Then, you can extract the substance you want by chromatography.

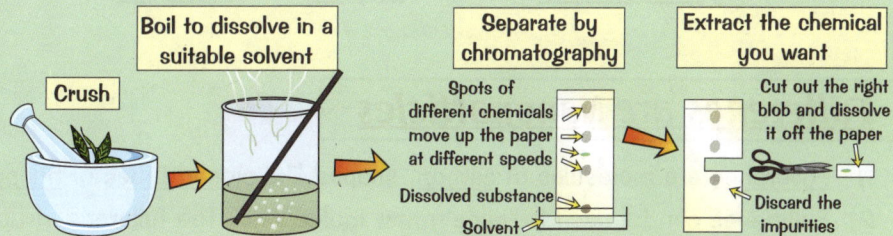

Crush

Boil to dissolve in a suitable solvent

Separate by chromatography

Spots of different chemicals move up the paper at different speeds

Dissolved substance

Solvent

Extract the chemical you want

Cut out the right blob and dissolve it off the paper

Discard the impurities

Test For Purity Using Chromatography And Boiling and Melting Points

You might be given data on a purity test and asked what it shows. Don't worry, it's fairly straightforward.

1) Pure substances won't be separated by chromatography — it'll all move as one blob.

2) Pure substances have a specific melting point and boiling point (e.g. pure ice melts at 0 °C, and pure water boils at 100 °C). If a substance is impure, the melting point will be too low and the boiling point will be too high (so if some ice melts at −2 °C, it's probably got an impurity in it e.g. salt).

I wish they'd find a drug to cure exams...

£900 million. You could buy yourself an island. And one for your mum. And a couple for your mates...

Allotropes of Carbon

Allotropes are just different <u>structural forms</u> of the same element in the same <u>physical state</u>, e.g. they're all solids. Carbon has quite a few allotropes, and you get to learn all about them. You lucky thing.

Diamond is Used in Jewellery and Cutting Tools

1) Diamonds are <u>lustrous</u> (sparkly) and <u>colourless</u>. Ideal for jewellery.
2) Each carbon atom forms <u>four covalent bonds</u> in a <u>very rigid</u> giant covalent structure, which makes diamond <u>really hard</u>. This makes diamonds ideal as cutting tools.
3) All those <u>strong covalent bonds</u> take a lot of energy to break and give diamond a <u>very high melting point</u>. Its high melting point is another reason diamond is so useful as a <u>cutting tool</u>.
4) It <u>doesn't conduct electricity</u> because it has <u>no free electrons</u> or ions.

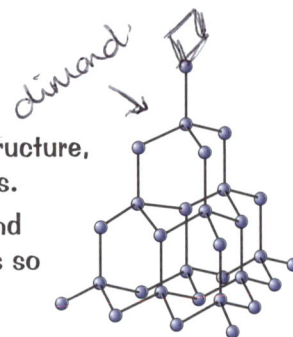

Graphite Makes the Lead of Your Pencil

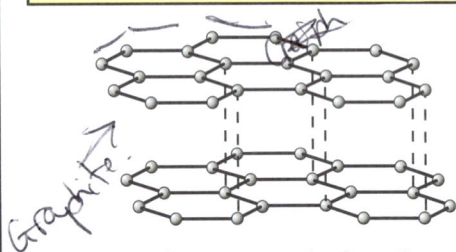

1) Graphite is <u>black</u> and <u>opaque</u>, but still kind of <u>shiny</u>.
2) Each carbon atom only forms <u>three covalent bonds</u>, creating <u>sheets of carbon atoms</u> which are free to <u>slide over each other</u>.
3) The layers are held together weakly so they are slippery and can be <u>rubbed off</u> onto paper to leave a black mark — that's how a pencil works. This also makes graphite ideal as a <u>lubricating material</u>.
4) Graphite's got a <u>high melting point</u> — the covalent bonds need <u>loads of energy</u> to break.
5) Since only three out of each carbon's four outer electrons are used in bonds, there are lots of <u>delocalised</u> (spare) <u>electrons</u> that can move. This means graphite <u>conducts electricity</u>.

Diamond and Graphite are Giant Molecular Structures

1) Because <u>carbon</u> can form lots of covalent bonds <u>with itself</u>, it can form <u>giant molecular structures</u> like diamond and graphite sheets.
2) Because of all the covalent bonds, <u>giant molecular structures</u> are <u>strong</u>, have <u>high melting points</u> and <u>don't dissolve</u> in water.
3) Giant molecular structures usually <u>don't conduct electricity</u> because there aren't any <u>free electrons</u> or ions — <u>graphite</u> is an <u>exception</u> to this.

Fullerenes are Nanoparticles

Nanoparticles are only a few nanometres (nm) across (1 nm = 0.000 000 001 m).

1) <u>Fullerenes</u> are molecules of <u>carbon</u>, shaped like <u>closed tubes</u> or <u>hollow balls</u>.
2) Fullerenes can be used to 'cage' other molecules. The fullerene structure forms around another atom or molecule, which is then trapped inside. This could be a new way of <u>delivering a drug</u> into the body, e.g. for slow release.
3) Fullerenes can be joined together to form <u>nanotubes</u> — tiny hollow carbon tubes.

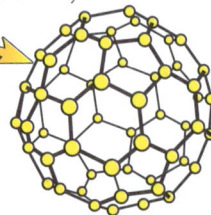

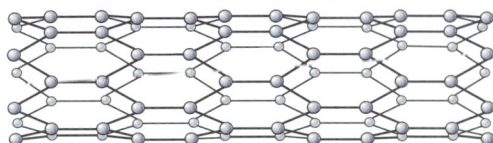

Nanotubes have a <u>huge surface area</u>, so they could help make great industrial <u>catalysts</u> — individual catalyst molecules could be attached to the nanotubes (the bigger the surface area the better).

Carbon is a girl's best friend...

Nanoparticles. Confused? Just think of it as knitting teeny weeny atomic footballs, and you'll be fine...

Revision Summary for Module C3

Some more tricky questions to stress you out. The thing is though, why bother doing easy questions?
These meaty monsters find out what you really know, and worse, what you really don't. Yeah, I know, it's
kinda scary, but if you want to get anywhere in life you've got to face up to a bit of hardship.
That's just the way it is. Take a few deep breaths and then try these.

1)* A molecule has the molecular formula $CH_3(CH_2)_4CH_3$. How many C and H atoms does it contain?

2)* Write down the displayed formula for a molecule with the molecular formula C_3H_8.

3) Write down the symbol equation for magnesium reacting with oxygen.

4)* Balance this equation which shows sodium reacting with water: $Na + H_2O \rightarrow NaOH + H_2$.

5) Give an example of: a) an endothermic reaction, b) an exothermic reaction.

6) Is bond breaking an exothermic or an endothermic reaction?

7) Give the formula that you would use to find the amount of energy transferred to the water in a
calorimetric experiment.

8) Give three things you should do in order to make sure a calorimetric experiment
is as accurate as possible.

9) How might you measure the rate of the reaction between calcium carbonate and hydrochloric acid?

10) Explain how increasing the collision frequency affects the rate of a chemical reaction.

11) What four things affect the rate of a reaction?

12) Why do gases react faster when they're under higher pressure?

13) Why do fine combustible powders sometimes explode?

14)* A piece of magnesium is added to a dilute solution of hydrochloric acid, and hydrogen gas is
produced. The experiment is repeated with a more concentrated hydrochloric acid. How can you
tell from the experiment which concentration of acid produces a faster rate of reaction?

15)* Find A_r or M_r for each of these (use the periodic table inside the front cover):
a) Ca   b) Ag   c) CO_2 d) $MgCO_3$ e) $Al(OH)_3$
f) ZnO   g) Na_2CO_3 h) sodium chloride

16)* Write down the three steps of the method for calculating reacting masses.
a) What mass of magnesium oxide is produced when 112.1 g of magnesium burns in air?
b) What mass of sodium is needed to produce 108.2 g of sodium oxide (Na_2O)?
c) What mass of carbon will react with hydrogen to produce 24.6 g of propane (C_3H_8)?

17) Write the equation for calculating the atom economy of a reaction.

18) Explain why it is important to use industrial reactions with a high atom economy.

19) What is the formula for percentage yield? How does percentage yield differ from actual yield?

20) Name four factors that prevent the percentage yield being 100%

21) What are 'batch production' and 'continuous production'?

22) Explain the advantages of using batch production to make pharmaceutical drugs.
What are the disadvantages?

23) It can take 12 years and about £900 million to bring a new drug to market. Explain why.

24) In terms of intermolecular bonds, explain why diamond makes a good cutting tool.

25) Why does graphite conduct electricity?

26) Do giant molecular structures have low or high melting points?

27) How might fullerenes be used to deliver drugs to the body?

* Answers on page 116.

Speed and Distance

Reckon you can speed on through this module? On your marks. Get set. Go...

Speed *is Just the* Distance *Travelled in a Certain* Time

1) To find the speed of an object, you need to measure the distance it travels (in metres or km) and the time it takes (in seconds or hours). Then the speed is calculated in metres per second (m/s) or kilometres per hour (km/h).

2) The greater the speed of an object, the further the distance it can travel in a certain time, or the shorter the time it takes to go a certain distance.

3) Speed, distance and time are related by the formula: ➤ | Distance = Speed × Time |

4) If an object is speeding up (or slowing down) then you might need to find the average of its speed over the journey: ➤ | Average Speed = $\dfrac{(u + v)}{2}$ |

5) If you put these equations together you get:

$$\text{Distance} = \frac{\text{Average}}{\text{Speed}} \times \text{Time} = \frac{(u + v)}{2} \times t$$

u is the speed at the start
v is the speed at the end

(You need to get pretty slick at using this formula.)

EXAMPLE: A ferret speeds up from 0 to 60 km/h in a time of half an hour. What distance does it cover in this time?

ANSWER: u = 0 km/h and v = 60 km/h, t = 0.5 h, so, distance = ((0 + 60) ÷ 2) × 0.5 = 30 × 0.5 = 15 km.

6) You might need to change the units:

EXAMPLE: A swimmer takes 8 hours to swim across the English Channel. She starts swimming at a speed of 2 m/s and gradually slows down to a speed of 0.5 m/s. How far did she swim? Give your answer in km.

ANSWER: u = 2 m/s, v = 0.5 m/s, t = 8 h, but t needs to be in seconds, so 8 × 3600 = 28 800 s. Distance = ((2 + 0.5) ÷ 2) × 28 800 = 1.25 × 28 800 = 36 000 m. Give answer in km = 36 000 ÷ 1000 = 36 km.

Distance-Time Graphs

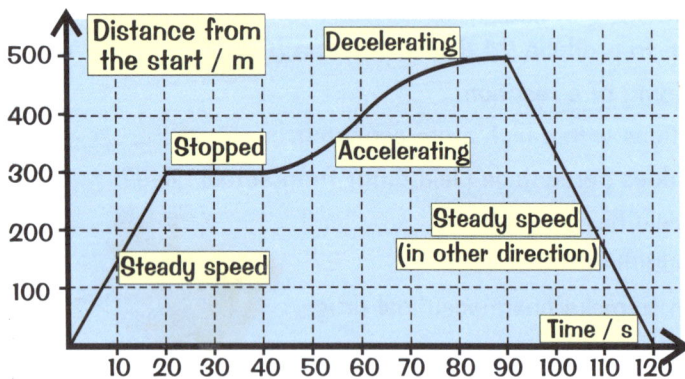

Very Important Notes:

1) GRADIENT = SPEED.

2) Flat sections are where it's stopped.

3) The steeper the gradient, the faster it's going.

4) 'Downhill' sections (negative gradient) mean it's changed direction and is coming back toward its starting point.

5) Curves represent acceleration or deceleration.

6) A steepening curve means it's speeding up (increasing gradient).

7) A levelling off curve means it's slowing down (decreasing gradient).

Calculating Speed *from a* Distance-Time *Graph —* It's Just the Gradient

For example, the speed of the return section of the graph is:

$$\text{Speed} = \text{gradient} = \frac{\text{vertical}}{\text{horizontal}} = \frac{500}{30} = 16.7 \text{ m/s}$$

Don't forget that you have to use the scales of the axes to work out the gradient. Don't measure in cm.

Miles (of revision) to go before I sleep...

You might have to draw graphs in an exam too, so have a peek at page 7 for a bit more on how to go about it.

Speed and Acceleration

Speed-time graphs allow you to calculate <u>acceleration</u> (which is how fast the speed is <u>changing</u>). Fun times.

Acceleration is How Quickly You're Speeding Up

1) Acceleration is <u>how quickly</u> the speed is <u>changing</u>.
2) You also accelerate when you <u>change direction, with</u> or <u>without changing speed</u>.   The 'Δv' means
'<u>change in speed</u>'.
3) A <u>decrease</u> in speed is a <u>deceleration</u> — a <u>negative acceleration</u>.
4) The <u>units</u> of acceleration (or deceleration) are <u>m/s^2</u>.

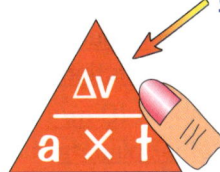

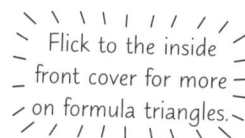

$$\text{Acceleration} = \frac{\text{Change in Speed}}{\text{Time Taken}}$$

$$\frac{\Delta v}{a \times t}$$

Flick to the inside front cover for more on formula triangles.

EXAMPLE: A skulking cat <u>decelerates</u> at 0.5 m/s^2 for 5.6 s until it reaches a speed of 2.5 m/s. Find its initial speed <u>before</u> it started to decelerate.

ANSWER: Find <u>change in speed</u> using the formula triangle: $\Delta v = a \times t = 0.5$ m/s^2 $\times 5.6$ s = <u>2.8 m/s</u>. Because the cat <u>decelerated</u>, its initial speed must be <u>2.8 m/s MORE</u> than its end speed. So initial speed = 2.5 m/s + 2.8 m/s = <u>5.3 m/s</u>.

Speed-Time Graphs

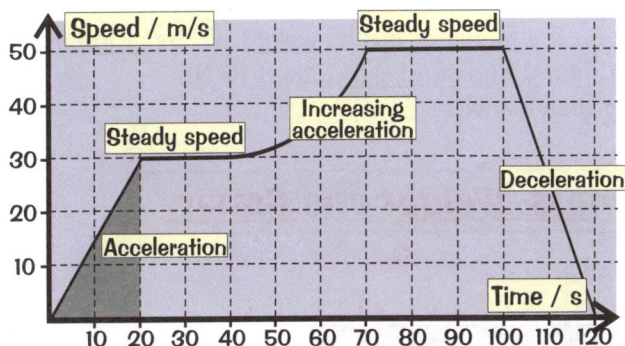

Very Important Notes:

1) <u>GRADIENT = ACCELERATION</u>.
2) <u>Flat sections</u> represent <u>steady speed</u>.
3) The <u>steeper</u> the gradient, the <u>greater</u> the <u>acceleration</u> or <u>deceleration</u>.
4) <u>Uphill</u> sections (/), +ve gradient, are <u>acceleration</u>.
5) <u>Downhill</u> sections (\), −ve gradient, are <u>deceleration</u>.
6) The <u>area</u> under any section of the graph is the <u>distance travelled</u> in that <u>time interval</u>.
7) A <u>curve</u> means <u>non-uniform</u> (<u>changing</u>) acceleration or deceleration.

Calculating Acceleration, Speed and Distance from a Speed-Time Graph

1) The <u>acceleration</u> in the <u>first section</u> of the graph = <u>gradient</u> = $\frac{\text{vertical}}{\text{horizontal}} = \frac{30}{20} =$ <u>1.5 m/s^2</u>

2) The <u>speed</u> at any point is simply found by <u>reading the value</u> off the <u>speed axis</u>.

3) The <u>distance travelled</u> in any time interval is equal to the <u>area</u> under the graph. E.g. the distance travelled in the first acceleration period is equal to the <u>shaded area</u> = ½ × 20 × 30 = <u>300 m</u>.

Speed is Just a Number, but Velocity Has Direction Too

1) The <u>speed</u> of an object is just <u>how fast</u> it's going — the <u>direction isn't important</u>. E.g. speed = 30 mph.
2) <u>Velocity</u> describes both the <u>speed and direction</u> of an object. E.g. velocity = 30 mph due north.
3) You can have <u>negative velocities</u>. If a car travelling at <u>20 m/s</u> then <u>turns around</u> to go in the opposite direction, the <u>speed</u> is still <u>20 m/s</u> but the <u>velocity</u> becomes <u>−20 m/s</u>.
4) If <u>two objects</u> are moving <u>parallel</u> to each other, their <u>relative velocity</u> is the <u>difference</u> in their velocities. E.g. two cars travelling at speeds of <u>30 m/s</u> in <u>opposite directions</u> have a <u>relative velocity</u> of <u>60 m/s</u> — because the <u>difference</u> between their <u>velocities</u> (30 and −30) is <u>60</u>.

Speed-time graphs — more fun than gravel (just)...

The tricky thing about graphs is that they can look the same but show <u>totally different</u> things. Make sure you can calculate both <u>speed</u> and <u>acceleration</u>, as well as being able to <u>rearrange the formulas</u> to calculate other things.

Mass, Weight and Gravity

Gravity attracts everything with mass, but you only notice it when one of the masses is really really big, like a planet. The weight of something depends on its mass, and how much gravity there is pulling it down.

Gravity is the Force of Attraction Between All Masses

1) On the surface of a planet, gravity makes all things accelerate towards the ground, all with the same acceleration, g.

2) So g is the acceleration due to gravity and it's also known as the gravitational field strength.

3) The value of g is about 10 m/s² (or 10 N/kg) on Earth. It's different on other planets though, and can even vary slightly in different places on Earth (e.g. g will be slightly different down a mineshaft compared to on top of a mountain). It's not affected by changes in the atmosphere though.

4) Gravity gives an object its weight — which is different from its mass.

5) Mass is just the amount of 'stuff' in an object. For any given object this will have the same value anywhere in the Universe.

6) Weight is caused by the pull of gravity.

7) Weight is a force measured in newtons (N). Mass is not a force. It's measured in kilograms.

8) An object has the same mass whether it's on Earth or on the Moon — but its weight will be different. A 1 kg mass will weigh less on the Moon (about 1.6 N) than it does on Earth (about 10 N), simply because the force of gravity pulling on it is less (see below).

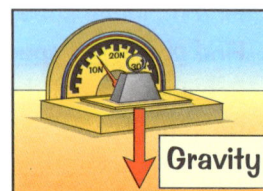

The Very Important Formula Relating Mass, Weight and Gravity

1) You need to know how to use this hideously easy formula:

$$\text{weight} = \text{mass} \times \text{gravitational field strength}$$

$$W = m \times g$$

EXAMPLE: What is the weight, in newtons, of a 5 kg chicken, both on Earth (g = 10 m/s²) and on the Moon (g = 1.6 m/s²)?

ANSWER: W = m × g
On Earth: Weight = 5 × 10 = 50 N
On the Moon: Weight = 5 × 1.6 = 8 N

2) You need to know how to rearrange it too:

EXAMPLE: The 5 kg chicken has a weight of 20 N on a mystery planet. What is the gravitational field strength of the planet?

ANSWER: Using the formula triangle: g = W ÷ m
So gravitational field strength = 20 ÷ 5 = 4 m/s²

(Remember — g is a measure of acceleration, so the units are m/s². Or you can use N/kg.)

Learn about gravity now — no point in "weighting" around...

Often the only way to "understand" something is to learn all the facts about it. And that's certainly true here. "Understanding" the difference between mass and weight is no more than learning all the facts about them. When you've learnt all those facts properly, you'll understand it. And make sure you can use that formula too.

Forces

A <u>force</u> is simply a <u>push</u> or a <u>pull</u>. There are only <u>six different forces</u> for you to know about:

1) GRAVITY or WEIGHT (see previous page) always acting <u>straight downwards</u>.
2) REACTION FORCE from a <u>surface</u>, usually acting <u>straight upwards</u>.
3) THRUST or PUSH or PULL due to an engine or rocket <u>speeding something up</u>.
4) DRAG or AIR RESISTANCE or FRICTION which is <u>slowing the thing down</u>.
5) LIFT due to an <u>aeroplane wing</u>.
6) TENSION in a <u>rope</u> or <u>cable</u>.

And there are basically only <u>five different force diagrams</u>:

1) Stationary Object — All Forces in Balance

1) The force of GRAVITY (or weight) is acting <u>downwards</u>.
2) This causes a REACTION FORCE from the surface <u>pushing up</u> on the object.
3) This is the <u>only way</u> it can be in BALANCE — balanced force arrows are <u>equal</u> in <u>size</u>.
4) <u>Without</u> a reaction force, it would <u>accelerate downwards</u> due to the pull of gravity.
5) Any HORIZONTAL forces must be <u>equal and opposite</u> otherwise the object will <u>accelerate sideways</u>.

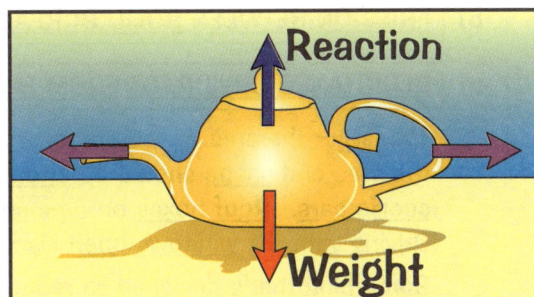

2) Steady Horizontal Speed — All Forces in Balance!

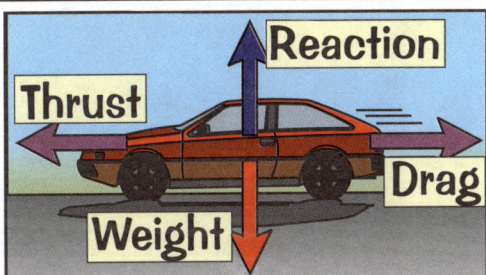

3) Steady Vertical Speed — All Forces in Balance!

This skydiver is free-falling at 'terminal speed' (see next page).

<u>Take note</u> — to move with a <u>steady speed</u> the forces must be in <u>balance</u>. If there is an <u>unbalanced force</u> then you get <u>acceleration</u>, not steady speed. That's <u>rrrreally important</u>.

4) Horizontal Acceleration — Unbalanced Forces

1) You only get <u>acceleration</u> with an overall <u>resultant</u> (unbalanced) <u>force</u>.
2) The <u>bigger</u> this <u>unbalanced force</u>, the <u>greater</u> the <u>acceleration</u>.
3) On a <u>force diagram</u> the <u>arrows</u> will be <u>unequal</u>.

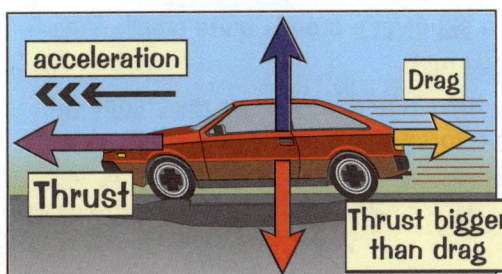

Note that the forces in the other direction (up and down) are still balanced (equal).

If drag was bigger than thrust you'd get deceleration.

5) Vertical Acceleration — Unbalanced Forces

Just after dropping out of the plane, the skydiver accelerates — see next page.

Accelerate your learning — force yourself to revise...

So, things <u>only accelerate</u> in a particular direction if there's an <u>overall force</u> in that direction. Simple.

Friction Forces and Terminal Speed

Imagine a world without <u>friction</u> — you'd be sliding around all over the place. Weeeeeeeeee.... Ouch.

Friction <u>WILL</u> Slow Things Down

1) When an object is <u>moving</u> (or trying to move) friction acts in the direction that <u>opposes movement</u>.

2) The frictional force will <u>match</u> the size of the <u>force</u> trying to move it, <u>up to a point</u>
   — after this the friction will be <u>less</u> than the other force and the object will <u>move</u>.

3) <u>Friction</u> will act to make the moving object <u>slow down and stop</u>.

4) So to travel at a <u>steady speed</u>, things always need a <u>driving force</u> to overcome the friction.

5) Friction occurs in <u>three main ways</u>:

   a) <u>FRICTION BETWEEN SOLID SURFACES WHICH ARE GRIPPING</u>   (static friction)

   b) <u>FRICTION BETWEEN SOLID SURFACES WHICH ARE SLIDING PAST EACH OTHER</u>

   c) <u>RESISTANCE OR "DRAG" FROM FLUIDS (LIQUIDS OR GASES</u>, e.g. AIR)

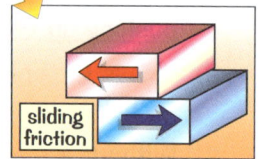
static friction

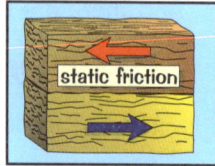
sliding friction

The larger the area of the object, the greater the drag. So, to <u>reduce drag</u>, the area and <u>shape</u> should be <u>streamlined</u> and <u>reduced</u>, like <u>wedge-shaped sports cars</u>. <u>Roof boxes</u> on cars <u>spoil this shape</u> and so <u>slow them down</u>. Driving with the <u>windows open</u> also <u>increases drag</u>.

Something that's designed to reduce your speed, e.g. a <u>parachute</u>, often has a <u>large area</u> to give a <u>high drag</u> to slow you down. For a given thrust, the <u>higher</u> the <u>drag</u>, the <u>lower</u> the <u>top speed</u> (see below). In a <u>fluid</u>: <u>FRICTION (DRAG) ALWAYS INCREASES AS THE SPEED INCREASES</u> — and don't forget it.

Moving Objects Can Reach a Terminal Speed

1) When objects <u>first set off</u> they have <u>much more</u> force <u>accelerating</u> them than <u>resistance</u> slowing them down.

2) As the <u>speed</u> increases, the resistance <u>increases</u> as well.

3) This gradually <u>reduces</u> the <u>acceleration</u> until the <u>resistance force</u> (friction or drag) is <u>equal</u> to the <u>accelerating force</u> (weight or thrust) so it can't accelerate any more. The forces are <u>balanced</u>.

4) It will have reached its maximum speed or <u>terminal speed</u>.

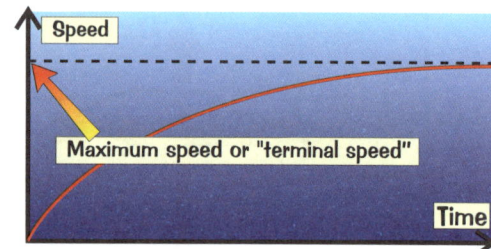
Speed

Maximum speed or "terminal speed"

Time

The Terminal Speed of Moving Objects Depends on Their Drag

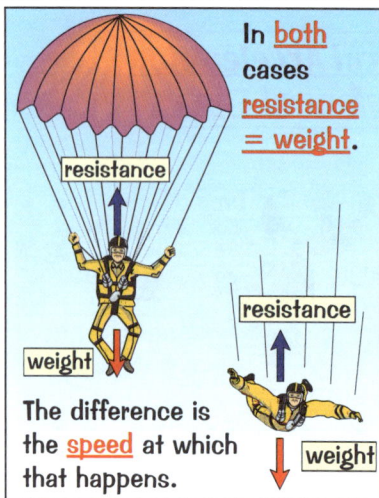

In <u>both</u> cases <u>resistance = weight</u>.

resistance

resistance

weight

weight

The difference is the <u>speed</u> at which that happens.

1) The <u>terminal speed</u> of <u>any moving object</u> depends on its <u>drag</u> compared to its <u>driving force</u> (weight for a falling object, thrust for, e.g. a car).

2) The <u>greater the drag</u>, the <u>lower the terminal speed</u> of the object, and the drag depends on its <u>shape and area</u>.

3) For example, think about a skydiver falling to Earth — the <u>driving (accelerating) force</u> acting on <u>all falling objects</u> is <u>gravity</u> and the <u>drag</u> (<u>air resistance</u>) depends on the skydiver's shape and area.

4) <u>Without</u> his parachute open, a <u>skydiver's</u> area is quite <u>small</u>. His <u>terminal speed</u> is about <u>120 mph</u>.

5) But with the parachute <u>open</u>, there's much more <u>air resistance</u> (at any given speed) but the <u>same force</u> (his weight) pulling him down.

6) This means his <u>terminal speed</u> comes right down to about <u>15 mph</u>, which is a <u>safe speed</u> to hit the ground at.

In space, where there's <u>no air</u>, everything falls at the <u>same speed</u>.

Air resistance — it can be a real drag...

Without friction, you wouldn't be able to walk or run or skip or write... hmm, not all bad then.

Forces and Acceleration

Things only underline accelerate or change direction if you give them a push. Makes sense.

A Balanced Force Means Steady Speed and Direction

> If the forces on an object are all BALANCED, then it'll keep moving at the SAME SPEED in the SAME DIRECTION (so if it starts off still, it'll stay still).

1) When an object is moving at a constant speed, without changing direction, then the forces on it must all be balanced (arrows are equal).

2) Things definitely DON'T need a constant overall force to keep them moving — NO NO NO NO!

3) To keep going at a steady speed, there must be zero resultant (overall) force.

An Unbalanced Force Means Acceleration

> If there is an UNBALANCED FORCE, the object will ACCELERATE in the direction of the force. The size of the acceleration is decided by: F = ma. This is NEWTON'S 2ND LAW OF MOTION.

1) An unbalanced force will always produce acceleration (or deceleration).

2) This 'acceleration' can take five different forms: starting, stopping, speeding up, slowing down and changing direction.

3) The arrows on a force diagram will be unequal:

The Overall Unbalanced Force is Often Called the Resultant Force

1) Any resultant force will produce acceleration and this is the formula for it:

$$\text{Force} = \text{mass} \times \text{acceleration}$$

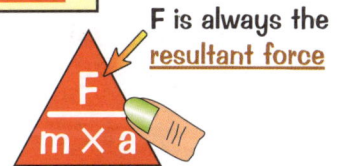

F is always the resultant force

2) In most real situations there are at least two forces acting on an object along any direction.

3) If the forces are parallel, the resultant force is found by just adding or subtracting them.

EXAMPLE: A car with a mass of 1750 kg has an engine which provides a driving force of 5200 N.
At 70 mph the drag force acting on the car is 5150 N.
Find its acceleration a) when first setting off from rest b) at 70 mph.

ANSWER: First draw a force diagram for both cases (no need to show the vertical forces):

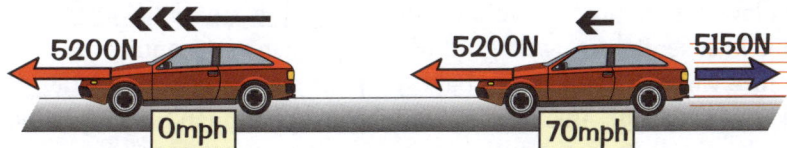

Remember — force is measured in newtons (N).

5200N   0mph

5200N   70mph   5150N

Work out the resultant force in each case, and use the formula triangle to find a.

a) Resultant force = 5200 N
a = F ÷ m
= 5200 ÷ 1750 = 3.0 m/s²

b) Resultant force = 5200 − 5150 = 50 N
a = F ÷ m
= 50 ÷ 1750 = 0.03 m/s²

Resultant force... I'm pretty sure that's a Steven Seagal film...

* Answer on page 116.

A 70 kg runner accelerates at 1.2 m/s². 8 N of drag are acting on the runner. Find the runner's driving force*.

Stopping Distances

The stopping distance of a car is the distance covered in the time between the driver first spotting a hazard and the car coming to a complete stop. Examiners are pretty keen on this stuff, so make sure you learn it.

Many Factors Affect Your Total Stopping Distance

The longer it takes to stop after spotting a hazard, the higher the risk of crashing into whatever's in front. The distance it takes to stop a car is divided into the THINKING DISTANCE and the BRAKING DISTANCE:

STOPPING DISTANCE = THINKING DISTANCE + BRAKING DISTANCE

1) Thinking Distance

"The distance the car travels in the time between the driver noticing the hazard and applying the brakes."

It's affected by TWO MAIN FACTORS:

a) **How FAST you're going** — obviously. Whatever your reaction time, the faster you're going, the further you'll go.

b) **How DOPEY you are** — This is affected by tiredness, drugs, alcohol, distractions, a lack of concentration and a careless blasé attitude.

Clown Hazard Ahead

2) Braking Distance

"The distance taken to stop once the brakes have been applied."

It's affected by FOUR MAIN FACTORS.
These are all to do with changes in speed, mass, braking force and friction:

a) **How FAST you're going** — The faster you're going, the further it takes to stop (see next page).

b) **How HEAVILY LOADED the vehicle is** — With the same brakes, the heavier the vehicle the longer it takes to stop. E.g. a car won't stop as quickly when it's full of people and luggage and towing a caravan.

c) **How good your BRAKES are** — Braking depends on how much force you apply — a little tap won't slow you down as much as if you put your foot down hard. Brakes must be checked and maintained regularly. If your brakes are worn or faulty you won't be able to brake with as much force, which will let you down catastrophically just when you need them the most, i.e. in an emergency.

d) **How good the GRIP is** — This depends on THREE THINGS:

1) Road surface — Leaves and diesel spills and muck on t'road are serious hazards.

2) Weather conditions — Wet or icy roads are always much more slippy than dry roads, but often you only discover this when you try to brake hard!

3) Tyres — By law, tyres should have a minimum tread depth of 1.6 mm. This is essential for getting rid of the water in wet conditions. A tyre without tread (i.e. a bald tyre) will simply ride on a layer of water and skid very easily. This is called 'aquaplaning' and isn't nearly as cool as it sounds.

Whatever the reason, if there's less friction between the car and the road then it takes longer to stop and the braking distance increases.

Bad visibility can also be a major factor in accidents — lashing rain, thick fog, bright oncoming lights, etc. might mean that a driver doesn't notice a hazard until they're quite close to it — so they have a much shorter distance available to stop in.

Stop right there — and learn this page...

Makes you think, doesn't it. Learn the details and write yourself a mini-essay to see how much you really know.

More on Stopping Distances

So now you know what affects <u>stopping distances</u>, let's have a look at the <u>facts and figures</u>.

Leave Enough Space to Stop

1) The figures below for <u>typical stopping distances</u> are from the <u>Highway Code</u>.
It's frightening to see just how far it takes to stop when you're going at 70 mph.

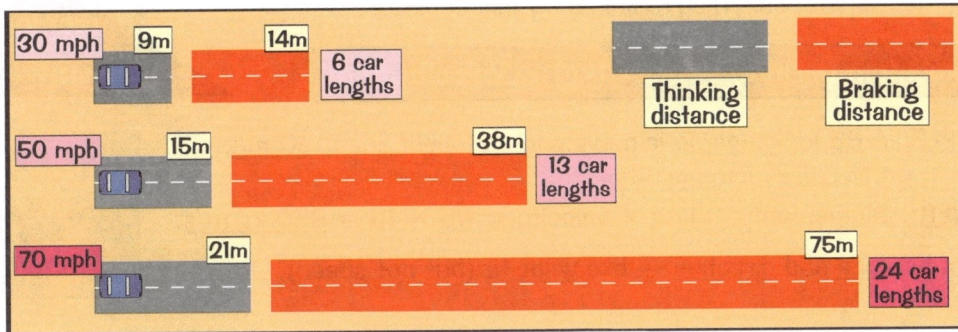

30 mph | 9m | 14m | 6 car lengths

Thinking distance | Braking distance

50 mph | 15m | 38m | 13 car lengths

70 mph | 21m | 75m | 24 car lengths

2) To <u>avoid an accident</u>, drivers need to leave <u>enough space</u> between their car and the one in front so that if they had to <u>stop suddenly</u> they would have time to do so <u>safely</u>. 'Enough space' means the <u>stopping distance</u> for whatever speed they're going at.

3) So even at <u>30 mph</u>, you should drive no closer than <u>6 or 7 car lengths</u> away from the car in front — just in case.

4) <u>Speed limits</u> are really important because <u>speed</u> affects the stopping distance so much — some <u>residential areas</u> are now <u>20 mph zones</u>.

Don't forget — things like bad weather and road conditions will make stopping distances even longer (see previous page).

Speed Affects Braking Distance More Than Thinking Distance

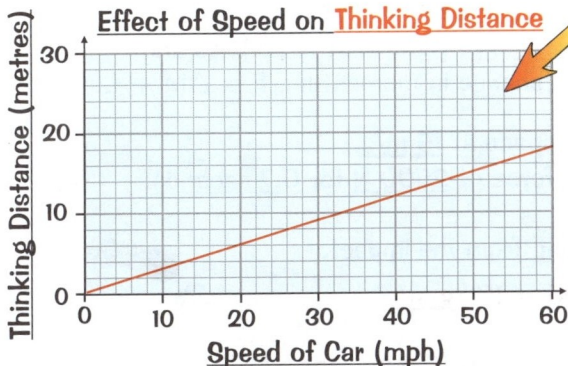

Effect of Speed on Thinking Distance

(graph: Thinking Distance (metres) vs Speed of Car (mph), linear line)

1) As a car <u>speeds up</u>, the <u>thinking distance increases</u> at the <u>same rate</u> as <u>speed</u>. The graph is <u>linear</u> (a <u>straight line</u>).

2) This is because the <u>thinking time</u> (how long it takes the driver to apply the brakes) stays pretty <u>constant</u> — but the higher the speed, the <u>more distance</u> you cover in that <u>same time</u>.

3) <u>Braking distance</u>, however, <u>increases faster</u> the <u>more</u> you <u>speed up</u>.

4) The <u>relationship</u> between <u>speed</u> and <u>braking distance</u> is a <u>squared</u> relationship.

5) This means as speed <u>doubles</u>, braking distance increases <u>4-fold</u> (2^2). And if speed <u>trebles</u>, braking distance increases <u>9-fold</u> (3^2). <u>Why</u> is explained on p.55.

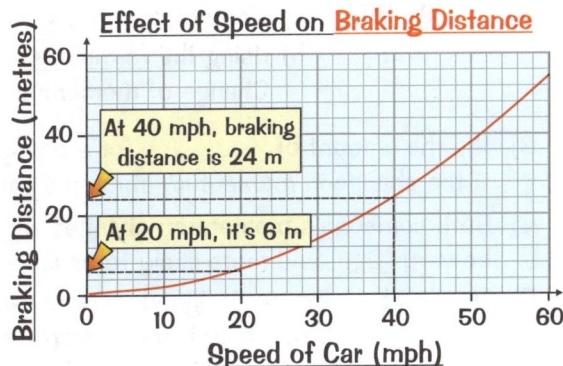

Effect of Speed on Braking Distance

(graph: Braking Distance (metres) vs Speed of Car (mph), curved line)

At 40 mph, braking distance is 24 m

At 20 mph, it's 6 m

Momentum

A <u>large</u> rugby player running very <u>fast</u> is going to be a lot harder to stop than a scrawny one out for a Sunday afternoon stroll — that's momentum for you.

Momentum = Mass × Velocity

1) The <u>greater</u> the <u>mass</u> of an object and the <u>greater</u> its <u>velocity</u>, the <u>more momentum</u> the object has. They're linked by this equation:

$$\text{Momentum (kg m/s)} = \text{Mass (kg)} \times \text{Velocity (m/s)}$$

$$\frac{\text{momentum}}{\text{mass} \times \text{velocity}}$$

EXAMPLE: A <u>65 kg</u> kangaroo is moving in a straight line at <u>10 m/s</u>. Calculate its <u>momentum</u>.

ANSWER: Momentum = mass × velocity = 65 × 10 = <u>650 kg m/s</u>.

2) Momentum has <u>size</u> and <u>direction</u> — like <u>velocity</u> (but not speed).

Forces Cause Changes in Momentum

1) When a <u>force</u> acts on an object, it causes a <u>change in momentum</u>.

$$\text{Force acting (N)} = \frac{\text{Change in momentum (kg m/s)}}{\text{Time taken for change to happen (s)}}$$

$$\frac{\Delta M}{F \times t}$$

2) You can use <u>Newton's 2nd Law</u> of motion (<u>force = mass × acceleration</u> — see p.49) to explain this:

- Any <u>force</u> applied to an object increases its <u>acceleration</u>, $F = m \times a$.
- And <u>acceleration</u> is just <u>change in velocity</u> over <u>time</u>, $a = \Delta v/t$ (see p.45).
- So a force applied to an object changes its <u>velocity</u> over <u>time</u>, $F = m \times \Delta v/t$.
- A <u>change in momentum</u> can be caused by a <u>change in velocity</u> ($\Delta M = m \times \Delta v$), so any <u>force applied</u> to an object over a certain time causes a change in momentum, $F = \Delta M \div t$.

EXAMPLE: A rock with mass <u>1 kg</u> is travelling through space at <u>15 m/s</u>. A comet hits the rock, giving it a resultant force of <u>2500 N</u> for <u>0.7 seconds</u>. Calculate a) the rock's <u>initial momentum</u>, and b) the <u>change</u> in its momentum resulting from the impact.

ANSWER: a) Momentum = mass × velocity = 1 × 15 = <u>15 kg m/s</u>
b) Using the <u>formula triangle</u>,
Change of momentum = force × time = 2500 × 0.7 = <u>1750 kg m/s</u>.

3) It's the amount of <u>time taken</u> for a change in momentum that determines how big or small the force is. If the change in momentum stays the same and <u>t is small</u>, <u>F will be big</u>, but if <u>t is big</u>, <u>F will be small</u>.

4) So if someone's momentum changes <u>very quickly</u> (like in a <u>car crash</u>), the <u>forces</u> on the body will be very <u>large</u>, and more likely to cause <u>injury</u>.

5) This is why cars are designed to slow people down over a <u>longer time</u> when they have a crash — the <u>longer</u> it momentum, the <u>smaller</u> the <u>force</u>, (see next page).

You can also think of a car crash as being a very fast deceleration (just a negative acceleration, remember). Because F = ma, any <u>large</u> deceleration causes a large force, which can lead to injury.

Car Safety

Cars have many <u>safety features</u> that are designed to <u>reduce the forces</u> acting on people involved in an accident. Smaller forces can mean <u>less severe injuries</u>.

Car Safety Features *Reduce the Forces Acting* in Accidents

1) In a collision, the <u>force</u> on an object can be lowered by <u>slowing the object down</u> over a <u>longer time</u>. This is because the <u>longer</u> it takes for a <u>change in momentum</u>, the <u>smaller the forces</u> acting (see previous page). Some <u>injuries</u> are caused by a <u>rapid deceleration</u> of parts of the body. Increasing the collision time <u>reduces deceleration</u> too (because $a = \Delta v \div t$).

2) These <u>safety features increase</u> the <u>collision time</u> to <u>reduce the forces</u> and <u>deceleration</u> to try and reduce injury.

- **CRUMPLE ZONES** crumple and <u>change shape</u> on impact, <u>increasing the time</u> taken for the car to stop.
- **SEAT BELTS** stretch slightly, <u>increasing</u> the <u>time taken</u> for the wearer to stop. This <u>reduces the forces</u> acting on the chest. (They need to be <u>replaced</u> after a crash though — they're <u>not as strong</u> once they've been stretched.)
- **AIR BAGS** also slow you down more <u>gradually</u>.

3) These safety features also <u>change shape</u> during a crash, which helps <u>absorb</u> some of the <u>kinetic energy</u> of the moving car.

4) They can also <u>reduce injuries</u> by <u>stopping</u> people <u>hitting hard surfaces</u> inside the car.

5) <u>Roads</u> can also be made safer by placing structures like <u>crash barriers</u> and <u>escape lanes</u> in dangerous locations (like on sharp bends or steep hills). These structures are designed to <u>increase the time</u> and <u>distance</u> of any collision — which means the <u>collision force</u> is <u>reduced</u>.

ABS Brakes *Help Drivers* Take Control *in an Emergency*

1) <u>ABS</u> (anti-lock braking system) <u>brakes</u> help drivers <u>keep control</u> of the car's <u>steering</u> when <u>braking hard</u>.

2) When a driver <u>brakes hard</u> (e.g. to avoid a <u>hazard</u>), <u>ordinary</u> brakes <u>lock the wheels</u> so they can't turn, which can cause the car to <u>skid</u>.

3) <u>ABS</u> brakes <u>automatically pump on and off</u> to stop the wheels locking and <u>preventing skidding</u>.

4) They can also give the car a <u>shorter braking distance</u> which could prevent a collision with a car in front.

Safety Features *Save Lives*

1) Safety features are <u>rigorously tested</u> to see how <u>effectively</u> they <u>save lives</u> or <u>stop injuries</u> in an accident.

2) Testing involves <u>crashing cars</u> containing <u>crash test dummies</u>, both <u>with and without</u> the safety feature in place, and watching <u>slow motion film footage</u> to see the results. The dummies have <u>sensors</u> at different places on their 'bodies' to show <u>where</u> a real person would be <u>injured</u>, and <u>how bad</u> the injury would be.

3) The tests are <u>repeated</u> using <u>different cars</u>, at <u>different speeds</u>, and using <u>different sized dummies</u>.

4) The results are then compared with <u>real data</u> on the <u>deaths</u> and <u>severe injuries</u> from <u>actual road accidents</u>. All this should be taken into account when deciding whether to fit or use a particular safety feature (although seatbelts are required by <u>law</u>).

5) <u>Crash tests</u> have shown that wearing a <u>seat belt</u> reduces the number of <u>fatalities</u> (deaths) in car accidents by about 50% and that <u>airbags</u> reduce the number of fatalities by about 30% — so they're well worth using.

6) The Department for Transport produce reports each year on <u>road traffic accidents</u> in the UK. They show a significant <u>reduction</u> in the number of deaths and serious injuries since the 1980s — probably due to the wide range of <u>safety features</u> found in cars since then.

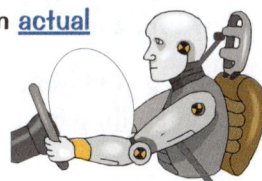

You might have to evaluate the effectiveness of different safety features. Think about the pros and cons and use any data you're given (see pages 6-8 for data analysis).

Belt up and start revising...

Back seat passengers who don't wear a seat belt will hit the front seat with a force of between <u>30 to 60 times</u> their body's weight in an accident at 30 mph — this is like the force you'd feel if you were sat on by an <u>elephant</u>.

Work Done and Gravitational Potential Energy

Time to get some work done on... er... <u>work done</u>. You'll need to muster up some <u>energy</u> too.

Work *is* Done **When a** *Force Moves an Object*

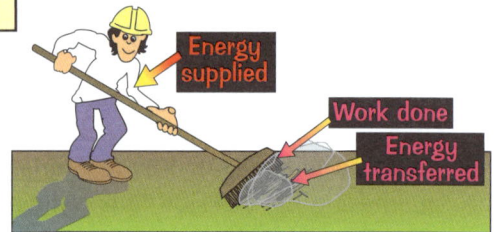

> When a **FORCE** makes an object **MOVE**,
> **ENERGY IS TRANSFERRED** and **WORK IS DONE**.

1) Whenever something <u>moves</u>, something else is providing some sort of '<u>effort</u>' to move it.

2) The thing putting the <u>effort</u> in needs a <u>supply</u> of energy (like <u>fuel</u> or <u>food</u> or <u>electricity</u> etc.).

3) It then does '<u>work</u>' by <u>moving</u> the object — and <u>transfers</u> the energy it receives (as fuel) into <u>other forms</u>.

4) Whether this energy is transferred '<u>usefully</u>' (e.g. by <u>lifting a load</u>) or is '<u>wasted</u>' (e.g. lost as <u>heat</u> through <u>friction</u>), you can still say that '<u>work is done</u>'. Just like Batman and Bruce Wayne, '<u>work done</u>' and '<u>energy transferred</u>' are indeed '<u>one and the same</u>'. (And they're both given in <u>joules</u>.)

5) The <u>formula</u> to calculate the <u>amount of work done</u> is:

$$\text{Work Done} = \text{Force} \times \text{Distance}$$

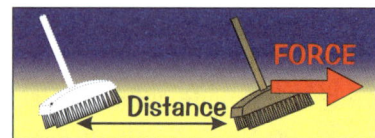

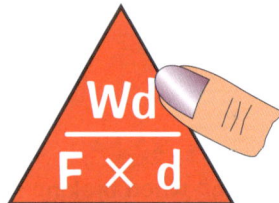

<u>EXAMPLE:</u> Some hooligan kids drag an old tractor tyre <u>5 m</u> over rough ground. They pull with a total force of <u>340 N</u>. a) Find the <u>energy transferred</u> dragging the tyre. b) <u>How far</u> could they pull the tyre using the same force but using <u>5100 J</u> of energy?

<u>ANSWER:</u> a) $Wd = F \times d = 340 \times 5 = \underline{1700 \text{ J}}$.
b) Using the formula triangle, $d = Wd \div F$, so $d = 5100 \div 340 = \underline{15 \text{ m}}$.

Gravitational Potential Energy **is Energy** *Due to Height*

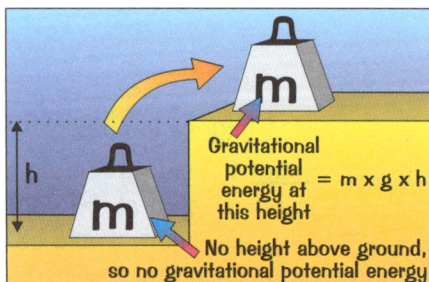

Gravitational potential energy at this height = m x g x h

No height above ground, so no gravitational potential energy

1) <u>Gravitational potential energy</u> (G.P.E.) is the energy that something has because of its <u>height</u> above the ground. The energy used to <u>raise</u> it is '<u>stored</u>', and can be <u>changed</u> to <u>kinetic energy</u> if it <u>falls</u>.

2) For example, a <u>lift</u> has a lot <u>more G.P.E.</u> on the <u>top floor</u> than it does at lower floors, because it is <u>higher</u> above the ground.

3) There are <u>other</u> types of <u>potential</u> energy too — e.g. <u>elastic</u> and <u>chemical</u>. G.P.E. is all about <u>height</u>.

4) G.P.E. can be found using this <u>formula</u>:

$$\text{G.P.E.} = \text{mass} \times g \times \text{height}$$

5) The <u>g</u> in the formula is <u>gravitational field strength</u> (see p.46). On <u>Earth</u>, g is about 10 m/s^2 (or <u>10 N/kg</u>).

<u>EXAMPLE:</u> A sheep of mass <u>47 kg</u> is slowly raised through <u>6.3 m</u>. Find its gain in gravitational potential energy.

<u>ANSWER:</u> Just plug the numbers into the formula:
G.P.E. = mgh = $47 \times 10 \times 6.3 = \underline{2961 \text{ J}}$.
(<u>Joules</u> because it's <u>energy</u>.)

Revise work done — what else...

Remember "<u>energy transferred</u>" and "<u>work done</u>" are the same thing. If you need a force to make something speed up (p.49), all that means is that you need to give it a bit of energy. Makes sense.

Kinetic Energy

Anything that's <u>moving</u> has <u>kinetic energy</u>. There's a slightly <u>tricky formula</u> for it, so you have to concentrate a little bit <u>harder</u> for this one. But hey, that's life — it can be real tough sometimes.

Kinetic Energy is Energy of Movement

1) The <u>kinetic energy</u> (<u>K.E.</u>) of something is the energy it has when <u>moving</u>.

2) The <u>kinetic energy</u> of something depends on both its <u>mass</u> and <u>speed</u>.

3) The <u>greater its mass</u> and the <u>faster it's going</u>, the <u>bigger</u> its kinetic energy will be.

4) For example, a <u>high-speed train</u>, or a <u>speedboat</u>, will have <u>lots of kinetic energy</u> — but your gran doing the weekly shop on her <u>little scooter</u> will only have a <u>little bit</u>.

5) You need to know how to use the <u>formula</u>:

$$\text{Kinetic Energy} = \tfrac{1}{2} \times \text{mass} \times \text{speed}^2$$

$$\frac{\text{K.E.}}{\tfrac{1}{2} \times m \times v^2}$$

EXAMPLE: A car of mass <u>1450 kg</u> is travelling at <u>28 m/s</u>. Calculate its kinetic energy.

ANSWER: It's pretty easy. You just plug the numbers into the formula — but watch the 'v^2'!
K.E. = $\tfrac{1}{2}mv^2$ = $\tfrac{1}{2} \times 1450 \times 28^2$ = <u>568 400 J</u>. (<u>Joules</u> because it's <u>energy</u>.)

6) If you <u>double the mass</u>, the <u>K.E. doubles</u>. If you <u>double the speed</u>, though, the <u>K.E. quadruples</u> (increases by a factor of <u>4</u>) — it's because of the 'v^2' in the formula.

small mass, not fast low kinetic energy	big fast lorries Ltd	big mass, real fast high kinetic energy

Stopping Distances Increase Alarmingly with Extra Speed
— Mainly Because of the v^2 Bit in the K.E. Formula

1) To stop a car, the <u>kinetic energy</u>, $\tfrac{1}{2}mv^2$, has to be <u>converted to heat energy</u> at the <u>brakes and tyres</u>:

$$\text{Kinetic Energy Transferred} = \text{Work Done by Brakes}$$
$$\tfrac{1}{2} \times m \times v^2 \qquad = \qquad F \times d$$

v = <u>speed</u> of car   F = maximum <u>braking force</u>   d = <u>braking distance</u>

2) The <u>braking distance</u> (d) increases as <u>speed squared</u> (v^2) increases — it's a <u>squared relationship</u>.

3) This means if you <u>double the speed</u>, you double the value of <u>v</u>, but the <u>v^2</u> means that the <u>K.E.</u> is then increased by a factor of <u>four</u>.

4) Because 'F' is always the <u>maximum possible</u> braking force (which <u>can't</u> be increased), <u>d</u> must increase by a factor of <u>four</u> to make the equation <u>balance</u>.

5) In other words, if you go <u>twice as fast</u>, the <u>braking distance</u> must increase by a <u>factor of four</u> to convert the <u>extra K.E.</u>

6) Increasing the speed by a <u>factor of 3</u> increases the K.E. by a factor of 3^2 (= <u>9</u>), so the braking distance becomes <u>9 times as long</u>.

7) <u>Doubling the mass</u> of the object <u>doubles the K.E.</u> it has — which will <u>double the braking distance</u>. So a big heavy lorry will need <u>more space to stop</u> than a small car.

Look back at pages 50-51 for more on braking distances.

Kinetic energy — just get a move on and learn it, OK...

So <u>that's</u> why braking distance goes up so much with speed. Bet you've been dying to find that out — and now you know. What you probably <u>don't</u> know yet, though, is that rather lovely formula at the top of the page. I mean, gosh, it's got more than two letters in it. So I'd hurry up and get it learnt if I were you.

Falling Objects and Roller Coasters

What goes up must come down — and transfer its <u>gravitational potential energy</u> to <u>kinetic energy</u> on the way.

Falling Objects Convert G.P.E. into K.E.

1) When something falls, its <u>gravitational potential energy</u> (G.P.E) is <u>converted</u> into <u>kinetic energy</u> (K.E.).

2) So the <u>further</u> it falls, the <u>faster</u> it goes.

3) You just need to remember this <u>simple</u> and <u>really quite obvious formula</u>:

> Kinetic Energy <u>gained</u> = Gravitational Potential Energy <u>lost</u>
> $$\tfrac{1}{2}mv^2 \qquad = \qquad mgh$$

EXAMPLE: A sheep of mass <u>52 kg</u> falls from the top of a building <u>30 m</u> high. Find the <u>speed</u> it hits the ground at (ignoring air resistance).

ANSWER: $\tfrac{1}{2}mv^2 = mgh$, so $\tfrac{1}{2} \times 52 \times v^2 = 52 \times 10 \times 30$
$26v^2 = 15\ 600$, so $v^2 = 15\ 600 \div 26 = 600$,
so $v = \sqrt{600} = \underline{24.5\ m/s}$.

Remember g is about 10 m/s².

G.P.E. ↓ K.E.

4) When a falling object reaches <u>terminal speed</u> (see p.48) its <u>speed can't increase</u> anymore, so its <u>K.E. doesn't increase</u>. Instead, the G.P.E. is transferred to <u>internal energy</u> of the object, or it's used <u>heating up</u> the <u>air particles</u> through <u>friction</u> — so it's turned into <u>thermal</u> energy. (This can happen even if it's not at terminal speed, but you're usually told to ignore air resistance in the exam question — so always use the formula above).

5) The formula can be <u>rearranged</u> to give: $\boxed{h = v^2 \div 2g}$ which will work for most things <u>falling to Earth</u>. As long as the <u>mass</u> of the object <u>doesn't change</u> while it's falling, the '<u>m</u>' on both sides of the equation will <u>cancel</u> out, leaving you with $\tfrac{1}{2}v^2 = gh$. Then <u>divide both sides</u> by <u>g</u> to get $h = v^2 \div 2g$.

6) This version can be used to easily find the <u>height</u> something needs to fall from to reach a <u>certain speed</u>, e.g. when designing a <u>roller coaster</u> (see below).

Roller Coasters Transfer Energy

1) At the top of a roller coaster (position A) the carriage has lots of <u>gravitational potential energy</u>.

2) As the carriage descends to position B, G.P.E. is transferred to <u>kinetic energy</u> and the carriage speeds up.

3) Between positions B and C the carriage keeps <u>accelerating</u> as its G.P.E. is converted into K.E.

4) If you <u>ignore</u> any <u>air resistance</u> or <u>friction</u> between the carriage and the track, then the carriage will have as much <u>energy</u> at C as it did at A. That energy must have been converted from G.P.E. to K.E. So at C the carriage has <u>minimum G.P.E.</u> and <u>maximum K.E.</u>

5) In a real roller coaster (that <u>does</u> have friction to deal with), the carriage has to have enough <u>kinetic energy</u> at point C to carry it up the hill again to D.

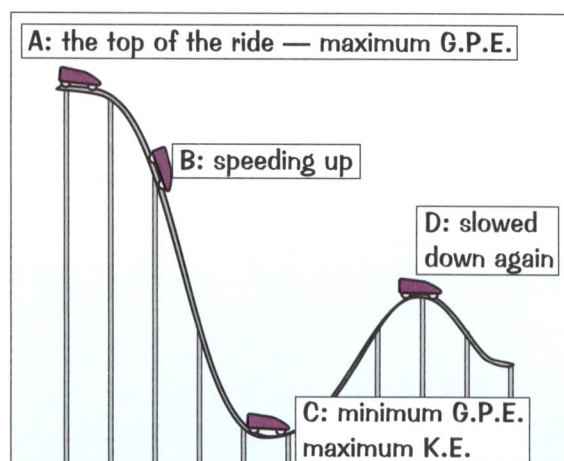

A: the top of the ride — maximum G.P.E.

B: speeding up

D: slowed down again

C: minimum G.P.E. maximum K.E.

Life is a roller coaster — just gotta ride it...

Now then, who said physics couldn't be fun? This has been a pretty <u>adrenaline-fuelled</u> section so far — I hope you're enjoying the ride. Even if you're not, you still need to know all this stuff for the exam, so get learning.

Power

Whenever I think of 'power', I have to stop myself saying things like 'mua haa haaarrr' and furtively plotting world domination whilst stroking a cat. It's hard being an evil genius (sigh).

Power *is the 'Rate of Doing Work' — i.e. How Much per Second*

POWER is not the same thing as force, nor energy. Power is a measure of how quickly work is being done.

A powerful machine is not necessarily one which can exert a strong force (though it usually ends up that way).

A POWERFUL machine is one which transfers A LOT OF ENERGY IN A SHORT SPACE OF TIME.

This is the very easy formula for power:

You might need to be able to answer questions where you have to calculate the work done first, so make sure you know how — see page 54.

$$\text{Power} = \frac{\text{Work done}}{\text{Time taken}}$$

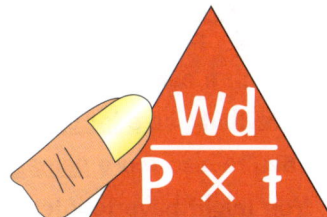

$$\frac{Wd}{P \times t}$$

MOTOR

4.8 kJ of useful energy in 2 minutes

EXAMPLE: A motor transfers 4.8 kJ of useful energy in 2 minutes. Find:
a) its power output, and b) how much work it could do in an hour.

ANSWER: a) 4.8 kJ = 4800 J, and 2 mins = 120 s. So
P = Wd / t = 4800/120 = 40 W (or 40 J/s — see below).
b) Using the formula triangle, Wd = P × t
P is 40 W (from a) and t = 1 h = 3600 s, so
Wd = 40 × 3600 = 144 000 J.

Power *is Measured in Watts (or J/s)*

The proper unit of power is the watt (W). 1 W = 1 J of energy transferred per second.

Power means 'how much energy per second', so watts are the same as 'joules per second' (J/s).

Don't ever say 'watts per second' — it's nonsense.

Power *is Also Force × Speed*

Sometimes you want to find the power of something based on force and speed.
The formula above can be written in a slightly different way to allow for this:

1) We know that work done is force × distance moved (see p.54).

2) And distance ÷ time is another way of writing speed (see p.44).

3) So combining these gives another formula for power:

$$\text{Power} = \text{Force} \times \text{Speed}$$

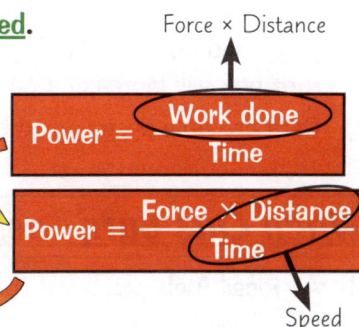

Force × Distance

$$\text{Power} = \frac{\text{Work done}}{\text{Time}}$$

$$\text{Power} = \frac{\text{Force} \times \text{Distance}}{\text{Time}}$$

Speed

EXAMPLE: A car's engine exerts a driving force of 1900 N when travelling at a speed of 25 m/s. Find its power output.

ANSWER: Power = Force × Speed = 1900 × 25 = 47 500 W (= 47.5 kW).

Watt are you waiting for — revise this stuff now...

The power of a car isn't always measured in watts — sometimes you'll see it in a funny unit called brake horsepower. James Watt defined 1 horsepower as the work done when a horse raises a mass of 550 lb (250 kg) through a height of 1 ft (0.3 m) in 1 second... as you do. I'd stick to watts if I were you.

Fuel Consumption and Emissions

A lot of us use cars to get us around and about, and lorries transport stuff around the country — but these forms of transport would be pretty useless if they didn't have any fuel to get them moving...

Fuel Consumption is All About the Amount of Fuel Used

1) The size and design of car engines determine how powerful they are.

2) The larger or more powerful an engine, the more energy it transfers from its fuel every second, so (usually) the higher the fuel consumption.

3) The fuel consumption of a car is usually stated as the distance travelled using a certain amount of fuel. Fuel consumption is often given in miles per gallon (mpg) or litres per 100 km (l/100 km) — e.g. a car with a fuel consumption of 5 l/100 km will travel 100 km on 5 litres of fuel.

4) Cars that use a lot of fuel compared to other cars are more expensive to run, because fuel costs money.

5) They're also more damaging to the environment, because fossil fuels pollute — see below and next page.

6) You might have to interpret data on fuel consumption — watch out for the units. A car with a low value for 'l/100 km' has a low fuel consumption — it doesn't need much fuel to travel 100 km. But a car with a low value for 'mpg' has a high fuel consumption — it means it won't travel very far on a gallon of fuel.

20 mpg = bad   60 mpg = good

Different Things Can Affect Fuel Consumption

1) A car's fuel consumption depends on many different things — e.g. the size of the engine, how the car is driven, the mass of the car, the speed it's driven at, the road conditions etc.

2) To move a car, the energy from the fuel needs to be changed into kinetic energy (K.E.). Since K.E. = ½mv² (see p.55), the higher the mass of the car (m) or the higher the speed you want it to go (v), the higher the K.E. will be — and so the more energy you need from fuel to give it that K.E.

3) So, in general, heavy cars have a higher fuel consumption than lighter cars, and the faster you drive the car the greater the fuel consumption too.

4) Cars work more efficiently at some speeds compared to others though — the most efficient speed is usually between 40 and 55 mph.

5) Driving style will also affect the fuel consumption — faster accelerations need more energy and so use more fuel. Frequent braking and acceleration (e.g. when driving in a town) will increase the fuel consumption. Driving in different road conditions can affect how much you need to brake too.

6) The energy from the fuel is also needed to do work against friction — e.g. between the tyres and the road, and between the car itself and the air around it. So, things like opening the windows or having a roof box will increase a car's fuel consumption because it increases air resistance and drag (see p.48).

7) Cars are now designed to be more fuel efficient — e.g. more efficient engines, more streamlined.

When Cars Burn Fuel they Release Emissions

1) As fossil fuels are burnt they release emissions — gases like CO_2, nitrogen dioxide (NO_2) and water vapour.

2) These emissions can cause environmental problems like acid rain and global warming.

3) In general, the higher the fuel consumption, the greater the emissions, and the worse for the environment.

4) But car manufacturers are changing the design of car engines to try and reduce emissions. Older cars often have worse fuel consumption and/or emission figures.

5) If you have to interpret data on emissions make sure you carefully read all the data given and check the units (there are lots of different ones that could be used, e.g. grams per unit distance like g/mile or g/km).

I bet this page has fuelled your enthusiasm...

You might get asked how to reduce the fuel consumption of a car, so it's important that you remember the different things that can affect fuel consumption — e.g. speed, friction, mass, driving style and conditions etc.

Fuels for Cars

We can't keep filling our fuel tanks with petrol and diesel forever.
Not only are they running out fast, but they're also bad for the environment. Eeep!

Most Cars Run on Fossil Fuels

1) All vehicles need a fuel to make them move — e.g. most cars and lorries use petrol or diesel.

2) Petrol and diesel are fuels that are made from oil, which is a fossil fuel. The emissions released when these fuels are burnt can cause environmental problems like acid rain and climate change.

3) Climate change is linked to an increase in greenhouse gases, such as carbon dioxide (CO_2), in the atmosphere. Fossil fuels produce a lot of carbon dioxide when they're burnt.

4) Fossil fuels are also non-renewable, so one day they'll run out — not good news if your car runs on them.

5) In the future we may have to rely on renewable sources of energy such as biofuels or solar power to power our vehicles (see below).

Some Cars Run On Biofuels

1) To get around some of the problems with petrol and diesel fuels, scientists are developing engines that run on alternative types of fuel, such as biofuels.

2) Biofuels are made from plants and organic waste, and are renewable — they won't run out because we can keep growing more.

3) Like fossil fuels, biofuels give off carbon dioxide when they're burnt. BUT because plants (grown to make the biofuel) also take in CO_2 when they're growing, there is no overall increase in the amount of CO_2 in the atmosphere when the biofuels are burnt. So if we switch from fossil fuels to biofuels, the overall CO_2 emissions could be reduced.

4) Burning biofuels when driving the cars doesn't produce as much other pollution (pollution at the point of use) as burning fossil fuels either.

5) BUT the cars themselves still have to be produced though and pollution is created in their production.

Electric Cars Need To Be Recharged

1) A few vehicles use large batteries to power electric motors.

2) These vehicles don't release any pollution at the point of use when they're driven, but their batteries need to be charged using electricity.

3) This electricity is likely to come from power stations that do pollute though — most power stations currently just burn fossil fuels to produce electricity.

4) One way around this is to use solar power — vehicles can have solar panels which change the energy from the sun into electricity to power the motor.

5) Solar-powered vehicles produce no pollution at the point of use, and there's also no pollution from making the electricity in this way. So solar panels could reduce overall CO_2 emissions from vehicles.

6) But electric cars and solar panels are expensive to make and buy, and pollution is created during their production too.

7) Currently, electric cars have limited performance compared to ordinary fossil fuel cars. But that is changing — newer, better designs are coming out all the time.

Make sure you can describe arguments for and against electrically-powered cars.

"I pity the fuel" — Mr T, campaigner for electric vehicles...

Almost done for another section — just one lovely little page of questions to go. Make sure you learn this page first though. You need to know about the ways we can power our cars without fossil fuels — biofuels, batteries and solar panels — and how they can reduce pollution. Of course, the humble bicycle is always an option too...

Revision Summary for Module P3

Well done, you've made it to the end of this section. There are loads of bits and bobs about forces, motion and fast cars which you definitely have to learn — and the best way to find out what you know is to get stuck in to these lovely revision questions, which you're going to really enjoy (honest)...

1)* A partly chewed mouse starting from rest reaches a speed of 0.08 m/s in 35 seconds. How far does it travel in that time?

2) Explain how to calculate speed from a distance-time graph.

3)* What's the acceleration of a soggy pea flicked from rest to a speed of 14 m/s in 0.4 seconds?

4) Explain how to find speed, distance and acceleration from a speed-time graph.

5) Explain the difference between mass and weight. What's the formula for weight?

6) Draw and label a diagram to show the forces acting on a stationary owl sat on a (stationary) rock.

7) Describe the effect on the top speed of a car of adding a roof box. Explain your answer.

8) Describe how air resistance is affected by speed.

9) What is "terminal speed"? What two main factors affect the amount of drag on a falling object?

10) If an object has zero resultant force on it, can it be moving? Can it be accelerating?

11)* A force of 30 N pushes a trolley of mass 4 kg. What will be its acceleration?

12) What are the two different parts of the overall stopping distance of a car?

13) List all the factors which affect each of the two parts of the stopping distance.

14) How does thinking distance change as speed increases?

15) If speed doubles, what happens to the braking distance?

16)* A 6 kg ferret has a momentum of 45 kg m/s. What is its velocity?

17)* The same ferret is hit by a speeding vole with a force of 70 N for 0.5 s. Calculate the ferret's change in momentum.

18) Explain how seat belts, crumple zones and air bags are useful in a crash.

19) How do ABS brakes make driving safer?

20)* A crazy dog drags a big branch 12 m over the next-door neighbour's front lawn, pulling with a force of 535 N. How much work was done?

21)* Calculate the increase in gravitational potential energy when a box of mass 12 kg is raised by 4.5 m. (g = 10 N/kg.)

22)* Find the kinetic energy of a 78 kg sheep moving at 23 m/s.

23) How does the kinetic energy formula explain the effect of speed on the stopping distance of a car?

24)* At the top of a roller coaster ride a carriage has 150 kJ of G.P.E. Ignoring friction, how much K.E. will the carriage have at the bottom (where G.P.E. = 0)?

25)* Calculate the speed of a 78 kg sheep just as it hits the floor after falling 20 m. Ignore air resistance.

26)* An electric motor uses 540 kJ of electrical energy in 4.5 minutes. What is its power consumption?

27)* Calculate the power output of a sheep running at 20 m/s exerting a force of 500 N.

28) Describe the relationship between the power of a car's engine and its fuel consumption.

29) Give three factors that affect the fuel consumption of a car.

30) Electric vehicles don't give out polluting gases directly, but they still cause pollution. Explain why.

* Answers on page 116.

Estimating Population Sizes

1) A <u>POPULATION</u> is <u>all</u> the organisms of <u>one species</u> in a <u>habitat</u> (the place where an organism lives).

2) Populations of <u>different species</u> in a habitat make up a <u>COMMUNITY</u>.

Estimate Population Sizes by Scaling Up from a Small Sample Area

A <u>quadrat</u> is a square frame enclosing a known area. You can study the <u>small area</u> within a quadrat and <u>scale up</u> your findings to make <u>estimates</u> for <u>larger areas</u>:

1) Count all the organisms in a <u>1 m² quadrat</u>.

2) Multiply the number of organisms by the <u>total area</u> (in m²) of the habitat.

Example: Estimate the total populations of the various species in a 120 m² field if a 1 m² quadrat contained 90 grass plants, 30 buttercups and 25 daisies.

Answer: Multiply the figures for the 1 m² quadrat by 120 to estimate the populations in the whole field. So the field will contain about 10 800 grass plants, 3600 buttercups and 3000 daisies.

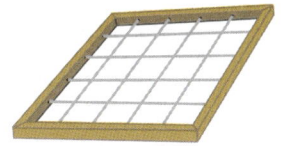

A quadrat

Estimate Population Sizes Using Capture-Recapture

To estimate <u>population size</u> using the capture-recapture method:

1) <u>Capture</u> a <u>sample</u> of the population and <u>mark</u> the animals in a <u>harmless</u> way.

2) <u>Release</u> them back into the environment.

3) <u>Recapture</u> another sample of the population. <u>Count</u> how many of this sample are marked.

4) <u>Estimate</u> population size using this equation:

$$\text{Population Size} = \frac{\text{number in first sample} \times \text{number in second sample}}{\text{number in second sample previously marked}}$$

Example: A pitfall trap was set up in an area of woodland. 30 woodlice were caught in an hour and marked on their shell, before being released back into the environment. The next day, 35 woodlice were caught in an hour, only 5 of which were marked. Estimate the population size.

A pitfall trap

Answer: Multiply the number of woodlice in the first sample by the number in the second sample, then divide the answer by the number that were marked in the second sample. So the area of woodland will contain about (30 × 35) ÷ 5 = 210 woodlice.

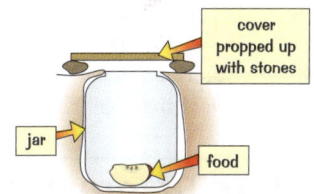

A Few Important Points About These Methods:

1) The <u>sample size</u> affects the <u>accuracy</u> of the estimate — the <u>bigger</u> your sample, the <u>more accurate</u> your estimate of the total population is likely to be.

2) When you're using <u>capture-recapture data</u> you have to make the following <u>assumptions</u>:

- There have been <u>no changes</u> in the population size due to <u>deaths</u>, <u>immigration</u> (individuals moving into the area) or <u>emigration</u> (individuals moving out of the area).
- The <u>sampling methods</u> for the capture and recapture were <u>identical</u> (e.g. the pitfall trap was set up in the same way each time).
- The <u>marking</u> hasn't affected the individuals' chances of <u>survival</u> (e.g. by making them more visible to predators).

Counting insects — avoid the pitfalls...

<u>Whenever</u> you're estimating the size of a population, you should make sure that your sample is <u>representative</u> of the whole population (i.e. what you find in your sample is broadly similar to what you'd find in the population).

Ecosystems and Distribution of Organisms

If you like getting down on your hands and knees and poking around at plants, you're in for a treat...

Ecosystems are Self-Supporting

1) An ecosystem is all the organisms living in a particular area, as well as all the non-living (abiotic) conditions, e.g. temperature, salinity and soil quality (see next page).

2) An ecosystem isn't the same as a habitat — a habitat is just the place where an organism lives.

3) Ecosystems are self-supporting — they contain (almost) everything they need to maintain themselves. Water, nutrients and essential elements like carbon all get recycled within the ecosystem.

4) The only thing that's needed from outside the ecosystem is an energy source. This is normally the Sun.

Transects are used to Investigate the Distribution of Organisms

1) Distribution is where organisms are found within a particular area.

2) You can investigate distribution using lines called transects.

3) To do a transect, you mark out a line using a tape measure and place quadrats next to each other all the way along the line. You then count and record the organisms you find in the quadrats.

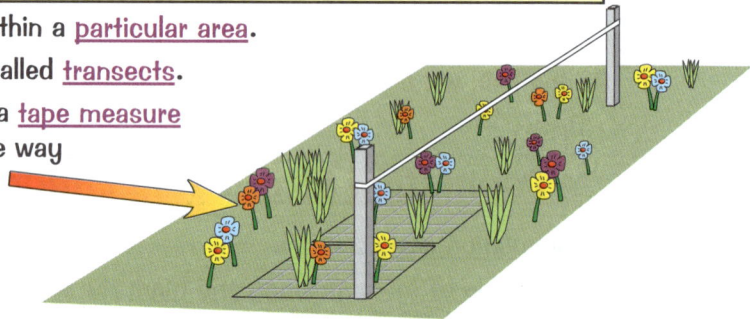

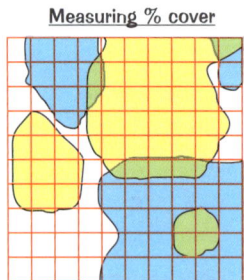

Measuring % cover

Organism Type A
42 squares
= 42%

Organism Type B
47 squares
= 47%

You count a square if it's more than half covered.

4) If it's difficult to count all the individual organisms in the quadrat (e.g. if they're grass) you can calculate the percentage cover. This means estimating the percentage area of the quadrat covered by a particular type of organism, e.g. by counting the number of little squares covered by the organisms.

5) You can plot the results of a transect in a kite diagram (see below). This allows you to map the distribution of organisms in an area.

Kite Diagrams Show the Abundance and Distribution of Organisms

The kite diagram below shows the distribution and abundance (number) of organisms along a transect in coastal sand dunes:

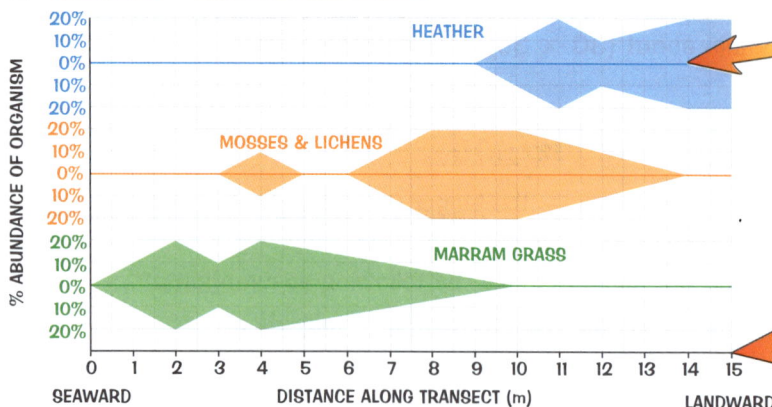

HEATHER

MOSSES & LICHENS

MARRAM GRASS

% ABUNDANCE OF ORGANISM

0 1 2 3 4 5 6 7 8 9 10 11 12 13 14 15
SEAWARD   DISTANCE ALONG TRANSECT (m)   LANDWARD

The abundance of each organism is shown by the thickness of the kite shape. The abundance is plotted above and below a central line to make the shape symmetrical.

The x-axis shows the distance along the transect line.

From the kite diagram you can see that marram grass was distributed between 0 and 10 m along the transect. At 2 m along the transect the abundance of marram grass was 20% (i.e. it covered 20% of the quadrat). At 7 m the abundance of marram grass was 10%.

Kite diagrams — to show your parents exactly how it got stuck in the tree...

Granted — this isn't the most adrenaline-fuelled wonder-page — but you still need to know it. Making sure you know the basics from this page and the previous one will make the rest of this section seem a lot easier.

Zonation

You need to know the factors that affect where organisms are found. You also need to know about a thing called zonation — thankfully, here's a page that'll tell you just that.

The Distribution of Organisms is Affected by Abiotic Factors

1) Abiotic factors are all the non-living, physical factors in an environment — e.g. light, temperature, water, oxygen, salinity (salt level) and soil quality.

2) The distribution of organisms is affected by abiotic factors because:

- Organisms are adapted to live in certain physical conditions. This means they're more likely to survive and reproduce in areas with these conditions. E.g. woodland ferns are adapted to living in shade, so you don't often find them growing in sunny, open spaces.
- Many organisms can only survive in the conditions they're adapted to. E.g. mosquitoes are adapted to live in warm climates — they can't survive in extreme cold.

Warm, sunny, by the sea — perfect abiotic conditions...

Changes in Abiotic Factors Can Lead to Zonation

ZONATION IS THE GRADUAL CHANGE IN THE DISTRIBUTION OF SPECIES ACROSS A HABITAT.

A gradual change in abiotic factors can lead to the zonation of organisms in a habitat. For example, in a coastal habitat, changes in salinity and soil depth result in zones where different types of plants grow:

1) Few plants can grow in zone 1 because salinity is very high — marram grass can grow because it is adapted to the salty conditions.

2) In zone 2, lichens and mosses can grow. They out-compete the marram grass because they're better adapted to the less saline conditions.

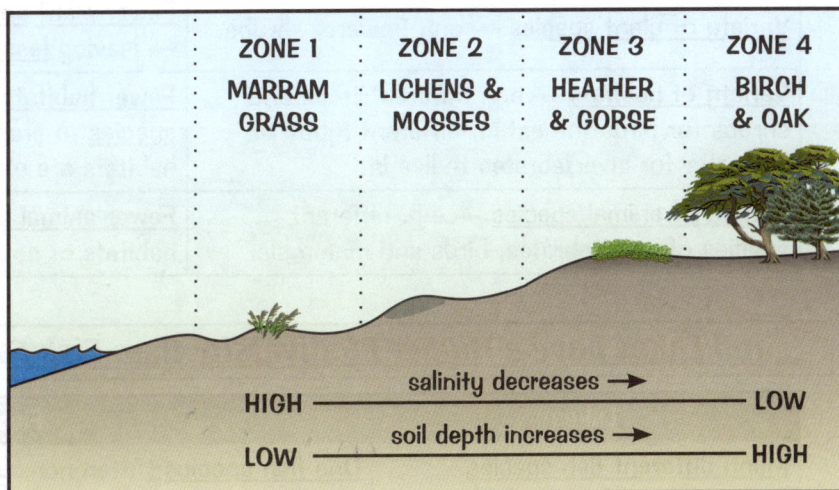

ZONE 1 — MARRAM GRASS

ZONE 2 — LICHENS & MOSSES

ZONE 3 — HEATHER & GORSE

ZONE 4 — BIRCH & OAK

HIGH —— salinity decreases → —— LOW

LOW —— soil depth increases → —— HIGH

3) In zone 3, shrubs such as heather and gorse can grow and they out-compete the lichens and mosses. This is because they're better adapted to the lower salinity and deeper soil further away from the shore.

4) In zone 4, trees such as birch and oak can grow and they out-compete the shrubs. This is because they're better adapted to the very low salinity and deep soil that's found even further inland.

Believe it or not — there's a reason that penguins don't live in the Sahara...

...and giraffes don't live in the sea. It sounds pretty straightforward, but make sure you can explain everything on this page — even the really tricky stuff, like the zonation bit. Sketching out the diagram should help.

Biodiversity

Biological + diversity = Biodiversity. Simple. There's a bit more to it than that actually — enjoy.

Biodiversity is a Measure of the Variety of Life in an Area

Biodiversity includes:

1) The amount of variation between individuals of the same species in an area.
2) The number of different species in an area.
3) The number of different habitats in an area.

Biodiversity is important — ecosystems with a high level of biodiversity are healthier than those without. This is because more diverse ecosystems are better able to cope with changes in the environment.

Natural Ecosystems have a Higher Biodiversity than Artificial Ones

1) Natural ecosystems maintain themselves without any major interference from humans — e.g. native woodlands and natural lakes.
2) Artificial ecosystems are created and maintained by humans — e.g. forestry plantations and fish farms.

Native Woodlands have a Higher Biodiversity than Forestry Plantations...

Native Woodlands	Forestry Plantations
Variety of tree species — e.g. birch, hazel, oak.	One species of tree (often non-native) is planted for timber — e.g. Corsican pine or Douglas fir.
Trees are different sizes and ages.	Blocks of trees are planted at the same time — so many trees are the same age.
Variety of plant species — e.g. flowers, shrubs.	Fewer plant species because trees are densely planted — leaving less room and light for other plants.
Variety of habitats — e.g. different trees and shrubs for birds to nest in, different types of leaf litter for invertebrates to live in.	Fewer habitats because there aren't enough plant species to create them. When trees are felled, habitats are also disturbed or destroyed.
Variety of animal species — e.g. different species of invertebrates, birds and mammals.	Fewer animal species because there aren't as many habitats or sources of food.

...and Lakes have a Higher Biodiversity than Fish Farms

Lakes	Fish Farms
Many different fish species.	One fish species (often non-native) is farmed for food.
Variety of plant species.	Fewer plant species. This is because fish food is added and the food waste can cause algal blooms (rapid algal growth). The blooms block out the light, killing plants.
Variety of animal species, e.g. invertebrates, birds, mammals.	Fewer animals species. Predators (e.g. herons, otters) are kept out and pests (e.g. fish lice) are killed. There's also less food and fewer habitats because of the lack of plants.

Biodiversity — sounds like a washing powder...

Getting your head around exactly what biodiversity actually is is really important. Lots of people make the mistake of thinking that it's just the total number of species in a particular habitat. Luckily — you know better.

Photosynthesis

There's a fair old bit to learn about photosynthesis, so make sure you've had a snack before you start.

Photosynthesis is a Two-Stage Process

1) Photosynthesis uses energy from the Sun to change carbon dioxide and water into glucose and oxygen.

2) It takes place in chloroplasts in plant cells — they contain pigments like chlorophyll that absorb light energy.

3) The overall balanced symbol equation for photosynthesis is:

carbon dioxide   water   glucose   oxygen

$$6CO_2 + 6H_2O \xrightarrow[\text{chlorophyll}]{\text{LIGHT ENERGY}} C_6H_{12}O_6 + 6O_2$$

4) Even though the equation above looks like a single chemical reaction, photosynthesis actually happens in two main stages.

5) First, light energy is used to split water into oxygen gas and hydrogen ions.

6) Carbon dioxide gas then combines with the hydrogen ions to make glucose and water.

7) Watch out though — water isn't one of the overall products of photosynthesis (because more gets used up in the first stage than is made in the second stage).

Glucose is Converted into Other Substances

Here's how plants use the glucose they make:

For Respiration ①

Plants use some of the GLUCOSE for RESPIRATION. This releases energy so they can convert the rest of the glucose into various other useful substances.

Stored in Seeds ③

GLUCOSE is turned into LIPIDS (fats and oils) for storing in seeds. Sunflower seeds, for example, contain a lot of oil — we get cooking oil and margarine from them.

Making Proteins ⑤

GLUCOSE is combined with nitrates (collected from the soil) to make amino acids, which are then made into PROTEINS. These are used for growth and repair.

② Making Cell Walls

GLUCOSE is converted into CELLULOSE for making cell walls, especially in a rapidly growing plant.

④ Stored as Starch

GLUCOSE is turned into STARCH and stored in roots, stems and leaves, ready for use when photosynthesis isn't happening, like at night.

STARCH is INSOLUBLE, which makes it good for storing. This is because:

- It can't dissolve in water and move away from storage areas in solution.

- It doesn't affect the water concentration inside cells — soluble substances would bloat the storage cells by drawing in water.

Convert this page into stored information...

Photosynthesis is important. All the energy we get from eating comes from it. When we eat plants, we're consuming the energy they've made, and when we eat meat, we're eating animals who got their energy from eating plants, or from eating animals that have eaten other animals who have... and so on.

Understanding Photosynthesis

We now know that plants get their food from photosynthesis — but it's taken us a while to work it out.

Greek Scientists Concluded That Plants Gain Mass from Soil Minerals

1) Around 350 BC Greek scientists (including Aristotle) studied plant growth.
2) They observed that the only thing touching plants was soil, so they decided that plants must grow and gain mass by taking in minerals from the soil (air touches plants too, but they couldn't see that).

Van Helmont Decided That Plants Gain Mass by Taking in Water

1) In 1648 Jan van Helmont set up the following experiment:
   • He dried some soil, weighed it, and put it in a pot.
   • He planted a willow tree weighing 2.2 kg in the soil.
   • He added rainwater to the pot whenever it was dry.
2) 5 years later van Helmont removed the tree from the pot:
   • The tree weighed 76.7 kg — so it had gained 74.5 kg of mass.
   • He dried the soil and weighed it — its mass had changed very little (it weighed about 60 g less).
3) Van Helmont concluded that because the weight of the soil had changed so little, the tree must have gained mass from another source. Because he only added water to the tree, he concluded the tree must have gained mass by taking in water.
4) Today we know that plants also gain mass using CO_2 from the air — but this experiment was important because it introduced the idea that plants don't just gain mass by taking in minerals from the soil.

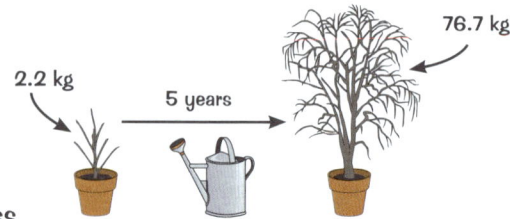

Priestley's Experiments Showed that Plants Produce Oxygen

1) In the early 1770s Joseph Priestley did the following experiment:
   • He placed a burning candle in a sealed container and observed that the flame went out after a short time. The candle couldn't be re-lit while in the container.
   • He then placed a burning candle and a living plant in the container. The flame went out after a short time, but after a few weeks the candle could be re-lit.
2) He decided that the burning candle used up something in the container — and that this made the flame go out. He also decided that the living plant 'restored the air' so the candle could burn again.
3) Priestley also did this experiment:
   • He filled a sealed container with exhaled air. He put a mouse in the container, and observed that it only survived for a few seconds.
   • He filled another sealed container with exhaled air. He put a living plant in the container and waited for a few days. He then put a mouse in the container — this time it survived for several minutes (lucky thing).
4) He thought that the mouse couldn't survive for long in the exhaled air because breathing had taken something out of the air. Again, he decided that the living plant 'restored the air' — this time allowing the mouse to survive for longer.
5) From these experiments, Priestley concluded that plants restore something to the air that burning and breathing take out. Today we know that this substance is oxygen — a product of photosynthesis.

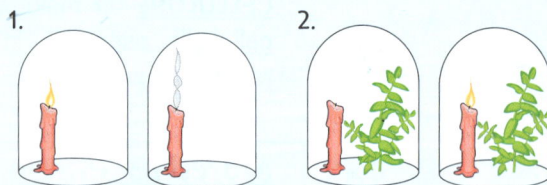

I don't understand 'Understanding Photosynthesis'...

Putting a mouse in a jar of carbon dioxide and noticing that it dies doesn't sound like a particularly cutting-edge investigation — but the experiments on this page all contributed hugely to our understanding of photosynthesis.

More on Photosynthesis

Here's some other wonderful stuff that scientists have worked out about photosynthesis.

The Oxygen Produced in Photosynthesis Comes From Water

1) Scientists realised that plants release oxygen during photosynthesis, but they didn't know whether the oxygen came from carbon dioxide or water (both of which contain oxygen atoms).

2) To find out where the oxygen came from, a scientist supplied plants with water containing an isotope of oxygen called oxygen-18. The carbon dioxide the plants received contained ordinary oxygen-16.

Isotopes are just different forms of the same element.

3) It was found that when the plants photosynthesised, they released oxygen-18.

4) This showed that the oxygen came from the water that was supplied to the plant, not the carbon dioxide.

There are Three Limiting Factors that Control the Rate of Photosynthesis

1) Not Enough LIGHT Slows Down the Rate of Photosynthesis

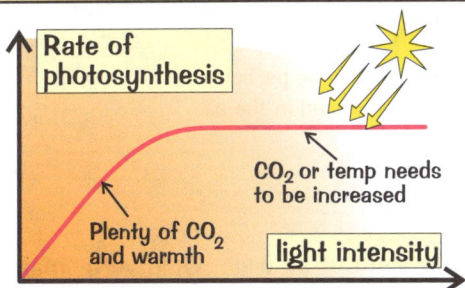
Rate of photosynthesis / CO_2 or temp needs to be increased / Plenty of CO_2 and warmth / light intensity

Light provides the energy needed for photosynthesis.

1) If the light level is raised, the rate of photosynthesis will increase, but only up to a certain point.

2) Beyond that, it won't make any difference because then it'll be either the temperature or the CO_2 level which is now the limiting factor.

2) Too Little CARBON DIOXIDE Also Slows It Down

CO_2 is one of the raw materials needed for photosynthesis — only 0.04% of the air is CO_2, so it's pretty scarce as far as plants are concerned.

1) As with light intensity, the amount of CO_2 will only increase the rate of photosynthesis up to a point. After this the graph flattens out, showing that CO_2 is no longer the limiting factor.

2) As long as light and CO_2 are in plentiful supply then the factor limiting photosynthesis must be temperature.

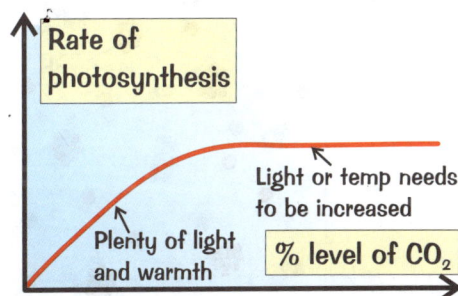
Rate of photosynthesis / Light or temp needs to be increased / Plenty of light and warmth / % level of CO_2

3) The TEMPERATURE Has to be Just Right

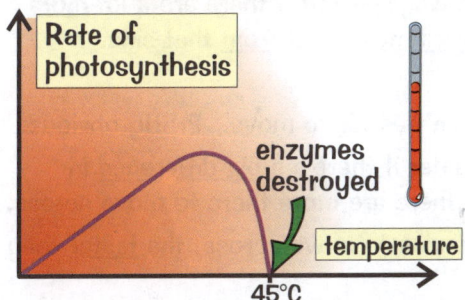
Rate of photosynthesis / enzymes destroyed / temperature / 45°C

Photosynthesis works best when it's warm but not too hot.

1) As the temperature increases, so does the rate of photosynthesis. But if the temperature is too high, the plant's enzymes will be denatured (see page 14), so the rate rapidly decreases.

2) This happens at about 45 °C (which is pretty hot for outdoors, though greenhouses can get that hot if you're not careful).

3) Usually though, if the temperature is the limiting factor it's because it's too low, and things need warming up a bit.

Life isn't all fun and sunshine...

There are three limiting factors, a graph for each and an explanation of why the rate of photosynthesis levels off or falls abruptly. After you've read over the page, cover it up and jot down the graphs and explain why they're the shapes that they are. It's not my idea of fun (honest) but it's the best way to get stuff lodged in your brain.

Diffusion

Particles <u>move about randomly</u>, and after a bit they end up <u>evenly spaced</u>. And that's how most things move about in our bodies — by "diffusion".

Don't be Put Off by the Fancy Word

"<u>Diffusion</u>" is simple. It's just the <u>gradual movement</u> of particles from places where there are <u>lots</u> of them to places where there are <u>fewer</u> of them. That's all it is — just the <u>natural tendency</u> for stuff to <u>spread out</u>. Unfortunately you also have to learn the fancy way of saying the same thing, which is this:

DIFFUSION is the NET MOVEMENT OF PARTICLES from an area of HIGHER CONCENTRATION to an area of LOWER CONCENTRATION

Diffusion happens in both <u>liquids</u> and <u>gases</u> — that's because the <u>individual particles</u> in these substances are free to <u>move about randomly</u>. The <u>simplest type</u> is when different <u>gases</u> diffuse through each other. This is what's happening when the smell of perfume diffuses through the air in a room:

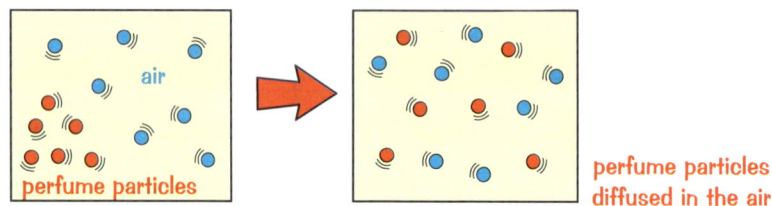

air

perfume particles

perfume particles diffused in the air

Cell Membranes are Kind of Clever...

They're clever because they <u>hold</u> the cell together <u>BUT</u> they let stuff <u>in and out</u> as well. Only very <u>small molecules</u> can <u>diffuse</u> through cell membranes though — things like <u>simple sugars</u>, <u>water</u> or <u>ions</u>. <u>Big</u> molecules like <u>starch</u> and <u>proteins</u> can't pass through the membrane.

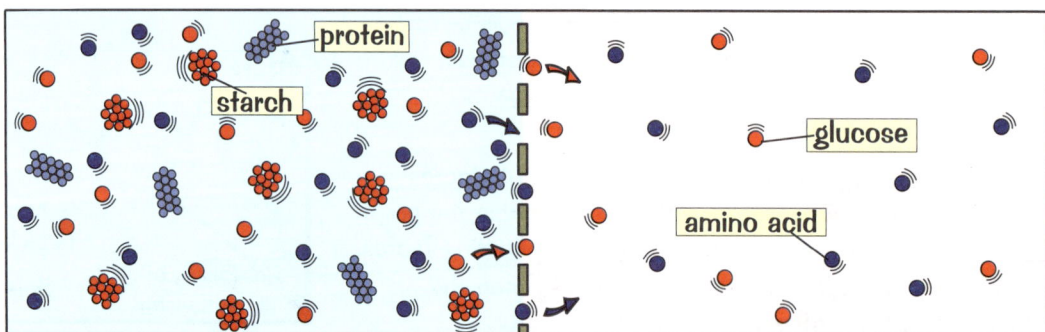

protein

starch

glucose

amino acid

1) Just like with diffusion in air, particles flow through the cell membrane from where there's a <u>higher concentration</u> (a lot of them) to where there's a <u>lower concentration</u> (not such a lot of them).

2) They're only moving about <u>randomly</u> of course, so they go <u>both</u> ways — but if there are a lot <u>more</u> particles on one side of the membrane, there's obviously an <u>overall</u> movement <u>from</u> that side.

3) The <u>rate</u> of diffusion depends on three main things:

a) <u>Distance</u> — substances diffuse <u>more quickly</u> when they haven't as <u>far</u> to move. Pretty obvious.

b) <u>Concentration difference</u> (<u>gradient</u>) — substances diffuse faster if there's a <u>big difference</u> in concentration. If there are <u>lots more</u> particles on one side, there are more there to move across.

c) <u>Surface area</u> — the <u>more surface</u> there is available for molecules to move across, the <u>faster</u> they can get from one side to the other.

Whoever smelt it dealt it... Whoever said the rhyme did the crime...

Because, of course, it's not just perfume that diffuses through a room. Anyway. All living cells have <u>membranes</u>, and their structure allows sugars, water and the rest to drift in and out as needed. Don't forget, the membrane doesn't <u>control</u> diffusion, it happens all by itself — but the membrane does stop <u>large molecules</u> passing through.

Leaves and Diffusion

This page is all about <u>leaves</u>, what they get up to in the <u>dark</u>, and how they <u>exchange gases</u>.

You Need to Learn The Structure of A Leaf

Let's start with the basics. You need to know all the different parts of a <u>typical leaf</u> shown on the diagram:

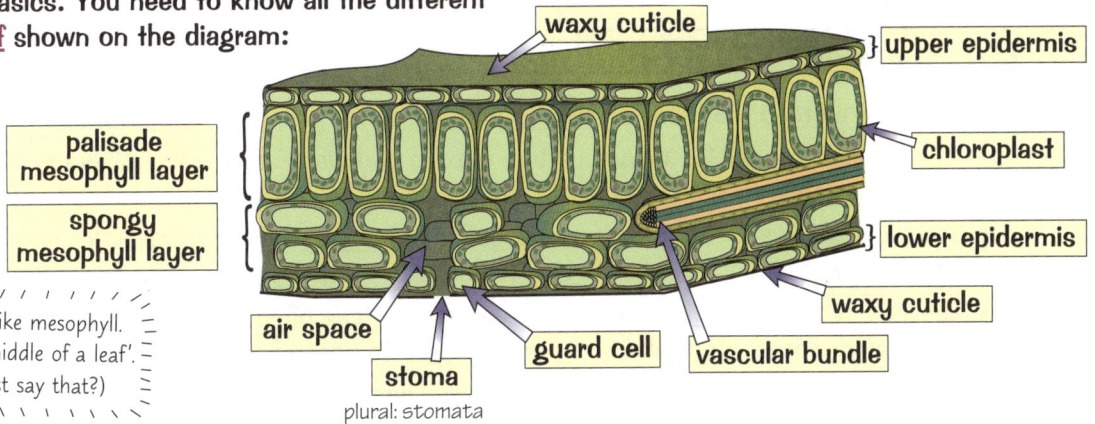

waxy cuticle · upper epidermis · chloroplast · lower epidermis · waxy cuticle · vascular bundle · guard cell · stoma (plural: stomata) · air space · spongy mesophyll layer · palisade mesophyll layer

Funny names here — like mesophyll. Mesophyll just means 'middle of a leaf'. (So why can't they just say that?)

Plants Carry Out Both Photosynthesis and Respiration

1) Photosynthesis and respiration are <u>opposite processes</u>:

Photosynthesis: carbon dioxide + water → glucose + oxygen (<u>Requires</u> energy)

Respiration: glucose + oxygen → carbon dioxide + water (Energy <u>released</u>)

2) <u>Photosynthesis</u> only happens during the <u>day</u> (i.e. when there's <u>light</u> available). But plants must <u>respire all the time</u>, day and night to get the <u>energy</u> they need to <u>live</u>.

3) During the <u>day</u>, plants <u>make</u> more <u>oxygen</u> by photosynthesis than they use in respiration. So in daylight, they <u>release oxygen</u> and <u>take in carbon dioxide</u>.

4) At <u>night</u> though, plants only <u>respire</u> — there's <u>no light</u> for photosynthesis. This means they <u>take in oxygen</u> and <u>release carbon dioxide</u> — just like us.

For more on respiration, see page 20.

Plants Exchange Gases by Diffusion

<u>Diffusion</u> of gases in the <u>leaves</u> is <u>vital</u> for both <u>photosynthesis</u> and <u>respiration</u>. Here's how it works:

PHOTOSYNTHESIS

1) When the plant is photosynthesising it uses up lots of <u>carbon dioxide</u>, so there's hardly any inside the leaf.

2) Luckily this makes <u>more</u> carbon dioxide move into the leaf by <u>diffusion</u> (from an area of <u>higher</u> concentration to an area of <u>lower</u> concentration).

3) At the same time lots of <u>oxygen</u> is being <u>made</u> as a waste product of photosynthesis.

4) Some is used in <u>respiration</u>, and the rest diffuses <u>out</u> of the leaf (moving from an area of <u>higher</u> concentration to an area of <u>lower</u> concentration).

RESPIRATION

1) At <u>night</u> it's a different story — there's <u>no photosynthesis</u> going on because there's <u>no light</u>. Lots of <u>carbon dioxide</u> is made in <u>respiration</u> and lots of <u>oxygen</u> is used up.

2) There's a lot of carbon dioxide in the leaf and not a lot of oxygen, so now it's mainly <u>carbon dioxide</u> diffusing <u>out</u> and <u>oxygen</u> diffusing <u>in</u>.

I tried really hard to leaf the dodgy jokes out of this page...

... and I got so close. Oh well — sorry about that. Remember: <u>photosynthesis</u> uses energy from light so it can only take place during the <u>day</u>. <u>Respiration</u> releases energy for life processes — it takes place <u>all the time</u>.

Leaves and Photosynthesis

Before you start, you'll definitely need to know a bit about the structure of a leaf — so have a quick squizz at the previous page if you haven't already.

Leaves are Adapted for Efficient Photosynthesis:

Leaves are Adapted for Diffusion

1) Leaves are broad, so there's a large surface area for gases to diffuse.

2) They're also thin, which means carbon dioxide and water vapour only have to diffuse a short distance to reach the photosynthesising cells where they're needed.

3) The lower surface is full of little holes called stomata. They're there to let gases like CO_2 and O_2 in and out. They also allow water to escape — which is known as transpiration (see page 73).

4) Leaves have guard cells surrounding each stoma (see page 74) to control when the stoma opens and closes. This allows the guards cells to control gas exchange.

5) There are air spaces in the spongy mesophyll layer. This allows gases like CO_2 and O_2 to move between the stomata and the photosynthesising cells. This also means there's a large surface area for gas exchange — the technical phrase for this is "they have a very big internal surface area to volume ratio".

Leaves are Adapted to Absorb Light

1) The leaves being broad also means there's a large surface area exposed to light.

2) Leaves contains lots of chloroplasts. Chloroplasts contain chlorophyll and other photosynthetic pigments to absorb light energy.

3) Different pigments absorb different wavelengths of light, so plant cells can make the most of the Sun's energy by absorbing as much of it as possible. The table below shows four different pigments found in plants and the wavelengths of light they absorb:

You might get asked to interpret data on the absorption of light in the exam.

Pigment:	Absorbs wavelengths of:
Chlorophyll a	400-450 nm and 650-700 nm
Chlorophyll b	450-500 nm and 600-650 nm
Carotene	400-550 nm
Xanthophyll	400-530 nm

'nm' stands for 'nanometre' — a really small unit of length.

4) The cells that contain the most chloroplasts are arranged in the palisade layer near the top of the leaf where they can get the most light.

5) The upper epidermis is transparent so that light can pass through it to the palisade layer.

Leaves Have a Network of Vascular Bundles

The vascular bundles are the transport vessels, xylem and phloem (see page 72). They deliver water and other nutrients to every part of the leaf and take away the glucose produced by photosynthesis. They also help to support the leaf structure.

If you don't do much revision, it's time to turn over a new leaf...

So how do they know all this stuff? Well, scientists know how leaves are adapted for photosynthesis because they've looked and seen the structure of leaves and the cells inside them. Not with the naked eye, of course — they used microscopes. So they're not just making it up, after all.

Osmosis

Trust me — osmosis really isn't as scary as it sounds. This page tells you everything you need to know.

Osmosis is a Special Case of Diffusion, That's All

> Osmosis is the net movement of water molecules across a partially permeable membrane from a region of higher water concentration (i.e. a dilute solution) to a region of lower water concentration (i.e. a concentrated solution).

1) A partially permeable membrane is just one with very small holes in it. So small, in fact, that only tiny molecules (like water) can pass through them, and bigger molecules (e.g. sucrose) can't.

2) The water molecules actually pass both ways through the membrane during osmosis. This happens because water molecules move about randomly all the time.

3) But because there are more water molecules on one side than on the other, there's a steady net flow of water into the region with fewer water molecules, i.e. into the stronger sucrose solution.

4) This means the concentrated sucrose solution gets more dilute. The water acts like it's trying to 'even up' the concentration either side of the membrane.

5) Osmosis is a type of diffusion — net movement of particles from an area of higher concentration to an area of lower concentration.

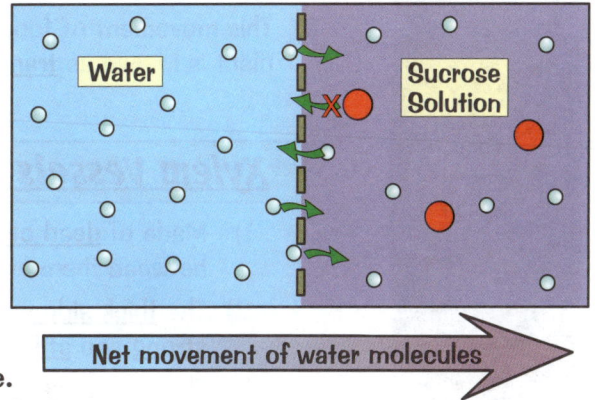

Net movement of water molecules

Turgor Pressure Supports Plant Tissues

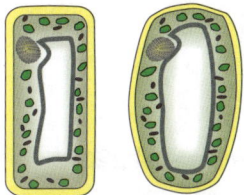

1) When a plant is well watered, all its cells will draw water in by osmosis and become plump and swollen. When the cells are like this, they're said to be turgid.

2) The contents of the cell push against the inelastic cell wall — this is called turgor pressure. Turgor pressure helps support the plant tissues.

3) If there's no water in the soil, a plant starts to wilt (droop). This is because the cells start to lose water and so lose their turgor pressure. They're then said to be flaccid.

4) If the plant's really short of water, the cytoplasm inside its cells starts to shrink and the membrane pulls away from the cell wall. The cell is now said to be plasmolysed. The plant doesn't totally lose its shape though, because the inelastic cell wall keeps things in position. It just droops a bit.

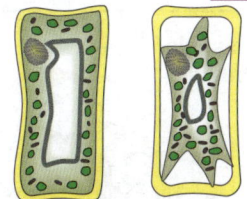

Normal Cell   Turgid Cell

Flaccid Cell   Plasmolysed Cell

Animal Cells Don't Have an Inelastic Cell Wall

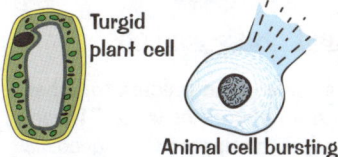

Turgid plant cell

Animal cell bursting

Plant cells aren't too bothered by changes in the amount of water because the inelastic cell wall keeps everything in place.

It's different in animal cells because they don't have a cell wall. If an animal cell takes in too much water, it bursts — this is known as lysis. If it loses too much water it gets all shrivelled up — this is known as crenation.

What all this means is that animals have to keep the amount of water in their cells pretty constant or they're in trouble, while plants are a bit more tolerant of periods of drought.

Revision by osmosis — you wish...

Wouldn't that be great — if all the ideas in this book would just gradually drift across into your mind, from an area of higher concentration (in the book) to an area of lower concentration (in your mind — no offence). Actually, that probably will happen if you read it again. Why don't you give it a go...

Transport Systems in Plants

Plants have <u>two</u> transport systems. They have <u>two</u> separate types of vessel — <u>xylem</u> and <u>phloem</u> — for transporting stuff around. <u>Both</u> types of vessel go to <u>every part</u> of the plant in a <u>continuous system</u>, but they're totally <u>separate</u>.

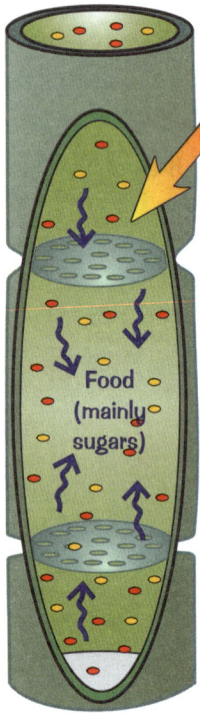

Phloem Tubes Transport Food:

1) Made of <u>columns</u> of <u>living cells</u> with <u>perforated end-plates</u> to allow stuff to flow through.

2) They transport <u>food substances</u> (mainly <u>sugars</u>) both <u>up</u> and <u>down</u> the stem to growing and storage tissues.

3) This movement of food substances around the plant is known as <u>translocation</u>.

Food (mainly sugars)

Xylem Vessels Take Water UP:

1) Made of <u>dead cells</u> joined end to end with <u>no</u> end walls between them and a hole (<u>lumen</u>) down the middle.

2) The <u>thick side walls</u> are made of <u>cellulose</u>. They're <u>strong</u> and <u>stiff</u>, which gives the plant <u>support</u>.

3) They carry <u>water</u> and <u>minerals</u> from the <u>roots</u> up the shoot to the leaves in the <u>transpiration stream</u> (see next page).

Water and minerals

You can Recognise Xylem and Phloem by Where They Are

1) They usually run <u>alongside</u> each other in <u>vascular bundles</u> (like veins).

2) <u>Where</u> they're found in each type of plant structure is related to <u>xylem</u>'s other function — <u>support</u>. You need to learn these <u>three examples</u>:

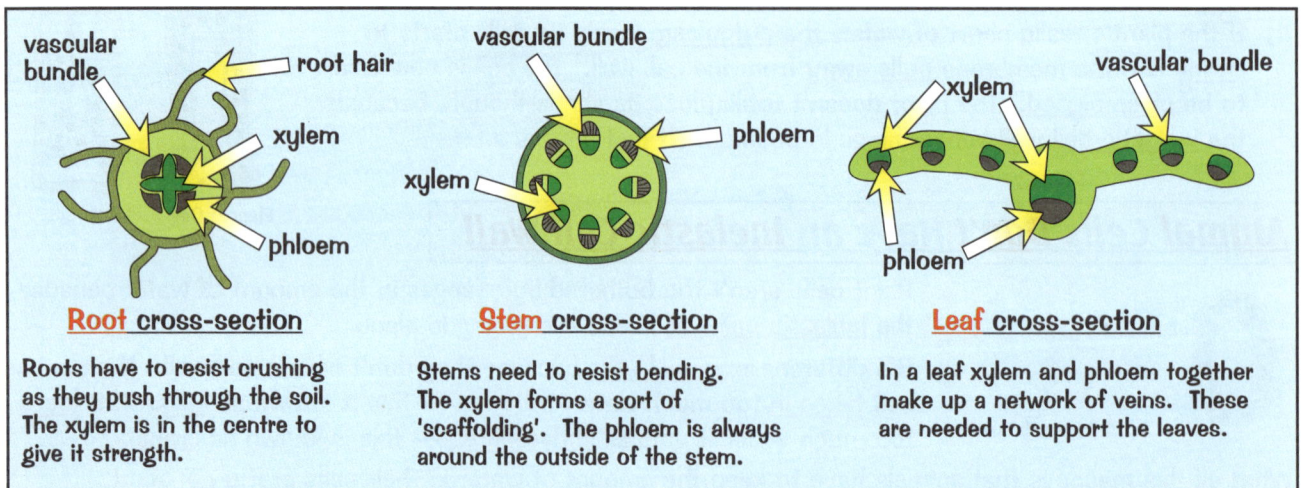

vascular bundle — root hair
xylem
phloem

Root cross-section

vascular bundle
phloem
xylem

Stem cross-section

xylem
vascular bundle
phloem

Leaf cross-section

Roots have to resist crushing as they push through the soil. The xylem is in the centre to give it strength.

Stems need to resist bending. The xylem forms a sort of 'scaffolding'. The phloem is always around the outside of the stem.

In a leaf xylem and phloem together make up a network of veins. These are needed to support the leaves.

Don't let revision stress you out — just go with the phloem...

You've probably done that really dull experiment where you stick a piece of <u>celery</u> in a beaker of water with red food colouring in it. Then you stare at it for half an hour, and once the time is up, hey presto, the red has reached the top of the celery. That's because it travelled there in the <u>xylem</u>. Unbelievable.

Water Flow Through Plants

If you don't water a house plant for a few days it starts to go all droopy. Then it dies, and the people from the Society for the Protection of Plants come round and have you arrested. Plants need water.

Root Hairs Take in Water by Osmosis

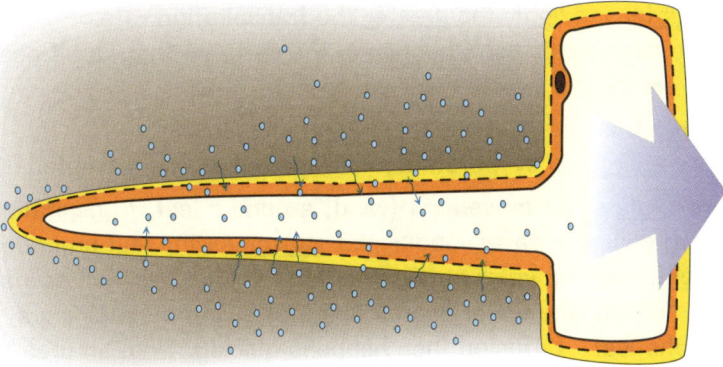

1) The cells on plant roots grow into long 'hairs' which stick out into the soil.

2) Each branch of a root will be covered in millions of these microscopic hairs.

3) This gives the plant a big surface area for absorbing water from the soil.

4) There's usually a higher concentration of water in the soil than there is inside the plant, so the water is drawn into the root hair cell by osmosis (see page 71).

Transpiration is the Loss of Water from the Plant

1) Transpiration is caused by evaporation and diffusion of water vapour from inside the leaves.

2) This creates a slight shortage of water in the leaf, and so more water is drawn up from the rest of the plant through the xylem vessels (see previous page) to replace it.

3) This in turn means more water is drawn up from the roots, and so there's a constant transpiration stream of water through the plant.

water evaporates from the leaves

water enters through the roots

Transpiration is just a side-effect of the way leaves are adapted for photosynthesis. They have to have stomata in them so that gases can be exchanged easily (see page 70). Because there's more water inside the plant than in the air outside, the water escapes from the leaves through the stomata.

The transpiration stream does have some benefits for the plants, however:

1) The constant stream of water from the ground helps to keep the plant cool.

2) It provides the plant with a constant supply of water for photosynthesis.

3) The water creates turgor pressure in the plant cells, which helps support the plant and stops it wilting (see page 71).

4) Minerals needed by the plant (see page 75) can be brought in from the soil along with the water.

Transpiration — the plant version of perspiration...

Here's an interesting fact — a biggish tree loses about a thousand litres of water from its leaves every single day. That's as much water as the average person drinks in a whole year, so the roots have to be very effective at drawing in water from the soil. Which is why they have all those root hairs, you see.

Water Flow Through Plants

If you thought that page on transpiration was interesting, you're not gonna believe your luck — here's another page all about water transport in plants.

Transpiration Rate is Increased by Four Main Things

1) **AN INCREASE IN LIGHT INTENSITY** — the brighter the light, the greater the transpiration rate. Stomata begin to close as it gets darker. Photosynthesis can't happen in the dark, so they don't need to be open to let CO_2 in. When the stomata are closed, water can't escape.

2) **AN INCREASE IN TEMPERATURE** — the warmer it is, the faster transpiration happens. When it's warm the water particles have more energy to evaporate and diffuse out of the stomata.

3) **AN INCREASE IN AIR MOVEMENT** — if there's lots of air movement (wind) around a leaf, transpiration happens faster. If the air around a leaf is very still, the water vapour just surrounds the leaf and doesn't move away. This means there's a high concentration of water particles outside the leaf as well as inside it, so diffusion doesn't happen as quickly. If it's windy, the water vapour is swept away, maintaining a low concentration of water in the air outside the leaf. Diffusion then happens quickly, from an area of high concentration to an area of low concentration.

4) **A DECREASE IN AIR HUMIDITY** — if the air around the leaf is very dry, transpiration happens more quickly. This is like what happens with air movement. If the air is humid there's a lot of water in it already, so there's not much of a difference between the inside and the outside of the leaf. Diffusion happens fastest if there's a really high concentration in one place, and a really low concentration in the other.

Plants Need to Balance Water Loss with Water Uptake

Transpiration can help plants in some ways (see previous page), but if it hasn't rained for a while and you're short of water it's not a good idea to have it rushing out of your leaves. So plants have adaptations to help reduce water loss from their leaves.

1) Leaves usually have a waxy cuticle covering the upper epidermis. This helps make the upper surface of the leaf waterproof.

2) Most stomata are found on the lower surface of a leaf where it's darker and cooler. This helps slow down diffusion of water out of the leaf (see above).

3) The bigger the stomata and the more stomata a leaf has, the more water the plant will lose. Plants in hot climates really need to conserve water, so they have fewer and smaller stomata on the underside of the leaf and no stomata on the upper epidermis.

Stomata Open and Close Automatically

Guard cells turgid — stoma opens

Guard cells flaccid — stoma closes

1) Stomata close automatically when supplies of water from the roots start to dry up.

2) The guard cells have a special kidney shape which opens and closes the stomata as the guard cells go turgid or flaccid (see page 71).

3) Thin outer walls and thickened inner walls make this opening and closing function work properly.

4) Open stomata allow gases in and out for photosynthesis.

5) They're sensitive to light, so they open during the day and close at night. This allows them to conserve water without losing out on photosynthesis.

It always helps if you're quick on the uptake...

In the exam they might ask you to interpret some data from experiments about transpiration rate. Don't panic — as long as you remember the four factors that affect the transpiration rate, you should be able to say something intelligent and get some valuable marks in the bag.

Minerals Needed for Healthy Growth

Plants are important in <u>food chains</u> and <u>nutrient cycles</u> because they can take <u>minerals</u> from the soil and <u>energy</u> from the Sun and turn it into food. And then, after all that hard work, we eat them.

Plants Need Three Main Minerals

Plants need certain <u>elements</u> so they can produce important compounds. They get these elements from <u>minerals</u> in the <u>soil</u>. If there aren't enough of these minerals in the soil, plants suffer <u>deficiency symptoms</u>.

1) Nitrates

Contain <u>nitrogen</u> for making <u>amino acids</u> and <u>proteins</u>. These are needed for <u>cell growth</u>. If a plant can't get enough nitrates, its <u>growth</u> will be <u>poor</u> and it'll have <u>yellow older leaves</u>.

2) Phosphates

Needed for <u>respiration</u> and <u>growth</u>. Contain <u>phosphorus</u> for making <u>DNA</u> and <u>cell membranes</u>. Plants without enough phosphate have <u>poor root growth</u> and <u>discoloured older leaves</u>.

3) Potassium

To help the <u>enzymes</u> needed for <u>photosynthesis</u> and <u>respiration</u>. If there's not enough potassium in the soil, plants have <u>poor flower and fruit growth</u> and <u>discoloured leaves</u>.

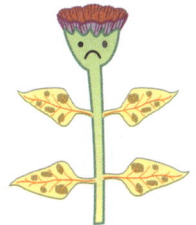

Magnesium is Also Needed in Small Amounts

The three main minerals are needed in fairly <u>large amounts</u>, but there are other elements which are needed in much <u>smaller</u> amounts. <u>Magnesium</u> is one of the most significant as it's required for making <u>chlorophyll</u> (needed for <u>photosynthesis</u>). Plants without enough magnesium have <u>yellow leaves</u>.

Root Hairs Take in Minerals Using Active Transport

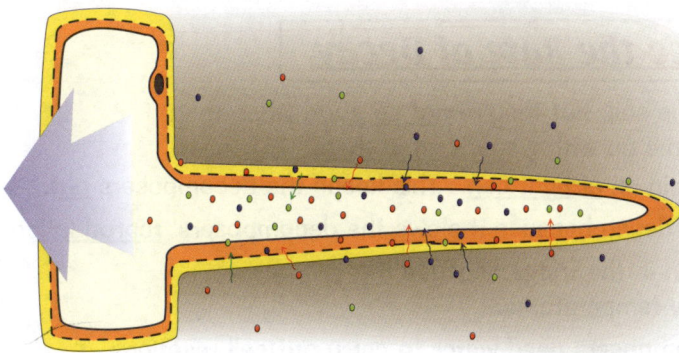

1) <u>Root hairs</u> (see page 73) give the plant a <u>big surface area</u> for absorbing minerals from the soil.

2) But the <u>concentration</u> of minerals in the <u>soil</u> is usually pretty <u>low</u>. It's normally <u>higher</u> in the <u>root hair cell</u> than in the soil around it.

3) So normal diffusion <u>doesn't</u> explain how minerals are taken up into the root hair cell.

4) They should go <u>the other way</u> if they followed the rules of diffusion.

5) The answer is that a different process called '<u>active transport</u>' is responsible.

6) Active transport uses <u>energy</u> from <u>respiration</u> to help the plant pull minerals into the root hair <u>against the concentration gradient</u> (from <u>low</u> concentrations to <u>high</u> concentrations).

Nitrogen and phosphorus and potassium — oh my...

When a farmer or a gardener buys <u>fertiliser</u>, that's pretty much what he or she is buying — <u>nitrates</u>, <u>phosphates</u> and <u>potassium</u>. A fertiliser's <u>NPK label</u> tells you the relative proportions of nitrogen (N), phosphorus (P) and potassium (K) it contains, so you can choose the right one for your plants and soil.

Module B4 — It's a Green World

Decay

Microorganisms are great because they break down plant and animal remains which are lying around and looking unsightly. But they also break down plant and animal remains that we just bought at the shops.

Things Decay Because of Microorganisms

1) Living things are made of materials they take from the world around them.

2) When they die and decompose, or release material as waste, the elements they contain are returned to the soil or air where they originally came from.

3) Nearly all decomposition is done by microorganisms like soil bacteria and fungi (known as decomposers).

4) The rate of decay depends on three main things:

   a) Temperature — a warm temperature makes things decay faster because it speeds up respiration in microorganisms.

   b) Amount of water — things decay faster when they're moist because microorganisms need water.

   c) Amount of oxygen (air) — decay is faster when there's oxygen available. The microorganisms can respire aerobically (see page 20), providing more energy.

5) When these factors are at optimum levels (i.e. warm, moist, plenty of O_2), microorganisms grow and reproduce more quickly. This means there'll be more of them to decay other living things.

Detritivores and Saprophytes Feed on Decaying Material

Detritivores and saprophytes are both types of organism that are important in decay. They're grouped into those two types depending on how they feed:

1) Detritivores feed on dead and decaying material (detritus). Examples of detritivores include earthworms, maggots and woodlice. As these detritivores feed on the decaying material, they break it up into smaller bits. This gives a bigger surface area for smaller decomposers to work on and so speeds up decay.

2) Saprophytes also feed on decaying material, but they do so by extracellular digestion — i.e. they feed by secreting digestive enzymes on to the material outside of their cells. The enzymes break down the material into smaller bits, which can then be absorbed by the saprophyte. Many saprophytes are fungi.

Food Preservation Methods Reduce the Rate of Decay

Decomposers are good for returning nutrients to the soil, but they're not so good when they start decomposing your lunch. So people have come up with ways to stop them:

1) Canning — basically, this involves putting food in an airtight can. This keeps the decomposers out.

2) Cooling — putting food in a fridge slows down decay because it slows the decomposers' reproduction rate.

3) Freezing — food lasts longer in the freezer than in the fridge because the decomposers can't reproduce at all at such low temperatures.

4) Drying — dried food lasts longer because decomposers need water to carry out cell reactions. Lots of fruits are preserved by drying them out, and sometimes meat is too.

5) Adding salt/sugar — if there's a high concentration of salt or sugar around decomposers, they'll lose water by osmosis. This damages them and means they can't work properly. Things like tuna and olives are often stored in brine (salt water).

6) Adding vinegar — mmm, pickled onions. Vinegar is acidic, and the acid kills the decomposers.

Decomposers — they're just misunderstood...

OK, so it's annoying when you go to the cupboard and find that everything has turned a funny green colour. But imagine the alternative — there'd be no nutrients in the soil and we'd be up to our eyes in dead things. Eww.

Intensive Farming

Farming's a noisy, tiring and often smelly pastime. You can understand why farmers would want to make it as efficient as possible — that's where intensive farming comes in. There are two sides to the story though...

Intensive Farming is Used to Produce More Food

Intensive farming means trying to produce as much food as possible from your land, animals and plants. Farmers can do this in different ways — the following methods all involve reducing the energy losses that happen at each stage in a food chain (making the transfer of energy between organisms in a food chain more efficient):

1) Using herbicides to kill weeds. This means that more of the energy from the Sun falling on fields goes to the crops, and not to any other competing plants that aren't wanted.

2) Using pesticides to kill insects that eat the crops. This makes sure no energy is transferred into a different food chain — it's all saved for growing the crops.

3) Battery farming animals. The animals are kept close together indoors in small pens, so that they're warm and can't move about. This saves them wasting energy as they move around, and stops them using up so much energy keeping warm.

Intensive farming allows us to produce a lot of food from less and less land, which means a huge variety of top quality foods, all year round, at cheap prices.

Hydroponics is Where Plants are Grown Without Soil

1) Hydroponics is another method of intensive farming. It's where plants are grown in nutrient solutions (water and fertilisers) instead of in soil.

2) Hydroponics is often used to grow glasshouse tomatoes on a commercial scale, as well as to grow plants in areas with barren soil.

3) There are advantages and disadvantages of growing plants using hydroponics rather than in soil:

ADVANTAGES	DISADVANTAGES
Mineral levels can be controlled more accurately.	Lots of fertilisers need to be added.
Diseases can be controlled more effectively.	There's no soil to anchor the roots and support the plants.

Intensive Farming Can Destroy the Environment

Intensive farming methods are efficient, but they sometimes raise ethical dilemmas because they can damage the world we live in, making it polluted, unattractive and devoid of wildlife. The main effects are:

1) Removal of hedges to make huge great fields destroys the natural habitat of wild creatures. It can also lead to serious soil erosion.

2) Careless use of fertilisers can pollute rivers and lakes (known as eutrophication).

3) Pesticides disturb food chains — see next page.

4) Lots of people think that intensive farming of animals such as battery-hens is cruel because they have very little space or freedom to move around.

Intensive farming — sounds like hard work...

So. Intensive farming allows us to produce lots of food, cheaply and efficiently, but it sometimes raises ethical dilemmas. For some environmentally friendly alternatives to these intensive farming methods, see page 79.

Pesticides and Biological Control

Biological control is growing more popular, as people get fed up with all the problems caused by pesticides.

Pesticides Disturb Food Chains

1) Pesticides are sprayed onto crops to kill the creatures that damage them (pests), but unfortunately they can also kill organisms that aren't pests, like bees and ladybirds.
2) This can cause a shortage of food for animals further up the food chain.
3) Some pesticides are persistent — they tend to stick around in ecosystems and are hard to get rid of.
4) There's a danger of pesticides being passed along the food chain and killing the animals further up.

This is well illustrated by the case of otters which were almost wiped out over much of crop-dominated southern England by a pesticide called DDT in the early 1960s. The diagram shows the food chain which ends with the otter. DDT (like most pesticides) can't be excreted — so it accumulates along the food chain and the otter ends up with most of the DDT collected by all the other animals.

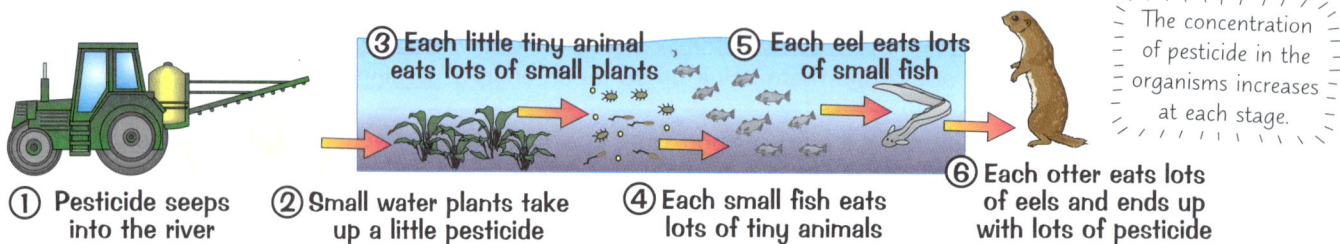

③ Each little tiny animal eats lots of small plants   ⑤ Each eel eats lots of small fish

The concentration of pesticide in the organisms increases at each stage.

① Pesticide seeps into the river   ② Small water plants take up a little pesticide   ④ Each small fish eats lots of tiny animals   ⑥ Each otter eats lots of eels and ends up with lots of pesticide

You Can Use Biological Control Instead of Pesticides

Biological control means using living things instead of chemicals to control a pest.
You could use a predator, a parasite or a disease to kill the pest. For example:

1) Aphids are a pest because they eat roses and vegetables. Ladybirds are aphid predators, so people release them into their fields and gardens to keep aphid numbers down.
2) Certain types of wasps and flies produce larvae which develop on (or in, yuck) a host insect. This eventually kills the insect host. Lots of insect pests have parasites like this.
3) Myxomatosis is a disease which kills rabbits. The Myxoma virus was released in Australia as a biological control when the rabbit population there grew out of control and ruined crops.

You need to be able to explain the advantages and disadvantages of biological control:
ADVANTAGES:
- No chemicals are used, so there's less pollution, disruption of food chains and risk to people eating the food that's been sprayed.
- There's no need to keep repeating the treatment — like you would with chemical pesticides.
DISADVANTAGES:
- The predator that you introduce might not eat the pest — making it useless.
- The predator could eat useful species e.g. pollinators or seed dispersers.
- The predator's population might increase and get out of control.
- The predator might not stay in the area where it's needed.

Remember that removing an organism from a food web, whether you use biological control or pesticides, can affect all the other organisms too. For example, if you remove a pest insect, you're removing a source of food from all the organisms that normally eat it. These might die out, and another insect that they normally feed on could breed out of control and become a pest instead. You have to be very careful.

Don't get bugged by biological pest control...

There's a fair ol' bit of information on this page, but you really do need to know it. So make sure you do.

Alternatives to Intensive Farming

Intensive farming can allow farmers to produce lots of food — but it isn't always possible and it isn't always the best approach. Some farmers are sticking with the good old fashioned 'hard graft' approach.

Lots of Farmers Use Organic Farming Methods

Modern intensive farming produces lots of food and we all appreciate it on the supermarket shelves. But traditional organic farming methods do still work (amazingly!), and they have their benefits too. You need to know about these organic farming techniques:

1) Use of organic fertilisers (i.e. animal manure and compost). This recycles the nutrients left in plant and animal waste. It doesn't work as well as artificial fertilisers, but it is better for the environment.

2) Crop rotation — growing a cycle of different crops in a field each year. This stops the pests and diseases of one crop building up, and stops nutrients running out (as each crop has slightly different needs). Most crop rotations include a nitrogen-fixing crop, such as legume plants (usually peas or beans). These help put nitrates back in the soil. *(See page 75 for more on nitrates.)*

Eeugh. I feel so dizzy.

Me too.

3) Weeding — this means physically removing the weeds, rather than just spraying them with a herbicide. Obviously it's a lot more labour intensive, but there are no nasty chemicals involved.

4) Varying seed planting times — sowing seeds later or earlier in the season will avoid the major pests for that crop. This means the farmer won't need to use pesticides.

5) Biological control — this is covered on the previous page.

Organic Farming Methods Have Their Advantages and Disadvantages

You also need to be able to explain the advantages and disadvantages of organic farming. Here are some of the main ones:

Advantages

1) Organic farming uses fewer chemicals, so there's less risk of toxic chemicals remaining on food.
2) It's better for the environment. There's less chance of polluting rivers with fertiliser. Organic farmers also avoid using pesticides, so don't disrupt food chains and harm wildlife.
3) For a farm to be classed as organic, it will usually have to follow guidelines on the ethical treatment of animals. This means no battery farming.

Disadvantages

1) Organic farming takes up more space than intensive farming — so more land has to be farmland, rather than being set aside for wildlife or for other uses.
2) It's more labour-intensive. This provides more jobs, but it also makes the food more expensive.
3) You can't grow as much food. But on the other hand, Europe over-produces food these days anyway.

Crop rotation — it's just like editing your digital photos...

Organic farming might be much better for the environment than intensive farming, but it still has its disadvantages. Make sure you're able to explain both the pros and the cons for the exam.

Revision Summary for Module B4

What a nice leafy section that was. Things started to get a bit mouldy at one point, but that's life I suppose. Now, just to make sure you've taken in all the leafiness and mouldiness, here's a little revision summary so you can check what you've learned. You know the routine by now — whizz through the questions and make a note of any you can't answer. Then go back and find the answer in the section. It's actually kind of fun, like a treasure hunt... well, okay, it's not — but it works.

1) Explain the terms 'community' and 'population'.
2)* Estimate the total ant population in a 4000 m^2 car park if a 1 m^2 area contained 80 ants.
3)* You catch 23 woodlice one day and mark their shells. The next day you catch 28 woodlice and find that four of them are marked. Estimate the population size.
4) Explain the meaning of the word 'ecosystem'. How is an ecosystem different to a habitat?
5) Describe how you'd carry out a transect to investigate the distribution of plant species in a field.
6) What are 'abiotic factors'?
7) What is zonation?
8) What is biodiversity?
9) Describe how the biodiversity is different in a native woodland compared to a forestry plantation.
10) Write down the balanced symbol equation for photosynthesis.
11) Explain why starch rather than glucose is used for storage in plants.
12) Describe van Helmont's experiment with a willow tree. What did it show?
13) What were the conclusions of Priestley's experiments with mice and plants?
14) Explain how experiments with isotopes have contributed to our understanding of photosynthesis.
15) What are the three limiting factors in photosynthesis? Sketch graphs to illustrate their effect on the rate of photosynthesis.
16) Write a definition of the word 'diffusion'.
17) Why can't starch pass through a partially permeable membrane?
18) What is usually found covering the upper epidermis layer of a leaf?
19) Why does oxygen tend to move into leaves during the night?
20) Describe how leaves are adapted for efficient diffusion.
21) Describe how leaves are adapted to absorb light energy.
22) Explain what osmosis is.
23) What is turgor pressure?
24) How are xylem vessels adapted to their function?
25) What do phloem tubes transport?
26) Where are the xylem and phloem found in a root?
27) What is the advantage to a plant of having root hairs?
28) Give three ways that the transpiration stream benefits a plant.
29) How is the transpiration rate affected by: a) increased temperature, b) increased air humidity?
30) What causes stomata to close when a plant is short of water? How does this benefit the plant?
31) Name the three main minerals plants need for healthy growth.
32) What is magnesium needed for in a plant?
33) Give an example of a detritivore.
34) Why does pickling food in vinegar help it to last for longer without decaying?
35) Give three ways that intensive farming methods reduce the energy lost at each stage in a food chain.
36) Give three problems associated with intensive farming.
37) Explain how pesticides can accumulate in a food chain.
38) List the advantages and disadvantages of biological pest control.
39) What is meant by the term 'hydroponics'?
40) Give two advantages and two disadvantages of organic farming methods.

* Answers on page 116.

The History of the Atom

If you cut up a cake you end up with slices. If you keep going you're gonna have crumbs. But what happens if you keep cutting... Just how small can you go and what would the stuff you end up with look like... Scientists have been trying to work it out for years...

The Theory of Atomic Structure Has Changed Throughout History

Atoms are the tiny particles of matter (stuff that has a mass) which make up everything in the universe...

1) At the start of the 19th century John Dalton described atoms as solid spheres, and said that different spheres made up the different elements.

2) In 1897 J J Thomson concluded from his experiments that atoms weren't solid spheres. His measurements of charge and mass showed that an atom must contain even smaller, negatively charged particles — electrons. The 'solid sphere' idea of atomic structure had to be changed. The new theory was known as the 'plum pudding model'.

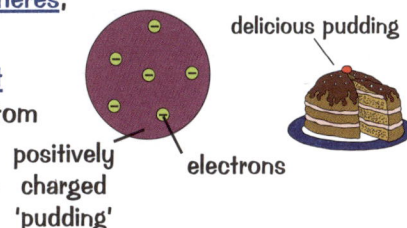

delicious pudding

positively charged 'pudding'

electrons

Rutherford Showed that the Plum Pudding Model Was Wrong

1) In 1909 Ernest Rutherford and his students Hans Geiger and Ernest Marsden conducted the famous gold foil experiment. They fired positively charged particles at an extremely thin sheet of gold.

2) From the plum pudding model, they were expecting most of the particles to be deflected by the positive 'pudding' that made up most of an atom. In fact, most of the particles passed straight through the gold atoms, and a very small number were deflected backwards. So the plum pudding model couldn't be right.

3) So Rutherford came up with an idea that could explain this new evidence — the theory of the nuclear atom. In this, there's a tiny, positively charged nucleus at the centre, surrounded by a 'cloud' of negative electrons — most of the atom is empty space.

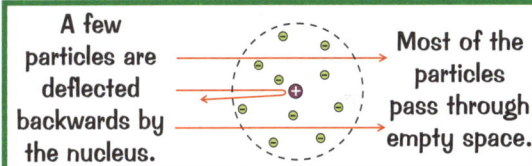

A few particles are deflected backwards by the nucleus.

Most of the particles pass through empty space.

The Refined Bohr Model Explains a Lot...

1) Scientists realised that electrons in a 'cloud' around the nucleus of an atom, as Rutherford described, would be attracted to the nucleus, causing the atom to collapse. Niels Bohr proposed a new model of the atom where all the electrons were contained in shells.

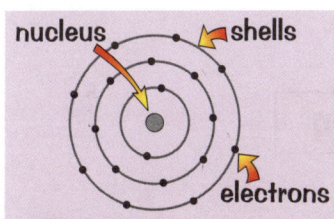

nucleus   shells

electrons

2) Bohr suggested that electrons can only exist in fixed orbits, or shells, and not anywhere in between. Each shell has a fixed energy.

3) Bohr's theory of atomic structure was supported by many experiments and it helped to explain lots of other scientists' observations at the time. It was pretty close to our currently accepted version of the atom (have a look at the next page to see what we now think atoms look like).

Scientific Theories Have to be Backed Up by Evidence

1) So, you can see that what we think the atom looks like now is completely different to what people thought in the past. These different ideas were accepted because they fitted the evidence available at the time.

2) As scientists did more experiments, new evidence was found and our theory of the structure of the atom was modified to fit it.

3) This is nearly always the way scientific knowledge develops — new evidence prompts people to come up with new, improved ideas. These ideas can be used to make predictions which if proved correct are a pretty good indication that the ideas are right.

4) Scientists also put their ideas and research up for peer review. This means everyone gets a chance to see the new ideas, check for errors and then other scientists can use it to help develop their own work.

I love a good model — Kate Moss is my favourite...

Scientists love a good theory but what they love more is trying to disprove their mate's one. That's how science works.

Atoms

There are quite a few <u>different</u> (and equally useful) <u>modern</u> models of the atom — but chemists tend to like this model best. You can use it to explain pretty much the whole of chemistry... which is nice.

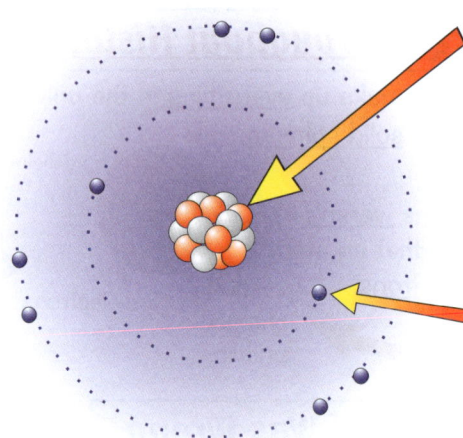

The Nucleus

1) It's in the <u>middle</u> of the atom.

2) It contains <u>protons</u> and <u>neutrons</u>.

3) It has a <u>positive charge</u> because of the protons.

4) Almost the <u>whole</u> mass of the atom (about 10^{-23} g) is <u>concentrated</u> in the nucleus.

The Electrons

1) Move <u>around</u> the nucleus in electron <u>shells</u>.

2) They're <u>negatively charged</u>.

3) They're <u>tiny</u>, but they cover <u>a lot of space</u>.

4) The <u>volume</u> of their orbits determines the size of the atom — atoms have a radius of about 10^{-10} m.

5) Electrons have virtually <u>no</u> mass.

Atoms are really tiny, don't forget. They're too small to see, even with a very high power microscope.

- <u>Protons</u> are <u>heavy</u> and <u>positively charged</u>
- <u>Neutrons</u> are <u>heavy</u> and <u>neutral</u>
- <u>Electrons</u> are <u>tiny</u> and <u>negatively charged</u>

PARTICLE	MASS	CHARGE
Proton	1	+1
Neutron	1	0
Electron	0.0005	−1

(<u>Electron mass</u> is often taken as <u>zero</u>.)

Number of Protons Equals Number of Electrons

1) Neutral atoms have <u>no charge</u> overall (unlike ions, see page 86).

2) This is because they have the <u>same number</u> of <u>protons</u> as <u>electrons</u>.

3) The <u>charge</u> on the electrons is the <u>same</u> size as the charge on the <u>protons</u>, but <u>opposite</u> — so the charges <u>cancel out</u>.

Atomic Number and Mass Number Describe an Atom

These two numbers tell you how many of each kind of particle an atom has.

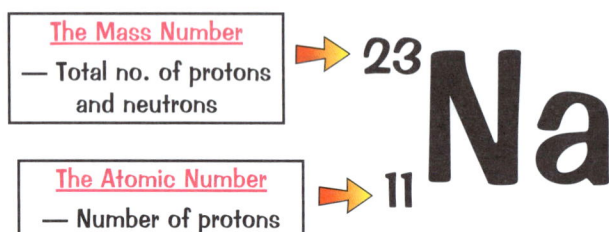

The Mass Number
— Total no. of protons and neutrons

The Atomic Number
— Number of protons

$$^{23}_{11}\text{Na}$$

1) The <u>atomic (proton) number</u> tells you how many <u>protons</u> there are.

2) Atoms of the <u>same</u> element all have the <u>same</u> number of <u>protons</u> — so atoms of <u>different</u> elements will have <u>different</u> numbers of protons.

3) To get the number of <u>neutrons</u>, just subtract the <u>atomic number</u> from the <u>mass number</u>.

4) The <u>mass (nucleon) number</u> is always the <u>biggest</u> number. On a periodic table the mass number is actually the <u>relative atomic mass</u> (see page 37).

Number of protons = number of electrons...

This stuff might seem a bit useless at first, but it should be permanently engraved into your mind. If you don't know these basic facts, you've got no chance of understanding the rest of chemistry. So <u>learn it now</u>, and watch as the Universe unfolds and reveals its timeless mysteries to you...

Elements and Isotopes

Elements are substances made up of only <u>one type</u> of atom, e.g. carbon is made up of <u>just</u> carbon atoms.

The Periodic Table is a Table of All Known Elements

The periodic table of elements is shown, with groups labelled Group 1 through Group 8, and a key showing: reactive metals, transition elements, post-transition metals, non metals, noble gases, and separates metals from non-metals. The key also shows mass number and atomic number using He Helium as an example.

1) There are 100ish elements, which all materials are made of. More are still being 'discovered'.

2) The <u>modern</u> periodic table shows the elements in order of ascending <u>atomic number</u>.

3) The periodic table is laid out so that elements with <u>similar properties</u> form <u>columns</u>.

4) These <u>vertical columns</u> are called <u>groups</u> and roman numerals are often (but not always) used for them.

5) The <u>group</u> to which the element belongs <u>corresponds</u> to the <u>number of electrons</u> it has in its <u>outer shell</u>.
E.g. <u>Group 1</u> elements have <u>1</u> outer shell electron, <u>Group 7</u> elements have <u>7</u> outer shell electrons and so on.
<u>Group 8</u> elements have <u>8</u> electrons in their outer shell — this means their outer shell is <u>full</u>.

6) The rows are called <u>periods</u>. Each new period represents another full <u>shell</u> of electrons (see page 85).

7) The period to which the element belongs corresponds to the <u>number of shells</u> of electrons it has.

Isotopes are the Same Except for an Extra Neutron or Two

> <u>Isotopes</u> are different forms of the same element, which have
> the <u>same number of protons</u> but a <u>different number of neutrons</u>.

1) Isotopes have the <u>same atomic number</u> but <u>different mass numbers</u>.

2) <u>If</u> they had <u>different</u> atomic numbers, they'd be <u>different</u> elements altogether.

3) A very popular pair of isotopes are <u>carbon-12</u> and <u>carbon-14</u>.

Carbon-12

$^{12}_{6}C$

6 PROTONS
6 ELECTRONS
6 NEUTRONS

Carbon-14

$^{14}_{6}C$

6 PROTONS
6 ELECTRONS
8 NEUTRONS

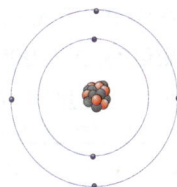

The number of neutrons is just the mass number minus the atomic number.

This table comes up periodically...

Scientists are still producing <u>new</u> elements in particle accelerators, but they're all <u>radioactive</u>.
Most only last a fraction of a second before they decay — they're up to element 118 at the moment.

History of the Periodic Table

We haven't always known as much about Chemistry as we do now. No sirree. Take the periodic table. Early chemists looked to try and understand patterns in the elements' properties to get a bit of understanding.

Döbereiner Tried to Organise Elements into Triads

Back in the 1800's the only thing they could measure was relative atomic mass, and so the known elements were arranged in order of atomic mass.

In 1828 a guy called Döbereiner started to put this list of elements into groups based on their chemical properties. He put the elements into groups of three, which he called triads. E.g. Cl, Br and I were one triad, and Li, Na and K were another.

The middle element of each triad had a relative atomic mass that was the average of the other two.

Element	Relative atomic mass
Lithium	7
Sodium	23
Potassium	39

$(7 + 39) \div 2 = 23$

Newlands' Law of Octaves Was the First Good Effort

A chap called Newlands had the first good stab at arranging things more usefully in 1864. He noticed that every eighth element had similar properties, and so he listed some of the known elements in rows of seven:

H	Li	Be	B	C	N	O
F	Na	Mg	Al	Si	P	S
Cl	K	Ca	Cr	Ti	Mn	Fe

These sets of eight were called Newlands' Octaves. Unfortunately the pattern broke down on the third row, with transition metals like titanium (Ti) and iron (Fe) messing it up.

It was because he left no gaps that his work was ignored. But he was getting pretty close, as you can see.

Newlands presented his ideas to the Chemical Society in 1865. But his work was criticised because:

1) His groups contained elements that didn't have similar properties, e.g. carbon and titanium.
2) He mixed up metals and non-metals e.g. oxygen and iron.
3) He didn't leave any gaps for elements that hadn't been discovered yet.

Dmitri Mendeleev Left Gaps and Predicted New Elements

1) In 1869, Dmitri Mendeleev in Russia, armed with about 50 known elements, arranged them into his Table of Elements — with various gaps as shown.

2) Mendeleev put the elements in order of atomic mass (like Newlands did). But Mendeleev found he had to leave gaps in order to keep elements with similar properties in the same vertical groups — and he was prepared to leave some very big gaps in the first two rows before the transition metals come in on the third row.

Mendeleev's Table of the Elements

```
H
Li  Be                                    B   C   N   O   F
Na  Mg                                    Al  Si  P   S   Cl
K   Ca  *   Ti  V   Cr  Mn  Fe Co Ni Cu Zn  *   *   As  Se  Br
Rb  Sr  Y   Zr  Nb  Mo  *   Ru Rh Pd Ag Cd In  Sn  Sb  Te  I
Cs  Ba  *   *   Ta  W   *   Os Ir Pt Au Hg Tl  Pb  Bi
```

3) The gaps were the really clever bit because they predicted the properties of so far undiscovered elements. When they were found and they fitted the pattern it was pretty smashing news for old Dmitri. The rogue.

4) Mendeleev's table made even more sense when later discoveries on atomic structure were made:
   - each element has an atomic number exactly one more than the previous element (see page 83).
   - the pattern in the periodic table — two elements in the first row, eight in the second and eight in the third, matches the way electrons are arranged in an atom — two in a first shell, eight in a second and eight in a third. There's more about this on the next page.

Julie Andrews' octaves — do-re-mi-fa-so-la-ti-do...

This is a good example of how science often progresses — even now. A scientist has a basically good (though incomplete) idea. Other scientists laugh and mock and generally deride. Eventually, the idea is modified a bit to take account of the available evidence, and voilà — into the textbooks it goes.

Electron Shells

Electron shells... orbits electrons zoom about in.

Electron Shell Rules:

1) Electrons always occupy shells (sometimes called energy levels).
2) The lowest energy levels are always filled first.
3) Only a certain number of electrons are allowed in each shell:

1st shell	2nd shell	3rd shell
2 electrons	8 electrons	8 electrons

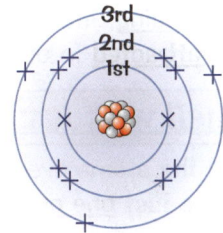

3rd shell still filling

Working Out Electron Configurations

You need to know the electron configurations for the first 20 elements. They're shown in the diagram below — but they're not hard to work out. For a quick example, take nitrogen. Follow the steps...

1) The periodic table tells you that nitrogen has seven protons... so it must have seven electrons.
2) Follow the 'Electron Shell Rules' above. The first shell can only take 2 electrons and the second shell can take a maximum of 8 electrons.
3) So the electron configuration for nitrogen must be 2,5 — easy peasy. Now you try it for argon.

The periodic table has a big gap here where the transition metals fit in on row four.

Answer: To calculate the electron configuration of argon, follow the rules. It's got 18 protons, so it must have 18 electrons. The first shell must have 2 electrons, the second shell must have 8, and so the third shell must have 8 as well. It's as easy as 2, 8, 8.

You can use the electronic configuration to work out the period, group and atomic number of an element.

- The period of the element is the same as the number of shells which contain electrons.
- The group number can be found by looking at how many electrons occupy the outer shell of the element.
  Example: Sodium has the electronic configuration 2,8,1. The period number is 3 as there are 3 shells occupied. The group number is 1 as there is 1 electron in the outer shell.
- The atomic number is found by adding up all the electrons. You can use it to identify elements. E.g. an electronic configuration of 2,8,2 gives an atomic number of 12, which tells you the element is Mg.

One little duck and two fat ladies — 2, 8, 8...

You need to know enough about electron shells to draw out that whole diagram at the bottom of the page without looking at it. Obviously, you don't have to learn each element separately, just learn the pattern.

Module C4 — The Periodic Table

Ionic Bonding

An ion is an atom or molecule which has lost or gained electrons to become <u>charged</u>.

Ionic Bonding — Transferring Electrons

In <u>ionic bonding</u>, atoms <u>lose or gain electrons</u> to form <u>charged particles</u> (or <u>ions</u>) which are then <u>strongly attracted</u> to one another (because of the attraction of opposite charges, + and −).

A Shell with Just One Electron is Well Keen to Get Rid...

1) All the atoms over at the <u>left-hand side</u> of the periodic table, such as sodium, magnesium etc., have just <u>one or two electrons</u> in their <u>outer shell</u>.

2) They're pretty keen to lose them, because then they'll only have <u>full shells</u> left, which is how they like it.

3) So given half a chance they do get rid, and that leaves the atom as a <u>positive ion</u> instead.

4) Ions are very reactive and will <u>leap</u> at the first passing ion with an <u>opposite charge</u> and stick to it like glue.

A Nearly Full Shell is Well Keen to Get That Extra Electron...

1) On the <u>other side</u> of the periodic table the elements in <u>Group 6</u> and <u>Group 7</u>, such as <u>oxygen</u> and <u>chlorine</u>, have outer shells which are <u>nearly full</u>.

2) They're obviously pretty keen to <u>gain</u> that <u>extra one or two electrons</u> to fill the shell up.

3) When they do they become <u>negative ions</u> and before you know it, <u>pop</u>, they've latched onto the atom (ion) that gave up the electron a moment earlier.

4) The reaction of sodium and chlorine is a <u>classic case</u>:

① The <u>sodium</u> atom <u>gives up</u> its <u>outer electron</u> and becomes an Na^+ ion.

② The <u>chlorine</u> atom <u>picks up</u> the <u>spare electron</u> and becomes a Cl^- ion.

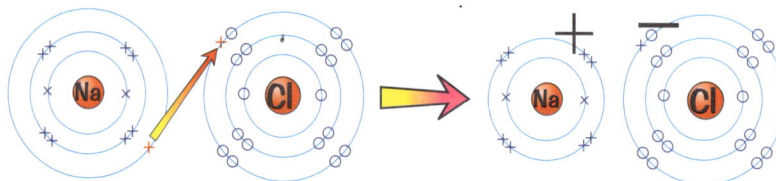

③ **POP!** An <u>ionic bond</u> is formed.

Ionic Compounds Form Giant Ionic Lattices

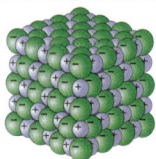

1) <u>Ionic bonds</u> form between <u>metals</u> and <u>non-metals</u> and always produce <u>giant ionic structures</u>.

2) The ions form a <u>closely packed</u> regular lattice arrangement. The ions are <u>not</u> free to move though, so these compounds do <u>not</u> conduct electricity when <u>solid</u>.

3) There are <u>very strong</u> chemical bonds between <u>all</u> the ions.

MgO and NaCl are Both Giant Ionic Structures

1) <u>Magnesium oxide</u> and <u>sodium chloride</u> both have high melting and boiling points. This is due to the <u>very strong</u> attraction between <u>oppositely charged ions</u> in the giant structures. To break the bonds you have to <u>overcome</u> these attractive forces — this takes a lot of energy.

2) MgO has a <u>higher melting point</u> than NaCl. It's made of Mg^{2+} and O^{2-} ions, which have <u>double the charge</u> of Na^+ and Cl^- ions, so the <u>attraction</u> between them is <u>harder to overcome</u>. O^{2-} ions are also <u>smaller</u> than Cl^- ions, so the ions in MgO can <u>pack together more closely</u>. This <u>also</u> makes the <u>attraction</u> between them <u>harder to overcome</u>.

Melted

Dissolved in Water

3) When MgO and NaCl <u>melt</u>, the ions are <u>free to move</u> and they'll conduct electricity.

4) NaCl <u>dissolves</u> to form a solution that <u>conducts electricity</u>. When dissolved the ions <u>separate</u> and are all <u>free to move</u> in the solution, so they can carry <u>electric current</u>.

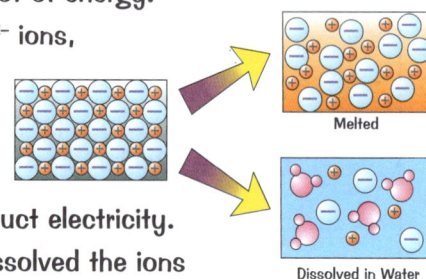

Giant ionic lattices — all over your chips...

Because they conduct electricity when they're dissolved in water, ionic compounds are used to make some types of <u>battery</u>. The solution used to leak all over the place but they can now make it into a <u>conductive paste</u>. Clever.

Ions and Ionic Compounds

Ions crop up all over the place in chemistry. You're gonna have to be able to work out <u>formulas</u> for compounds from their ions and draw some nifty <u>diagrams</u> to show it too. You'd better get on...

Simple Ions — Groups 1 & 2 and 6 & 7

1) <u>Ions</u> are <u>charged</u> particles — they can be <u>single atoms</u> (e.g. Cl^-) or <u>groups of atoms</u> (e.g. NO_3^-).

2) When <u>atoms</u> lose or gain electrons to form ions, all they're trying to do is get a <u>full outer shell</u> (also called a "<u>stable electronic structure</u>"). Atoms like full outer shells — it's atom heaven.

3) When <u>metals</u> form ions, they <u>lose</u> electrons to form <u>positive ions</u>.

4) When <u>non-metals</u> form ions, they <u>gain</u> electrons to form <u>negative ions</u>.

5) So when a <u>metal</u> and a <u>non-metal</u> combine, they form <u>ionic bonds</u>.

6) The <u>number</u> of electrons lost or gained is the same as the <u>charge</u> on the ion. E.g. If 2 electrons are <u>lost</u> the charge is 2^+. If 3 electrons are <u>gained</u> the charge is 3^-.

7) To work out the formula of an <u>ionic compound</u>, you have to <u>balance</u> the +ve and the –ve charges.

Potassium Chloride	Potassium oxide	Magnesium chloride
$K^+ + Cl^- \longrightarrow KCl$	$2K^+ + O^{2-} \longrightarrow K_2O$	$Mg^{2+} + 2Cl^- \longrightarrow MgCl_2$
The <u>potassium</u> ion is 1+, and the <u>chloride</u> ion is 1–, so they balance.	The <u>potassium</u> ion is 1+, and the <u>oxygen</u> ion is 2–, so you need <u>two</u> K^+ ions to balance the O^{2-} ion.	The <u>magnesium</u> ion is 2+, and the <u>chloride</u> ion is 1–, so you need <u>two</u> Cl^- ions to balance the Mg^{2+} ion.

Electronic Structure of Some Simple Ionic Compounds

'<u>Dot and cross</u>' diagrams show what happens to the electrons in <u>ionic bonds</u>:

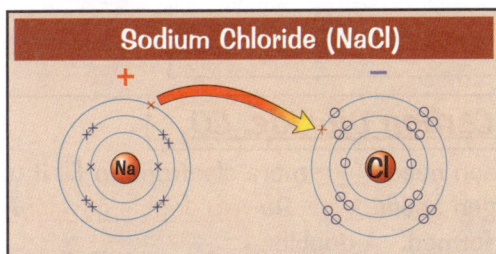

Sodium Chloride (NaCl)

The <u>sodium</u> atom gives up its outer electron, becoming an Na^+ ion. The <u>chlorine</u> atom picks up the electron, becoming a Cl^- (<u>chloride</u>) ion.

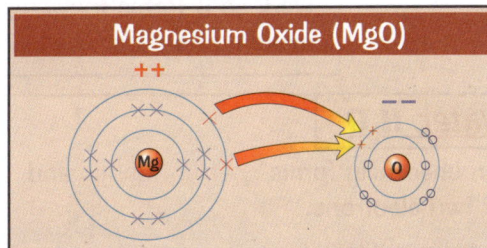

Magnesium Oxide (MgO)

The <u>magnesium</u> atom gives up its <u>two</u> outer electrons, becoming an Mg^{2+} ion. The <u>oxygen</u> atom picks up the electrons, becoming an O^{2-} (<u>oxide</u>) ion.

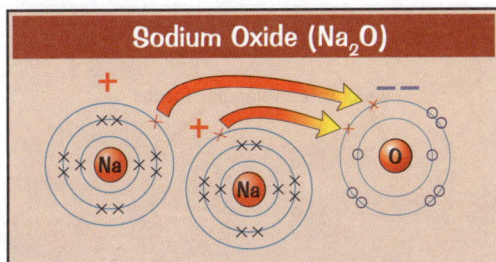

Sodium Oxide (Na₂O)

Two <u>sodium</u> atoms give up their outer electrons, becoming <u>two</u> Na^+ ions. The <u>oxygen</u> atom picks up the <u>two</u> electrons, becoming an O^{2-} ion.

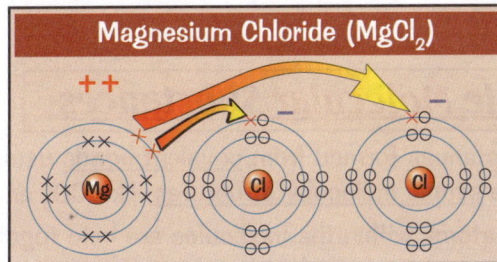

Magnesium Chloride (MgCl₂)

The <u>magnesium</u> atom gives up its <u>two</u> outer electrons, becoming an Mg^{2+} ion. The two <u>chlorine</u> atoms pick up <u>one electron each</u>, becoming <u>two</u> Cl^- ions.

Notice that <u>all</u> the atoms end up with <u>full outer shells</u> as a result of this giving and taking of electrons.

Full Shells — it's the name of the game...

Here's where you can get a little practice working out <u>formulas</u> for <u>molecules</u>. Remember to <u>balance</u> them, or you'll lose marks. Some elements like to gain electrons, some like to lose electrons, but they all want to have a <u>full outer shell</u>. Poor little electron shells, all they want in life is to be full...

Covalent Bonding

But wait — ionic bonding isn't the only way atoms can join together. Atoms can also <u>share</u> electrons to create very strong covalent bonds. Ah... aint that nice.

Covalent Bonds — Sharing Electrons

1) When <u>non-metal atoms</u> combine together they form <u>covalent bonds</u> by <u>sharing</u> pairs of electrons.
2) This way <u>both atoms</u> feel that they have <u>a full outer shell</u>, and that makes them happy.
3) <u>Each</u> covalent bond provides <u>one extra</u> shared electron for each atom.
4) Each atom involved has to make <u>enough</u> covalent bonds to <u>fill up</u> its outer shell.
5) <u>Learn</u> these important examples:

1) Hydrogen Gas, H_2

Hydrogen atoms have just one electron. They <u>only need one more</u> to complete the first shell...

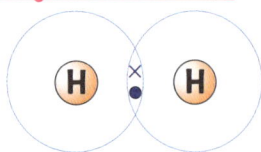

...so they often form <u>single covalent bonds</u> to achieve this.

2) Chlorine Gas, Cl_2

Each chlorine atom needs just <u>one more electron</u> to complete the outer shell...

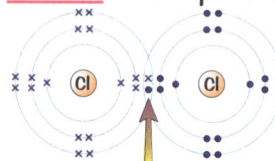

...so they form <u>a single covalent bond</u> and together share <u>one pair</u> of electrons.

3) Methane, CH_4

Carbon has <u>four outer electrons</u>, which is a <u>half-full</u> shell.

To become a 4+ or a 4– ion is hard work so it forms <u>four covalent bonds</u> to make up its outer shell.

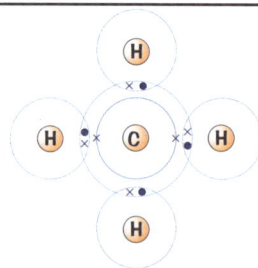

4) Water, H_2O

Oxygen cheerfully forms <u>covalent bonds</u> and <u>shares</u> two electrons.
Like in <u>water molecules</u>, where it <u>shares</u> electrons with the hydrogen atoms.

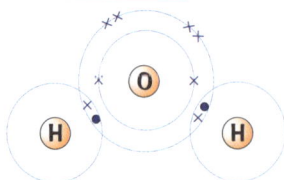

5) Carbon Dioxide, CO_2

Carbon needs <u>four</u> more electrons to fill it up, oxygen needs <u>two</u>. So <u>two double covalent bonds</u> are formed. A double covalent bond has <u>two shared pairs</u> of electrons.

Simple Molecular Substances

1) Substances formed from <u>covalent bonds</u> usually have <u>simple molecular structures</u>, like CO_2 and H_2O.
2) The atoms within the molecules are held together by <u>very strong covalent bonds</u>.
3) By contrast, the forces of attraction <u>between</u> these molecules are <u>very weak</u>.
4) The <u>result</u> of these <u>feeble intermolecular forces</u> is that the melting and boiling points are <u>very low</u>, because the molecules are <u>easily parted</u> from each other.
5) Most molecular substances are <u>gases or liquids</u> at room temperature.
6) Molecular substances <u>don't conduct electricity</u>, simply because there are <u>no free electrons</u> or ions.

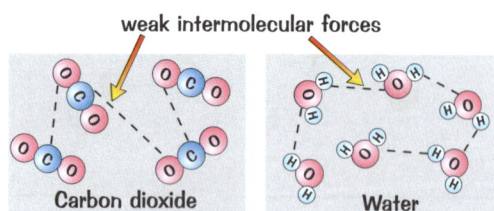

weak intermolecular forces

Carbon dioxide   Water

It's good to share — especially when it's somebody else's...

If a compound has a <u>simple molecular structure</u>, you need to be able to predict its properties. So remember — <u>low</u> melting and boiling points, so probably a <u>gas</u> or <u>liquid</u> at room temperature, and <u>doesn't conduct electricity</u>.

Group 1 — Alkali Metals

Welcome to the wonderful world of the <u>alkali metals</u>. May I introduce Li, Na, K, Rb, Cs and Fr...

Group 1 Metals are Known as the 'Alkali Metals'

Group 1 metals include lithium, sodium and potassium... know those three names real well. They could also ask you about rubidium and caesium.

> As you go <u>DOWN</u> Group 1, the alkali metals become <u>more reactive</u> — the <u>outer electron</u> is more easily <u>lost</u>, because it's further from the nucleus (the <u>atomic radius</u> is <u>larger</u>) so <u>less energy</u> is needed to remove it.

1) The alkali metals all have <u>ONE outer electron</u>.
   This makes them <u>very reactive</u> and gives them all <u>similar properties</u>.

2) They all have the following <u>physical properties</u>:
   - <u>Low melting point</u> and <u>boiling point</u> (compared with other metals).
   - <u>Low density</u> — lithium, sodium and potassium float on water.
   - <u>Very soft</u> — they can be cut with a knife.

3) The alkali metals always form <u>ionic</u> compounds. They are so keen to lose the outer electron there's no way they'd consider <u>sharing</u>, so covalent bonding is <u>out of the question</u>.

Oxidation is the Loss of Electrons

1) Group 1 metals are keen to <u>lose an electron</u> to form a <u>1⁺ ion</u> with a <u>stable electronic structure</u>.

2) The <u>more</u> reactive the metal the happier it is to <u>lose</u> an electron.

3) Loss of electrons is called <u>OXIDATION</u>.

$$Li - e^- \rightarrow Li^+$$

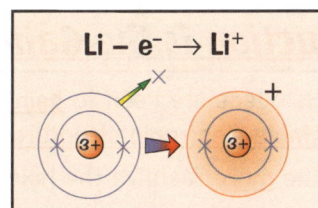

Reaction with Cold Water Produces Hydrogen Gas

1) When <u>lithium</u>, <u>sodium</u> or <u>potassium</u> are put in <u>water</u>, they react very <u>vigorously</u>.

2) They <u>move</u> around the surface, <u>fizzing</u> furiously and produce <u>hydrogen</u>.

3) The reactivity with water increases down the group — the reaction with potassium gets hot enough to <u>ignite</u> it.

4) Sodium and potassium <u>melt</u> in the heat of the reaction.

5) An <u>alkali</u> forms which is the <u>hydroxide</u> of the metal.

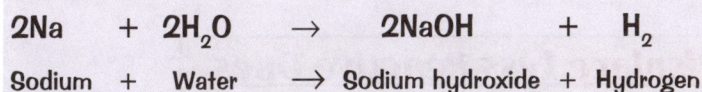

A lighted splint will <u>indicate</u> hydrogen by producing the notorious "<u>squeaky pop</u>" as the H_2 ignites.

$$2Na \quad + \quad 2H_2O \quad \rightarrow \quad 2NaOH \quad + \quad H_2$$

Sodium + Water $\rightarrow$ Sodium hydroxide + Hydrogen

Rubidium and caesium are even more reactive than potassium. This means they react more violently with water. They even explode when they get wet...

6) This happens with <u>all</u> the alkali metals (lithium forms LiOH, potassium forms KOH etc.). For the exam you could be asked about <u>any</u> of them so make sure you can write <u>balanced equations</u> for each one.

Alkali Metal Compounds Burn with Characteristic Colours

1) Dip a wire loop into some <u>hydrochloric acid</u> to clean and moisten it.

2) Put the loop into a <u>powdered</u> sample of the compound to be tested, then place the end in a <u>blue Bunsen flame</u>.

3) Alkali metal ions will give pretty coloured flames — the colour of the flame tells you which <u>alkali metal</u> is present.

<u>Lithium</u>:   <u>Red</u> flame
<u>Sodium</u>:   <u>Yellow/orange</u> flame
<u>Potassium</u>: <u>Lilac</u> flame

Red and orange and pink and green — or something like that...

Alkali metals are <u>really reactive</u>. They're so reactive in fact they have to be stored in oil — otherwise they just react with the air. Learn the <u>trends</u> and <u>characteristics</u> of alkali metals before turning over.

Group 7 — Halogens

Here's a page on another periodic group — the halogens...

Group 7 Elements are Known as the 'Halogens'

1) Group 7 is made up of fluorine, chlorine, bromine, iodine and astatine.
2) All Group 7 elements have 7 electrons in their outer shell — so they all react by gaining one electron to form a negative ion.
3) This means they've all got similar properties.

> As you go DOWN Group 7, the halogens become less reactive — there's less inclination to gain the extra electron to fill the outer shell when it's further out from the nucleus (there's a larger atomic radius).

4) As you go down group 7 the melting points and boiling points of the halogens increase.
5) This means that at room temperature:

- Chlorine (Cl_2) is a fairly reactive, poisonous, dense green gas (low boiling point).
- Bromine (Br_2) is a dense, poisonous, orange liquid.
- Iodine (I_2) is a dark grey crystalline solid (high boiling point).

Reduction is the Gain of Electrons

1) Halogens are keen to gain an electron to form a 1^- ion with a stable electronic structure.
2) The more reactive the halogen the happier it is to gain an electron.
3) Gain of electrons is called REDUCTION.

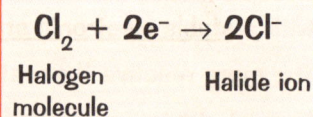

$$Cl_2 + 2e^- \rightarrow 2Cl^-$$

Halogen molecule   Halide ion

The Halogens React with Alkali Metals to Form Salts

The Halogens react vigorously with alkali metals (group 1 elements, see page 89) to form salts called 'metal halides'.

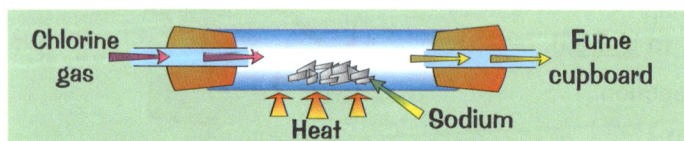

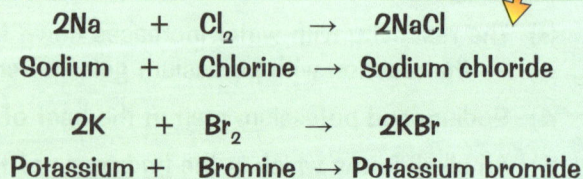

Make sure you can write equations for the reactions between all the group 1 and group 7 elements.

Chlorine gas   Fume cupboard

Heat   Sodium

$$2Na + Cl_2 \rightarrow 2NaCl$$
Sodium + Chlorine → Sodium chloride

$$2K + Br_2 \rightarrow 2KBr$$
Potassium + Bromine → Potassium bromide

More Reactive Halogens Will Displace Less Reactive Ones

Chlorine can displace bromine and iodine from a solution of bromide or iodide. Bromine will also displace iodine. You could be asked to predict the results of displacement reactions using other halogens — just remember, more reactive halogens displace less reactive ones.

Remember to balance the symbol equation properly or you'll lose marks in the exam.

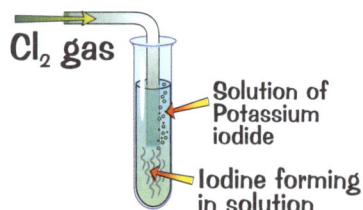

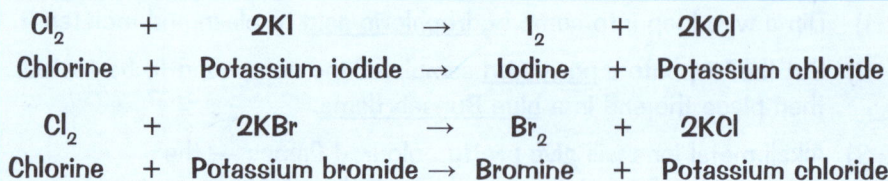

Cl_2 gas

Solution of Potassium iodide

Iodine forming in solution

$$Cl_2 + 2KI \rightarrow I_2 + 2KCl$$
Chlorine + Potassium iodide → Iodine + Potassium chloride

$$Cl_2 + 2KBr \rightarrow Br_2 + 2KCl$$
Chlorine + Potassium bromide → Bromine + Potassium chloride

Halogens — one electron short of a full shell...

The halogens are another group from the periodic table, and just like the alkali metals (p.89) you've got to learn their trends and the equations on this page. Learn them, cover up the page, scribble, check.

Metals

Loads of elements are metals and they all have really <u>useful properties</u>. Make sure you learn 'em well.

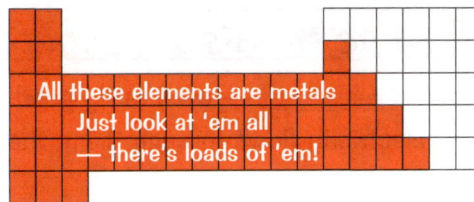

All these elements are metals
Just look at 'em all
— there's loads of 'em!

Metals Have a Crystal Structure

1) <u>All</u> metals have the <u>same</u> basic properties.
2) These are due to the <u>special type of bonding</u> that exists in metals.
3) Metals are held together with <u>metallic bonds</u>.
4) These special bonds allow the <u>outer electron(s)</u> of each atom to move freely.
5) This creates a '<u>sea</u>' of <u>delocalised</u> (free) <u>electrons</u> throughout the metal which is what gives rise to many of the properties of metals.

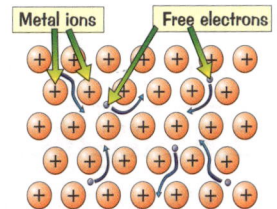

Metal ions   Free electrons

Most Have High Melting and Boiling Points, and High Density

1) Metals are very <u>hard</u>, <u>dense</u> and <u>lustrous</u> (i.e. shiny).
2) There's a <u>strong attraction</u> between the <u>delocalised electrons</u> and the closely packed <u>positive ions</u> — causing very <u>strong metallic bonding</u>.
3) Metals have <u>high melting</u> and <u>boiling points</u> because of these <u>strong metallic bonds</u>. You need to use a lot of <u>energy</u> to break them apart.
4) The <u>strength</u> of the metallic bond (and the <u>melting point</u>) <u>decreases</u> as <u>atomic radius increases</u>.

They're Strong, but Also Bendy and Malleable

1) Metals have a <u>high tensile strength</u> — in other words they're <u>strong</u> and <u>hard to break</u>.
2) But they can also be <u>hammered</u> into a different shape (they're malleable).

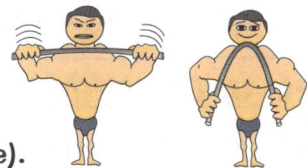

They're Good Conductors of Heat and Electricity

1) This is entirely due to the sea of <u>delocalised electrons</u> which move freely through the metal, carrying the <u>electrical current</u>.
2) They also carry the <u>heat energy</u> through the metal.

Don't try this at home. You'll die.

You've Got to be Able to Match the Metal to the Use

Use	Properties	Metal
Saucepans	Good conductor of heat, doesn't rust easily	Stainless Steel — and it's cheap too.
Electrical Wiring	Good conductor of electricity, easily bent	Copper. One of the best conductors around.
Aeroplanes	Low density (light), strong, doesn't corrode	Aluminium. Titanium's sometimes used, but it's a lot more expensive.
Bridges	Strong	Steel — this is mostly iron, but it's got a little bit of carbon in it, which makes it a lot less brittle.

In the exam you might have to suggest properties needed by a metal for a particular use.

Daniel Craig — he's definitely a strong Bond...

It's not just the main structure of an aeroplane that's made of aluminium — parts of the <u>engines</u>, the <u>seat supports</u> and even the cabin crew's <u>trolleys</u> are all made of aluminium. All this aluminium means the plane's light enough to fly.

Module C4 — The Periodic Table

Superconductors and Transition Metals

Oooooo, some interesting stuff...

At Very Low Temperatures, Some Metals are Superconductors

1) Normally, all metals have some electrical resistance — even really good conductors like copper.

2) That resistance means that whenever electricity flows through them, they heat up, and some of the electrical energy is wasted as heat.

3) If you make some metals cold enough, though, their resistance disappears completely. The metal becomes a superconductor.

4) Without any resistance, none of the electrical energy is turned into heat, so none of it's wasted.

5) That means you could start a current flowing through a superconducting circuit, take out the battery, and the current would carry on flowing forever.

So What's the Catch...

1) Using superconducting wires you can make:

   a) Power cables that transmit electricity without any loss of power (loss-free power transmission).

   b) Really strong electromagnets that don't need a constant power source.

   c) Electronic circuits that work really fast, because there's no resistance to slow them down.

2) But here's the catch — when I said cold, I meant REALLY COLD. Metals only start superconducting at less than −265 °C! Getting things that cold is very hard, and very expensive, which limits the use of superconductors.

3) Scientists are trying to develop room temperature superconductors now. So far, they've managed to get some weird metal oxide things to superconduct at about −135 °C, which is a much cheaper temperature to get down to. They've still got a long way to go though — ideally they need to develop superconductors that still work at 20 °C.

Metals in the Middle of the Periodic Table are Transition Metals

A lot of everyday metals are transition metals (e.g. copper, iron, zinc, gold, silver, platinum) — but there are loads of others as well. Transition metals have typical 'metallic' properties.

If you get asked about a transition metal you've never heard of — don't panic. These 'new' transition metals follow all the properties you've already learnt for the others. It's just that some folk get worried by the unfamiliar names.

These are the transition metals

| Sc | Ti | V | Cr | Mn | Fe | Co | Ni | Cu | Zn |

Transition Metals and Their Compounds Make Good Catalysts

1) Iron is the catalyst used in the Haber process for making ammonia.

2) Nickel is useful for the hydrogenation of alkenes (e.g. to make margarine).

The Compounds are Very Colourful

The compounds of transition elements are colourful due to the transition metal ion they contain. E.g. Iron(II) compounds are usually light green, iron(III) compounds are orange/brown (e.g. rust) and copper compounds are often blue.

Mendeleev and his amazing technicoloured periodic table...

Superconducting magnets are used in magnetic resonance image (MRI) scanners in hospitals. That way, the huge magnetic fields they need can be generated without using up a load of electricity. Great stuff...

Thermal Decomposition and Precipitation

There's an awful lot of stuff to learn on this page so you'd better get started...

1) Thermal Decomposition — Breaking Down with Heat

1) Thermal decomposition is when a substance breaks down into at least two other substances when heated.

2) Transition metal carbonates break down on heating. Transition metal carbonates are things like copper(II) carbonate ($CuCO_3$), iron(II) carbonate ($FeCO_3$), zinc carbonate ($ZnCO_3$) and manganese carbonate ($MnCO_3$), i.e. they've all got a CO_3 bit in them.

3) They break down into a metal oxide (e.g. copper oxide, CuO) and carbon dioxide. This usually results in a colour change.

EXAMPLE: The thermal decomposition of copper(II) carbonate.

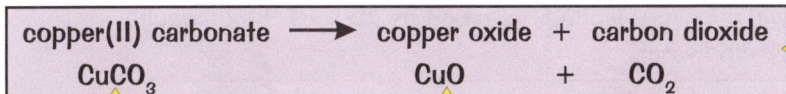

copper(II) carbonate	$\longrightarrow$	copper oxide	+	carbon dioxide
$CuCO_3$		CuO	+	CO_2

This is green... ...and this is black.

The reactions for the thermal decomposition of:
(i) iron(II) carbonate to iron oxide (FeO),
(ii) manganese carbonate to manganese oxide (MnO),
(iii) zinc carbonate to zinc oxide (ZnO),
are the same — although the colours are different.

4) You can easily check that the gas given off is carbon dioxide by bubbling it through limewater. If carbon dioxide is present the limewater turns milky.

2) Precipitation — A Solid Forms in Solution

1) A precipitation reaction is where two solutions react and an insoluble solid forms in the solution.

2) The solid is said to 'precipitate out' and, confusingly, the solid is also called 'a precipitate'.

3) Some soluble transition metal compounds react with sodium hydroxide to form an insoluble hydroxide, which then precipitates out. Here are some examples you need to know.

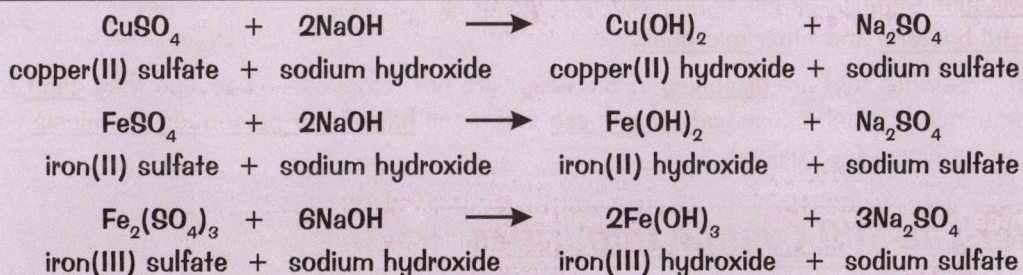

$CuSO_4$	+	2NaOH	$\longrightarrow$	$Cu(OH)_2$	+	Na_2SO_4
copper(II) sulfate	+	sodium hydroxide		copper(II) hydroxide	+	sodium sulfate
$FeSO_4$	+	2NaOH	$\longrightarrow$	$Fe(OH)_2$	+	Na_2SO_4
iron(II) sulfate	+	sodium hydroxide		iron(II) hydroxide	+	sodium sulfate
$Fe_2(SO_4)_3$	+	6NaOH	$\longrightarrow$	$2Fe(OH)_3$	+	$3Na_2SO_4$
iron(III) sulfate	+	sodium hydroxide		iron(III) hydroxide	+	sodium sulfate

4) You can also write the above equations in terms of ions, for example:

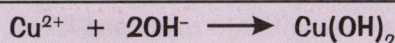

$$Cu^{2+} + 2OH^- \longrightarrow Cu(OH)_2$$

Use Precipitation to Test for Transition Metal Ions

1) Some insoluble transition metal hydroxides have distinctive colours.

2) You can use this fact to test which transition metal ions a solution contains.

Copper(II) hydroxide is a blue solid.
Iron(II) hydroxide is a grey/green solid.
Iron(III) hydroxide is an orange/brown solid.

3) For example, if you add sodium hydroxide to an unknown soluble salt, and an orange/brown precipitate forms, you know you've got iron(III) hydroxide and so have Fe^{3+} ions in the solution.

My duffel coat's worn out — thermal decomposition...

Wow. This page is packed full of chemistry. I'm afraid you're gonna have to learn all the equations for thermal decomposition and precipitation and the colours of the precipitates if you want to impress the examiner.

Module C4 — The Periodic Table

Water Purity

Water, water, everywhere... well, there is if you live in Cumbria.

There are a Variety of Limited Water Resources in the UK

1) As well as for drinking, we need water for loads of domestic uses (mainly washing things).
2) Industrially, water is important as a cheap raw material, a coolant (especially in power stations) and a solvent. Between half and two thirds of all the fresh water used in the UK goes into industry.

> In the UK, we get our water from:
> 1) SURFACE WATER: lakes, rivers and reservoirs (artificial lakes). In much of England and Wales, these sources start to run dry during the summer months.
> 2) GROUNDWATER: aquifers (rocks that trap water underground). In parts of the south-east where surface water is very limited, as much as 70% of the domestic water supply comes from groundwater.

All these resources are limited, depending on annual rainfall, and demand for water increases every year. Experts worry that, unless we limit our water use, by 2025 we might not have enough water to supply everybody's needs. So it's important to conserve water.

Water is Purified in Water Treatment Plants

How much purification the water needs depends on the source. Groundwater from aquifers is usually quite pure, but surface water needs a lot of treatment. The processes include:

1) Filtration — a wire mesh screens out large twigs etc., and then gravel and sand beds filter out any other solid bits.
2) Sedimentation — iron sulfate or aluminium sulfate is added to the water, which makes fine particles clump together and settle at the bottom.
3) Chlorination — chlorine gas is bubbled through to kill harmful bacteria and other microbes.

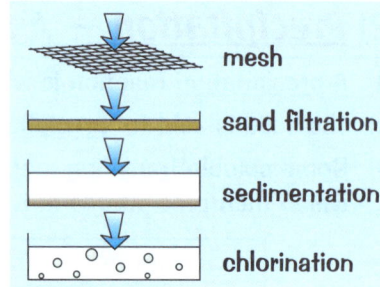

mesh

sand filtration

sedimentation

chlorination

Some soluble impurities that are dissolved in the water are not removed — because they can't be filtered out. These include minerals which cause water hardness and some harmful or poisonous chemicals such as pesticides and fertilisers (see below).

Tap Water Can Still Contain Impurities

The water that comes out of our taps has to meet strict safety standards, but low levels of pollutants are still found. These pollutants come from various sources:

1) Nitrate residues from excess fertiliser 'run-off' into rivers and lakes. If too many nitrates get into drinking water it can cause serious health problems, especially for young babies. Nitrates prevent the blood from carrying oxygen properly.
2) Lead compounds from old lead pipes. Lead is very poisonous, particularly in children.
3) Pesticide residues from spraying too near to rivers and lakes.

You Can Get Fresh Water by Distilling Sea Water

1) In some very dry countries, e.g. Kuwait, sea water is distilled to produce drinking water.
2) Distillation needs loads of energy, so it's really expensive and not practical for producing large quantities of fresh water.

Who'd have thought there'd be so much to learn about water...

In the UK we're very lucky to have clean water available at the turn of a tap — but it's not a never-ending supply. Learn how water is purified in the UK, and what pollutants get through the cleaning process. Cover. Scribble.

Testing Water Purity

Here's another page on water and an interesting fact to keep you going... Taking a five-minute shower uses more water than a typical person in a slum in a developing country uses in a whole day. Crazy stuff.

You Can Test Water for Various Dissolved Ions

Water companies have to test their water regularly to make sure that pollutant levels don't exceed strict limits. You can test for some dissolved ions very easily using precipitation reactions (where two dissolved compounds react to form an insoluble solid — see page 93).

Test for Sulfate Ions Using Barium Chloride

1) Add some dilute hydrochloric acid to the test sample.
2) Then add 10 drops of barium chloride solution.
3) If you see a white precipitate, there are sulfate ions in the sample.

barium ions + sulfate ions → barium sulfate
$$Ba^{2+} + SO_4^{2-} \rightarrow BaSO_4$$

add $BaCl_2$ solution
white precipitate of $BaSO_4$

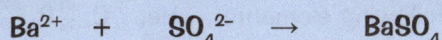

4) Here's an example where potassium sulfate is present in the sample:

barium chloride + potassium sulfate → barium sulfate + potassium chloride
$$BaCl_2 + K_2SO_4 \rightarrow BaSO_4 + KCl$$

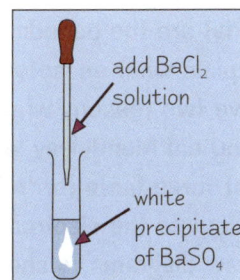

Test for Halide Ions Using Silver Nitrate

1) Add some dilute nitric acid to the test sample.
2) Then add 10 drops of silver nitrate solution.
3) If halide ions are present a precipitate will form.

- Chloride ions will produce a white precipitate.
- Bromide ions will produce a cream precipitate.
- Iodide ions will produce a pale yellow precipitate.

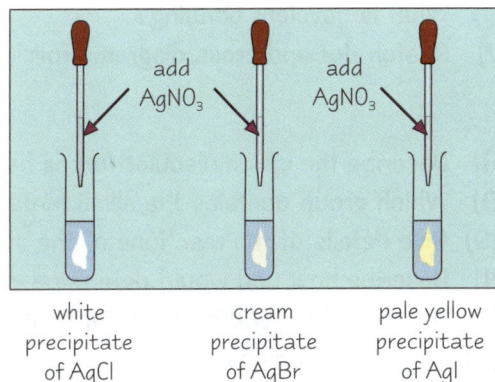

add $AgNO_3$ add $AgNO_3$
white precipitate of AgCl   cream precipitate of AgBr   pale yellow precipitate of AgI

4) These are the reactions you'll need to know for the exam:

silver nitrate + sodium chloride → silver chloride + sodium nitrate
$$AgNO_3 + NaCl \rightarrow AgCl + NaNO_3$$

silver nitrate + sodium bromide → silver bromide + sodium nitrate
$$AgNO_3 + NaBr \rightarrow AgBr + NaNO_3$$

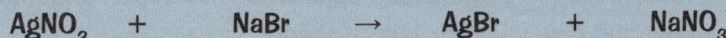

silver nitrate + sodium iodide → silver iodide + sodium nitrate
$$AgNO_3 + NaI \rightarrow AgI + NaNO_3$$

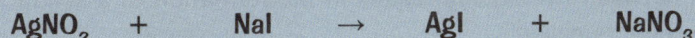

Two parts hydrogen, one part oxygen — hold the pollutants...

Water is amazingly important for us humans, but it's only safe to use if it's been tested properly for pollutants. One in eight people in the world don't have daily access to clean water and over two million people a year die from water related diseases. That's why it's so important for water companies to test their water regularly. Now, to brighten up your day, here comes a lovely revision summary. I know, I shouldn't have...

Module C4 — The Periodic Table

Revision Summary for Module C4

These certainly aren't the easiest questions you're going to come across. That's because they test what you know without giving you any clues. At first you might think they're impossibly difficult. Eventually you'll realise that they simply test whether you've learnt the stuff or not. If you're struggling to answer these then you need to do some serious learning.

1) Describe the famous 'gold foil experiment'. What did Rutherford conclude from it?
2) What are the three particles found in an atom? What are their relative masses and charges?
3) What do the mass number and atomic number represent?
4) What feature of atoms determines the order of the modern periodic table?
5) What are the periods and groups? Explain their significance in terms of electrons.
6) Explain what an isotope is. Give a well-known example.
7) Give two reasons why Newlands' Octaves were criticised.
8) Why did Mendeleev leave gaps in his Table of Elements?
9) List three facts (or 'rules') about electron shells.
10) Calculate the electron configuration for each of the following elements: $^{4}_{2}He$, $^{12}_{6}C$, $^{31}_{15}P$, $^{39}_{19}K$.
11) Draw diagrams to show the electron arrangements for the first 20 elements.
12) What is ionic bonding?
13) Draw a diagram of a giant ionic lattice and give three features of giant ionic structures.
14) How many electrons are lost or gained for atoms to form 1+, 1–, 2+ and 2– ions?
15) Sketch dot and cross diagrams for: a) sodium chloride
                                                     b) magnesium oxide
                                                     c) sodium oxide
                                                     d) magnesium chloride
16) What is covalent bonding?
17) Sketch dot and cross diagrams for: a) hydrogen gas
                                                  b) water
                                                c) carbon dioxide
18) Describe the intermolecular forces between simple molecular substances.
19) Which group contains the alkali metals? How many electrons do they each have in their outer shell?
20) Give details of the reactions of the alkali metals with water.
21) Describe how you would determine whether a powdered sample contained sodium or potassium.
22) Describe the trend in reactivity of the halogens as you go down the group.
23) What is reduction?
24)* Write word equations and balanced symbol equations for the reactions between:
    a) bromine and lithium,   b) chlorine and potassium,   c) iodine and sodium.
25) Give details, with an equation, of a displacement reaction involving the halogens.
26) Give two properties of metals. Explain these properties in terms of the structure of a metal.
27) Why is copper used for electrical wiring?
28) What is a superconductor? Describe some useful applications of superconductors.
29) Name six transition metals, and give uses for two of them.
30) What are thermal decomposition reactions?
31) What type of reaction between two liquids results in the formation of a solid?
    What are these solid products called?
32) Describe a way to test solutions for transition metal ions.
33) Describe three processes used during the purification of surface water.
34) A student adds dilute hydrochloric acid and barium chloride to a water sample and a white precipitate is produced. What ions are present in the water?

* Answers on page 116.

Static Electricity

Static electricity is all about charges which are <u>NOT</u> free to move. This causes them to build up in one place, and it often ends with a <u>spark</u> or a <u>shock</u> when they do finally move.

1) Build-up of Static is Caused by Friction

1) <u>Electrons</u> have a <u>negative</u> charge.

2) When two <u>insulating</u> materials are <u>rubbed</u> together, electrons will be <u>scraped off one</u> and <u>dumped</u> on the other.

3) This leaves a <u>positive</u> static charge on one due to a <u>lack</u> of electrons — it <u>lost</u> electrons (–), so this leaves it positively (+) charged.

4) And it leaves a <u>negative</u> static charge on the other due to an <u>excess</u> of electrons — it <u>gained</u> electrons (–).

5) <u>Which way</u> the electrons are transferred <u>depends</u> on the <u>two materials</u> involved.

6) Electrically charged objects <u>attract</u> small neutral objects placed near them. (Try this: rub a balloon on a woolly pullover — then put it near tiddly bits of paper and watch them jump.)

7) The classic examples are <u>polythene</u> and <u>acetate</u> rods being rubbed with a <u>cloth duster</u>, as shown in the diagrams.

With the <u>polythene rod</u>, electrons move <u>from the duster</u> to the rod.

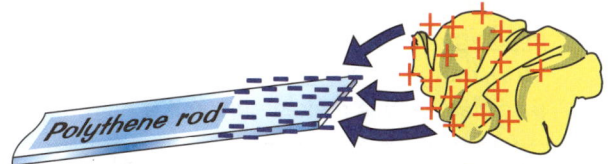

Polythene rod

Acetate rod

With the <u>acetate rod</u>, electrons move <u>from the rod</u> to the duster.

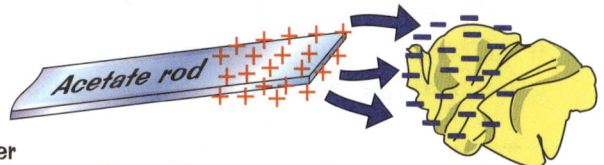

2) Only Electrons Move — Never the Positive Charges

1) <u>Watch out for this in exams</u>. Both +ve and –ve electrostatic charges are only ever produced by the movement of <u>electrons</u>.

2) The positive charges <u>definitely do not move</u>. A positive static charge is always caused by electrons <u>moving</u> away elsewhere, as shown above. Don't forget!

3) If enough static charge builds up, it can <u>suddenly move</u> which can cause <u>sparks</u> or <u>shocks</u> that can be dangerous (see next page).

4) A charged conductor can be <u>discharged safely</u> by connecting it to earth with a <u>metal strap</u>. This is called <u>earthing</u> (see next page).

5) The electrons flow <u>down</u> the strap to the ground if the charge is <u>negative</u> and flow <u>up</u> the strap from the ground if the charge is <u>positive</u>.

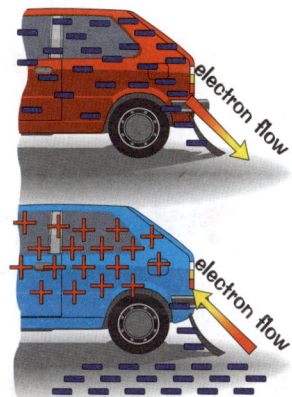

electron flow

electron flow

3) Like Charges Repel, Opposite Charges Attract

Hopefully this is <u>kind of obvious</u>.

1) Two things with <u>opposite</u> electric charges are <u>attracted</u> to each other.

2) Two things with the <u>same</u> electric charge will <u>repel</u> each other.

3) These forces get <u>weaker</u> the <u>further apart</u> the two things are.

4) <u>Atoms</u> or <u>molecules</u> that become <u>charged</u> are known as <u>ions</u>.

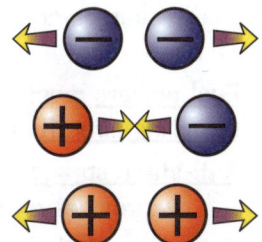

Come on, be +ve — this module's more interesting than the last one...

Static electricity's great fun. You must have tried it — rubbing a balloon against your clothes and trying to get it to stick to the ceiling. It really works... well, sometimes. And it's all due to the build-up of static. <u>Bad hair days</u> are also caused by static — it builds up on your hair, so your strands of hair repel each other. Conditioners try to decrease this, but they don't always work — so not as much fun as the jumper trick...

More on Static Electricity

They like asking you to give quite detailed examples in exams. Make sure you learn all these details.

Static Electricity Being a Nuisance:

1) Attracting Dust

Dust particles are charged and will be attracted to anything with the opposite charge. Unfortunately, many objects around the house are made out of insulators (e.g. TV screen, wood, plastic containers etc.) that get easily charged and attract the dust particles — this makes cleaning a nightmare.

2) Clothing Clings and Crackles

When synthetic clothes are dragged over each other (like in a tumble drier) or over your head, electrons get scraped off, leaving static charges on both parts, and that leads to the inevitable — attraction (they stick together and cling to you) and little sparks or shocks as the charges rearrange themselves.

3) Shocks From Door Handles

If you walk on a nylon carpet wearing shoes with insulating soles, charge builds up on your body. Then if you touch a metal door handle or water pipe, the charge flows via the conductor and you get a little shock.

Static Electricity Can be Dangerous:

1) A Lot of Charge Can Build Up on Clothes

1) A large amount of static charge can build up on clothes made out of synthetic materials if they rub against other synthetic fabrics (see above).

2) Eventually, this charge can become large enough to make a spark — which is really bad news if it happens near any inflammable gases or fuel fumes... KABOOM!

2) Grain Chutes, Paper Rollers and the Fuel Filling Nightmare

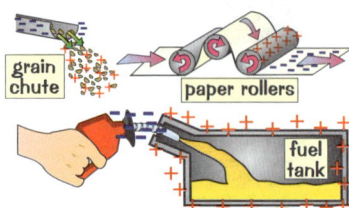

grain chute   paper rollers   fuel tank

1) As fuel flows out of a filler pipe, or paper drags over rollers, or grain shoots out of pipes, then static can build up.

2) This can easily lead to a spark and might cause an explosion in dusty or fumey places — like when filling up a car with fuel at a petrol station.

3) All these problems with sparks can be solved by earthing charged objects.

Objects Can be Earthed or Insulated to Prevent Sparks

1) Dangerous sparks can be prevented by connecting a charged object to the ground using a conductor (e.g. a copper wire) — this is called earthing and it provides an easy route for the static charges to travel into the ground. This means no charge can build up to give you a shock or make a spark.

2) Static charges are a big problem in places where sparks could ignite inflammable gases, or where there are high concentrations of oxygen (e.g. in a hospital operating theatre).

3) Fuel tankers must be earthed to prevent any sparks that might cause the fuel to explode — refuelling aircraft are bonded to their fuel tankers using an earthing cable to prevent sparks.

4) Anti-static sprays and liquids work by making the surface of a charged object conductive — this provides an easy path for the charges to move away and not cause a problem.

5) Anti-static cloths are conductive, so they can carry charge away from objects they're used to wipe.

6) Insulating mats and shoes with insulating soles prevent static electricity from moving through them, so they stop you from getting a shock.

Static electricity — it's really shocking stuff...

Lightning is an extreme case of a static electricity spark. It always chooses the easiest path between the sky and the ground — that's the nearest, tallest thing. That's why it's never a good idea to fly a kite in a thunderstorm...

Uses of Static Electricity

Static electricity isn't always a nuisance. It's got loads of applications in medicine and industry, and now's your chance to learn all about them, you lucky thing...

1) Paint Sprayers — Getting an Even Coat

1) Bikes and cars are painted using electrostatic paint sprayers.

2) The spray gun is charged, which charges up the small drops of paint.

3) Each paint drop repels all the others, since they've all got the same charge, so you get a very fine spray.

The spray gun can be charged either positive or negative. You've just got to remember to charge the object you're painting the opposite charge.

4) The object to be painted is given an opposite charge to the gun. This attracts the fine spray of paint.

5) This method gives an even coat and hardly any paint is wasted. Parts of the bicycle or car pointing away from the spray gun still receive paint too — there are no paint shadows.

6) In the diagram, the paint is negatively charged so it's gained electrons, and the bike is positively charged so it's lost electrons.

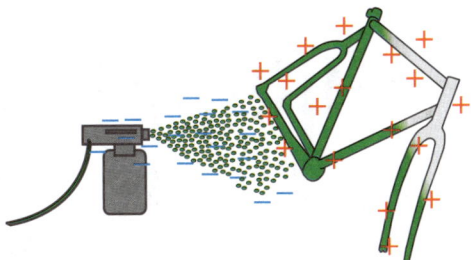

2) Dust Precipitators — Cleaning Up Emissions

Factories and power stations produce loads of smoke, which is made up of tiny particles. Fortunately, the smoke can be removed with a precipitator — here's a very simple one:

1) As smoke particles reach the bottom of the chimney, they meet a wire grid or rods with a high voltage and negative charge.

2) The dust particles gain electrons and become negatively charged.

3) The dust particles then induce a charge on the earthed metal plates (the negatively charged dust particles repel electrons on the plates, so that the plates become positively charged).

4) The dust particles are attracted to the metal plates, where they stick together to form larger particles.

5) When heavy enough, the particles fall off the plates or are knocked off by a hammer.

6) The dust falls to the bottom of the chimney and can be removed.

7) So the gases coming out of the chimney have very few smoke particles in them.

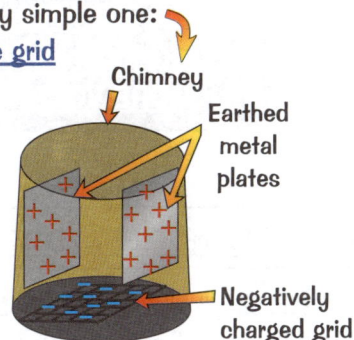

Chimney

Earthed metal plates

Negatively charged grid

3) Defibrillators — Restarting a Heart

1) The beating of your heart is controlled by tiny little electrical pulses inside your body. So an electric shock to a stopped heart can make it start beating again.

2) Hospitals and ambulances have machines called defibrillators which can be used to shock a stopped heart back into operation.

3) The defibrillator consists of two paddles connected to a power supply.

4) The paddles of the defibrillator are placed firmly on the patient's chest to get a good electrical contact and then the defibrillator is charged up.

5) Everyone moves away from the patient except for the defibrillator operator who holds insulated handles — so only the patient gets a shock.

6) The charge passes through the paddles to the patient to make the heart contract.

If this doesn't get your heart going — nothing will...

You can get your very own special defibrillator now. One to carry around in your handbag, just in case. No, really, you can (okay, maybe it wouldn't fit in your handbag unless you're Mary Poppins, but it's still handy).

Charge in Circuits

If you've got a complete loop (a circuit) of conducting stuff (e.g. metal) connected to an electric power source (like a battery), electricity flows round it. Isn't electricity great.

Charge Flows Around a Circuit

1) **CURRENT** is the flow of electrical charge around a circuit — basically the flow of electrons. It's measured in amps, A. More charge passes around a circuit when a higher current flows. Current will only flow through a component if there is a voltage across that component (unless the component is a superconductor).

2) **VOLTAGE** is the driving force that pushes the current round — kind of like "electrical pressure". Voltage is measured in volts, V.

3) **RESISTANCE** is anything in the circuit which slows the flow down. Resistance is measured in ohms, Ω.

4) **THERE'S A BALANCE**: the voltage is trying to push the current round the circuit, and the resistance is opposing it — the relative sizes of the voltage and resistance decide how big the current will be:

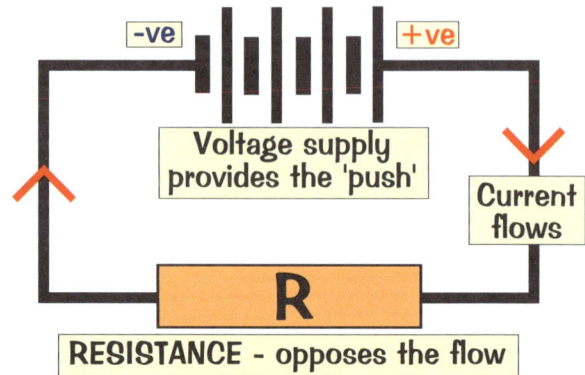

-ve   +ve

Voltage supply provides the 'push'

Current flows

R

RESISTANCE - opposes the flow

> If you increase the VOLTAGE — then MORE CURRENT will flow.
> If you increase the RESISTANCE — then LESS CURRENT will flow
> (or MORE VOLTAGE will be needed to keep the SAME CURRENT flowing).

It's Just Like the Flow of Water Around a Set of Pipes

1) The current is simply like the flow of water.

2) The voltage is like the force provided by a pump which pushes the stuff round.

3) Resistance is any sort of constriction in the flow, which is what the pressure has to work against.

4) If you turn up the pump and provide more force (or "voltage"), the flow will increase.

5) If you put in more constrictions ("resistance"), the flow (current) will decrease.

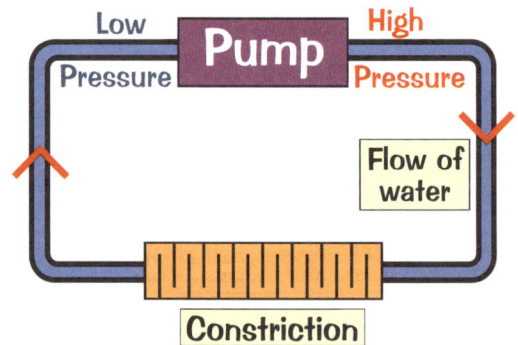

Low Pressure   **Pump**   High Pressure

Flow of water

Constriction

If You Break the Circuit, the Current Stops Flowing

1) Current only flows in a circuit as long as there's a complete loop for it to flow around. Break the circuit and the current stops.

2) Wire fuses and circuit breakers (resettable fuses) are safety features that break a circuit if there's a fault (see p.101).

Teachers — the driving force of revision...

The funny thing is — the electrons in circuits actually move from –ve to +ve... but scientists always think of current as flowing from +ve to –ve. Basically it's just because that's how the early physicists thought of it (before they found out about the electrons), and now it's become convention.

Plugs and Fuses

Now then, did you know... electricity is dangerous. It can kill you. Well just watch out for it, that's all.

All the Wires in a Plug are Colour Coded

In plugs, the correct coloured wire is connected to each pin, and firmly screwed in place so no bare wires show. You need to learn what each of the wires is there for:

1) The LIVE WIRE carries the voltage. It alternates between a high +ve and −ve voltage of about 230 V.

2) The NEUTRAL WIRE completes the circuit — electricity normally flows in through the live wire and out through the neutral wire. The neutral wire is always at 0 V.

3) The EARTH WIRE and fuse (or circuit breaker) are for safety and work together (see below).

4) All appliances with metal cases must be "earthed" to reduce the danger of electric shock. "Earthing" just means the case must be attached to an earth wire. An earthed conductor can never become live — the earth wire stops appliances becoming live.

5) If the appliance has a casing that's non-conductive (e.g. plastic) then it's said to be double insulated.

6) Anything with double insulation doesn't need an earth wire as it can't become live.

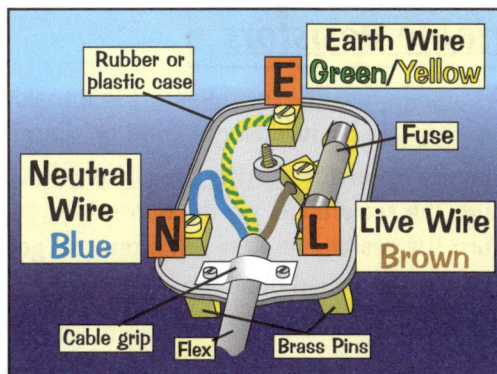

Earth Wire — Green/Yellow
Rubber or plastic case
E
Fuse
Neutral Wire — Blue
N
L
Live Wire — Brown
Cable grip — Flex — Brass Pins

Earthing and Fuses Prevent Fires and Shocks

1) If a fault develops in which the live wire somehow touches the metal case, then because the case is earthed, a big current flows in through the live wire, through the case and out down the earth wire.

2) The surge in current 'blows' the fuse and causes the wire inside it to melt. This cuts off the live supply because it breaks the circuit.

3) This isolates the whole appliance, making it impossible to get an electric shock from the case.

4) It also stops the flex overheating, which could cause a fire, and it prevents further damage to the appliance.

5) A circuit breaker works like a fuse but can be reset after it 'trips' and used again. Fuses break when they 'blow' and have to be replaced.

6) Fuses should be rated as near as possible but just higher than the normal operating current. If they were a lot higher, they wouldn't blow when the live wire touched the case or when a fault developed.

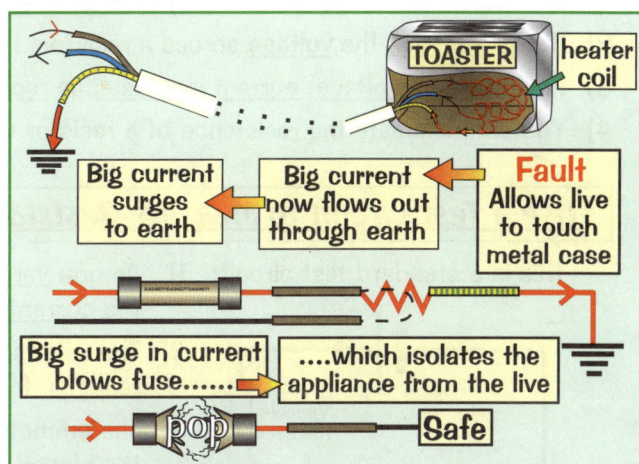

TOASTER — heater coil
Big current surges to earth
Big current now flows out through earth
Fault — Allows live to touch metal case
Big surge in current blows fuse......
....which isolates the appliance from the live
POP
Safe

Electrical Power and Fuse Ratings

1) The formula for electrical power is: **POWER = VOLTAGE × CURRENT** (P = V × I)

2) Most electrical goods show their power rating and voltage rating.

3) To work out the fuse needed, you need to work out the current that the item will use.

4) The fuse used should be rated just a little higher than the current.

5) Fuses come with fixed ratings, e.g. 3 A, 5 A and 13 A. Choose the first one that's just higher than the current the appliance uses.

$$\frac{P}{V \times I}$$

CGP books are ACE — well, I had to get a plug in somewhere...

Have you ever noticed how if anything doesn't work in the house, it's always due to the fuse. But it does make everything a whole load safer. Now have a go at this question: A kettle comes with a power rating of 1200 W and a voltage rating of 230 V. What current will the kettle use and what fuse is needed — 5 A, 7 A or 13 A?*

Resistance

A <u>resistor</u> is a component that reduces the current flowing in a circuit. The higher the <u>resistance</u>, the harder it is for the electricity to flow, and so the lower the <u>current</u>. If you get an electric shock, it's the current that does the damage, not the voltage. So the higher the resistance in a circuit, the smaller the risk of injury.

Variable Resistors

1) A <u>variable resistor</u> (or <u>rheostat</u>) is a resistor whose resistance can be <u>changed</u> by twiddling a knob or something.

2) They're great for <u>altering the current</u> flowing through a circuit.
   Turn the resistance <u>up</u>, the current <u>drops</u>.
   Turn the resistance <u>down</u>, the current goes <u>up</u>.

3) The old-fashioned ones are <u>huge coils of wire</u> with a <u>slider</u> on them.

4) As you move the slider, the <u>length of wire</u> that has <u>current</u> flowing through it <u>changes</u>.

5) <u>Longer</u> wires have <u>more resistance</u>, so have <u>less current</u> flowing through them. This is because the <u>longer</u> the wire, the <u>more material</u> electric charge has to flow through, which <u>increases</u> the <u>resistance</u>.

6) The <u>thickness</u> of a wire also matters — <u>thinner</u> wires have <u>more</u> resistance and so less current can flow.

7) The <u>thinner</u> the wire, the <u>less space</u> electric charge has to move through, which <u>increases</u> the <u>resistance</u>. It's like being on the motorway when only one lane's open — fewer cars make it down the road.

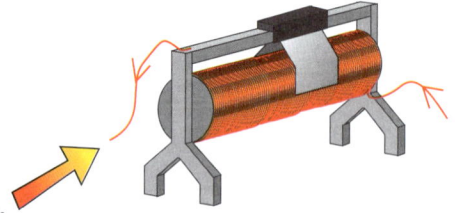

Calculating Resistance: R = V/I

1) The resistance of a (non-variable) resistor is <u>steady</u> (at constant temperature).

2) If you <u>increase</u> the <u>voltage</u> across a resistor, the <u>current increases</u> as well.

3) For the <u>same voltage</u>, <u>current increases</u> as <u>resistance decreases</u>.

4) You can calculate the resistance of a resistor using the formula:

$$\text{Resistance} = \frac{\text{Voltage}}{\text{Current}} \qquad \frac{V}{I \times R}$$

Use a Test Circuit to Measure Resistance

This is a standard test circuit:

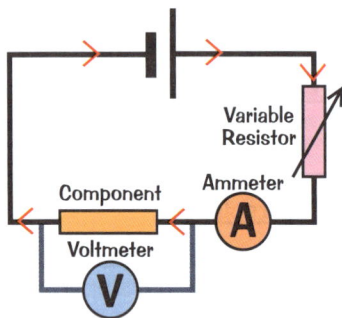

1) As you <u>vary</u> the <u>variable resistor</u> it alters the <u>current</u> flowing through the circuit.

2) This allows you to take several <u>pairs of readings</u> from the <u>ammeter</u> and <u>voltmeter</u>.

3) The ammeter measures the <u>current</u> (in <u>amps</u>) <u>through</u> the component. It's placed in <u>series</u> (in <u>line</u>) with the other components.

4) The voltmeter measures the <u>voltage</u> (in <u>volts</u>) <u>across</u> the component. It's placed in <u>parallel</u> around the component being <u>tested</u>.

5) The proper name for voltage is <u>potential difference</u>, <u>pd</u>.

Calculating Resistance — An Example

EXAMPLE. Voltmeter V reads 6 V and resistor R is 4 Ω. What is the current through ammeter A?

ANSWER. Rearrange the resistance formula to give: I = V/R.
Then put in the values: I = 6/4 which is 1.5 A.

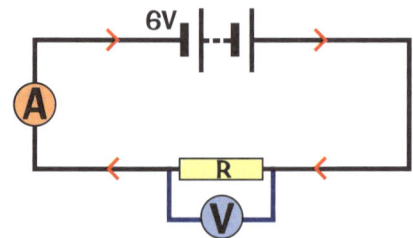

You have to learn this — resistance is futile...

Sometimes you can get funny light switches which <u>fade</u> the light in and out. Some of them work by resistance, and are perfect for getting that nice romantic atmosphere you want for your dinner for two. Handy.
Some questions to try: 1) Calculate the resistance of a resistor which draws 3 A of current from a 9 V battery.*
2) A resistor with a resistance of 2.5 Ω draws 6.4 A of current. What's the voltage of the power supply?*

Ultrasound Treatments and Scans

Ultrasound — it's used for more than looking at babies, you know. Learn all about it, right here...

Sound is a Longitudinal Wave

You need to know the features of longitudinal waves:

1) Sound waves squash up and stretch out the arrangement of particles in material they pass through, making compressions and rarefactions.

2) Compressions are the bits under high pressure (lots of particles) and rarefactions are the parts under low pressure (fewer particles).

3) The WAVELENGTH is a full cycle of the wave, e.g. from crest to crest, or from compression to compression.

4) FREQUENCY is how many complete waves there are per second (passing a certain point). Frequency is measured in hertz. 1 Hz is 1 complete wave per second. For sound, high frequency = high pitch.

A longitudinal wave in a spring (in spring).

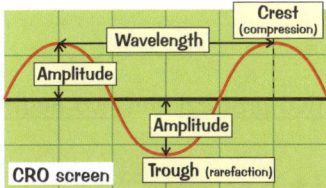

5) The AMPLITUDE tells you how much energy the wave is carrying, or how loud the sound is. You can see the amplitude of a sound on a CRO (oscilloscope). CRO displays show sounds as transverse waves so you can see what's going on. You measure the amplitude from the middle line to the crest, NOT from a trough to a crest.

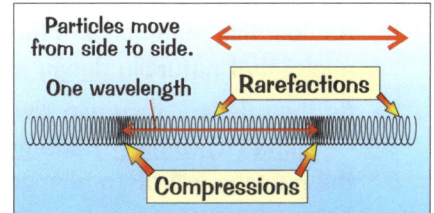

| In LONGITUDINAL waves the vibrations are along the SAME DIRECTION as the wave is travelling. | In TRANSVERSE waves the vibrations are at 90° to the DIRECTION OF TRAVEL of the wave. |

Ultrasound is Sound with a Higher Frequency Than We Can Hear

Electrical devices can be made which produce electrical oscillations of any frequency. These can easily be converted into mechanical vibrations to produce longitudinal (sound) waves beyond the range of human hearing (i.e. frequencies above 20 000 Hz). This is called ultrasound and it has loads of uses in hospitals:

1) Breaking Down Accumulations in the Body — Getting Rid of Kidney Stones

An important example is the removal of kidney stones... An ultrasound beam concentrates high energy waves at the kidney stone and turns it into sand-like particles. These particles then pass out of the body in urine. It's useful because the patient doesn't need surgery (it's non-invasive) and it's relatively painless.

2) For Body Scanning

Ultrasound waves can pass through the body, but whenever they reach a boundary between two different media (like fluid in the womb and the skin of the foetus) some of the wave is reflected back and detected, returning back from different depths at different times.

The exact timing and distribution of these echoes are processed by a computer to produce a video image of whatever is being scanned (for example, a foetus).

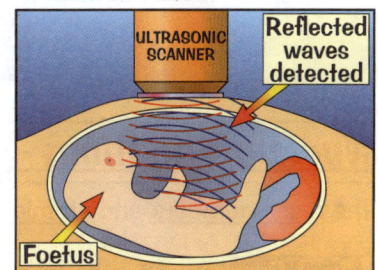

Ultrasound Has Advantages over X-Rays

1) X-rays pass easily through soft tissues like muscle and skin, so you can usually only use them to make images of hard things like bone. Ultrasound is great for imaging soft tissue.

2) The other advantage is that ultrasound is, we're pretty sure, safe — it doesn't damage living cells. X-rays are ionising radiation. They can damage living cells and cause cancer if you're exposed to too high a dose.

Looking at things with sound — weird if you ask me...

Pity that you can't see into peoples minds when they have headphones on... Well, you win some, you lose some.

Radioactive Decay

Phew. Now all that <u>electricity</u> and <u>sound</u> stuff is out of the way we can get onto more exciting stuff. Ooooh.

<u>Radioactivity</u> Comes From an <u>Unstable Nucleus</u>

1) Radioactive materials are made up of atoms with <u>unstable nuclei</u> that naturally <u>decay</u> at <u>random</u>.

2) As they decay, they can give out <u>three</u> forms of radiation — <u>alpha</u> (α), <u>beta</u> (β) and <u>gamma</u> (γ). During the decay, the nucleus will often change into a <u>new element</u>.

3) Gamma radiation happens <u>after</u> α and β emission if the nucleus has some <u>extra energy</u> to get rid of. It emits a γ-ray that has <u>no mass or charge</u>. This means the <u>atomic</u> and <u>mass</u> numbers <u>don't change</u>.

> All elements in the <u>periodic table</u> have <del>two</del> numbers:
> Relative atomic mass number (mass number) = number of protons and neutrons.
> Atomic number = number of protons. $^{23}_{11}Na$
> Atoms of the <u>same element</u> have the <u>same number</u> of <u>protons</u>, atoms of different elements have <u>different</u> numbers of protons. <u>Isotopes</u> are atoms with the <u>same</u> atomic number, but <u>different</u> mass numbers.

Alpha Radiation is a Helium Nucleus

1) An α-particle is a <u>helium nucleus</u>, <u>mass</u> 4 and <u>charge</u> of +2, made up of <u>two protons</u> and <u>two neutrons</u>.

2) So, when a nucleus emits an <u>alpha particle</u>:
   - The <u>mass number decreases by 4</u> — because it <u>loses</u> two protons and two neutrons.
   - The <u>atomic number decreases by 2</u> — because it has <u>two less</u> protons.
   - It forms a <u>new element</u> — because the number of protons has <u>changed</u>.

3) A typical <u>alpha emission</u>:

$^{226}_{88}Ra \longrightarrow {}^{222}_{86}Rn \longrightarrow {}^{4}_{2}\alpha$
Unstable isotope → New isotope → Alpha particle

> You need to remember the mass and atomic numbers for alpha and beta particles.

Beta Radiation is a Fast-Moving Electron

1) A β-particle is a fast-moving <u>electron</u>, with virtually <u>no mass</u> and a <u>charge of –1</u>.

2) So, when a nucleus emits a <u>beta particle</u>:
   - The <u>mass number doesn't change</u> — because it has <u>lost</u> a neutron but <u>gained</u> a proton.
   - The <u>atomic number increases by 1</u> — because it has <u>one more</u> proton.
   - It forms a <u>new element</u> — because the number of protons has <u>changed</u>.

3) A typical <u>beta emission</u>:

$^{14}_{6}C \longrightarrow {}^{14}_{7}N \longrightarrow {}^{0}_{-1}\beta$
Unstable isotope → New isotope → Beta particle

> Beta particles can be written as $^{0}_{-1}e$ too.

> A neutron turns into a proton and a β particle (electron) is emitted.

Nuclear Equations — Not Half as Bad as They Sound

The <u>mass numbers</u> and <u>atomic numbers</u> should <u>balance</u> on both sides.

> You can check a periodic table to find out the mass and atomic numbers, or the new element.

ALPHA EMISSION An α-particle has a mass of 4 and charge of +2: $^{4}_{2}\alpha$

A typical <u>alpha emission</u>: $^{226}_{88}Ra \longrightarrow {}^{222}_{86}Rn + {}^{4}_{2}\alpha$

mass number	$226 \longrightarrow 222 + 4 = 226$
atomic number	$88 \longrightarrow 86 + 2 = 88$

BETA EMISSION A β-particle has (virtually) no mass and a charge of –1: $^{0}_{-1}\beta$

A typical <u>beta emission</u>: $^{14}_{6}C \longrightarrow {}^{14}_{7}N + {}^{0}_{-1}\beta$

mass number	$14 \longrightarrow 14 + 0 = 14$
atomic number	$6 \longrightarrow 7 + (-1) = 6$

<u>Sorry, no clear equations on this page...</u>

The most important thing to remember is the symbol for each type of particle with its <u>atomic number</u> and <u>mass number</u>. As long as you know those, you should be able to write down an equation for alpha or beta decay.

Radioactivity and Half-Life

Radioactivity is measured in <u>becquerels</u> (<u>Bq</u>) or <u>counts per minute</u> (<u>cpm</u>). 1 Bq is <u>1 decay emitted per second</u>.

The Radioactivity of a Sample Always Decreases Over Time

1) Each time an unstable nucleus <u>decays</u> and emits radiation, that means one more <u>radioactive nucleus isn't there</u> to decay later.

2) As more <u>unstable nuclei</u> decay, the <u>radioactivity</u> of the source as a whole <u>decreases</u> — so the <u>older</u> a radioactive source is, the <u>less radiation</u> it emits.

3) <u>How quickly</u> the activity <u>decreases</u> varies a lot. For <u>some</u> isotopes it takes <u>just a few hours</u> before nearly all the unstable nuclei have <u>decayed</u>. For others it can take <u>millions of years</u>.

4) The problem with trying to <u>measure</u> this is that <u>the activity never reaches zero</u>, which is why we have to use the idea of <u>half-life</u> to measure <u>how quickly the activity decreases</u>.

5) Learn this <u>important definition</u> of <u>half-life</u>:

> **HALF-LIFE is the <u>TIME TAKEN</u> for <u>HALF</u> of the <u>radioactive nuclei</u> now present to <u>DECAY</u>.**

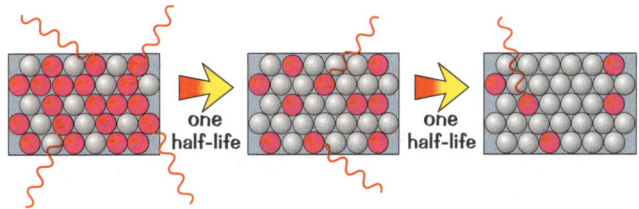

one half-life → one half-life →

6) A <u>short half-life</u> means the <u>activity falls quickly</u>, because <u>lots</u> of the nuclei decay in a <u>short time</u>.

7) A <u>long half-life</u> means the activity <u>falls more slowly</u> because <u>most</u> of the nuclei don't decay <u>for a long time</u> — they just sit there, <u>basically unstable</u>, but kind of <u>biding their time</u>.

Do Half-Life Questions Step by Step

Half-life can be confusing, but exam calculations are <u>straightforward</u> so long as you do them <u>STEP BY STEP</u>:

A Very Simple Example:

The activity of a radioactive sample is 640 Bq. Two hours later it has fallen to 40 Bq. Find its half-life.

ANSWER: Go through it in <u>short simple steps</u> like this:

INITIAL		after ONE		after TWO		after THREE		after FOUR
count:	(÷2) →	half-life:	(÷2) →	half-lives:	(÷2) →	half-lives:	(÷2) →	half-lives:
640		320		160		80		40

This careful <u>step-by-step method</u> shows that it takes <u>four half-lives</u> for the activity to fall from 640 to 40. So <u>two hours</u> represents <u>four half-lives</u> — so the half-life is 2 hours ÷ 4 = <u>30 MINUTES</u>.

You also need to be able to find the half-life of a sample from a <u>graph</u>. Relax, this is (almost) <u>fun</u>.

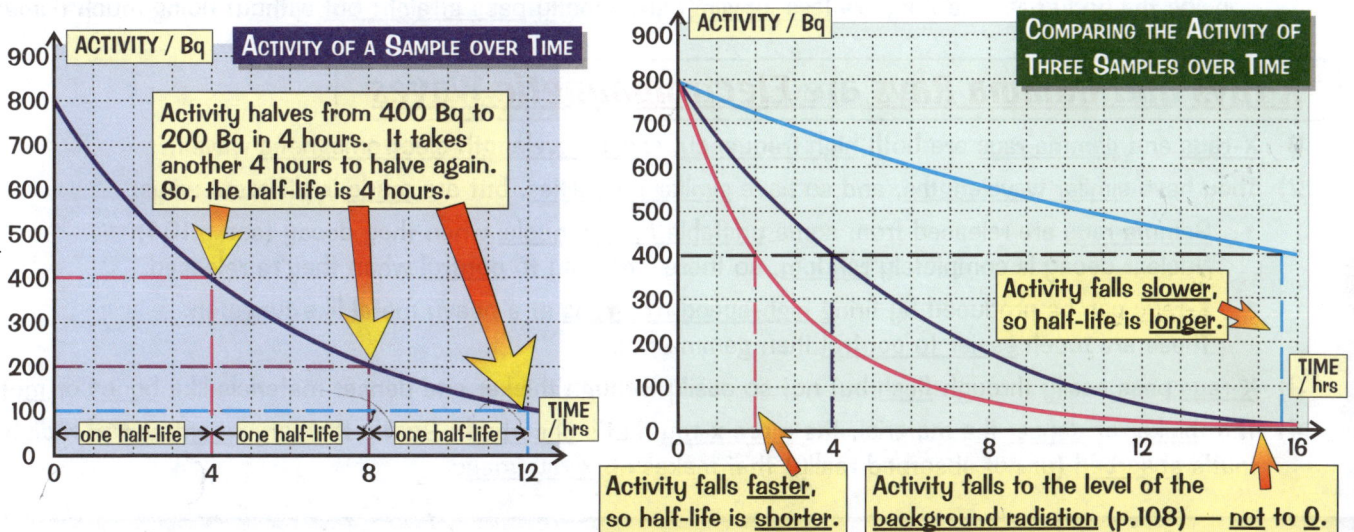

ACTIVITY / Bq — Activity of a Sample over Time

Activity halves from 400 Bq to 200 Bq in 4 hours. It takes another 4 hours to halve again. So, the half-life is 4 hours.

one half-life | one half-life | one half-life
TIME / hrs

ACTIVITY / Bq — Comparing the Activity of Three Samples over Time

Activity falls slower, so half-life is longer.

Activity falls faster, so half-life is shorter.

Activity falls to the level of the background radiation (p.108) — not to 0.

TIME / hrs

Half-life of a box of chocolates — about five minutes...

To measure half-life, you time how <u>long it takes</u> for the number of decays per second to <u>halve</u>. Simples.

Ionising Radiation

Nuclear radiation (alpha, beta and gamma) and X-rays are <u>ionising radiation</u> — they can <u>damage</u> living cells.

Ionising Radiation Harms Living Cells

1) <u>Nuclear radiation</u> (alpha α, beta β, gamma γ) and <u>X-rays</u> are ionising radiation.

2) Some materials <u>absorb</u> ionising radiation — it can <u>enter living cells</u> and <u>interact with molecules</u>.

3) These interactions cause <u>ionisation</u> — they produce <u>charged</u> particles called <u>ions</u>.

4) Ionisation occurs because the particle <u>gains</u> or <u>loses electrons</u>.

5) <u>X-rays and gamma rays</u> can <u>transfer energy</u> to electrons. The electrons then have enough energy to <u>escape</u> from the atom, ionising it and leaving it <u>positively</u> charged.

6) <u>Beta particles</u> can <u>remove electrons</u> from atoms or molecules they collide with, leaving them <u>positively charged</u>. A beta particle (an <u>electron</u>) can also <u>stick</u> to an atom, <u>ionising</u> it and making it <u>negatively charged</u>.

7) <u>Alpha particles</u> can <u>remove electrons</u> from atoms and molecules they pass by or hit, making them <u>positive</u>.

8) Alpha particles are <u>good ionisers</u> for two reasons:

   • They're relatively <u>large</u> — so it's easy for them to collide with atoms or molecules.
   • They're <u>highly charged</u> — so they can easily <u>remove</u> electrons from the atoms they pass or collide with.

8) <u>Lower doses</u> of ionising radiation tend to cause <u>minor damage</u> without <u>killing</u> the cell. This can give rise to <u>mutant cells</u> which <u>divide uncontrollably</u>. This is <u>cancer</u>.

9) <u>Higher doses</u> tend to <u>kill cells completely</u>, which causes <u>radiation sickness</u> if a lot of cells <u>all get blasted at once</u>.

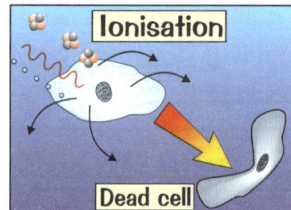

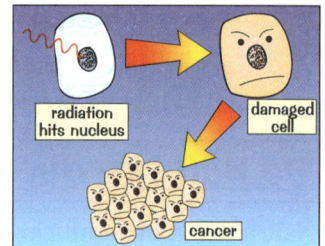

Which Radiation is the Most Dangerous Depends on Where it is

1) <u>OUTSIDE</u> the body, <u>beta</u> and <u>gamma</u> sources are the <u>most dangerous</u>.

2) This is because <u>beta and gamma</u> can still get <u>inside</u> to the delicate <u>organs</u> — they can <u>pass through</u> the <u>skin</u>.

3) Alpha is much <u>less dangerous</u> because it <u>can't penetrate the skin</u>.

4) <u>INSIDE</u> the body, an <u>alpha</u> source is the <u>most dangerous</u> because they do all their damage in a <u>very localised area</u>.

5) Beta and gamma sources on the other hand are <u>less dangerous</u> inside the body because they are <u>less ionising</u>, and mostly <u>pass straight out</u> without doing much damage.

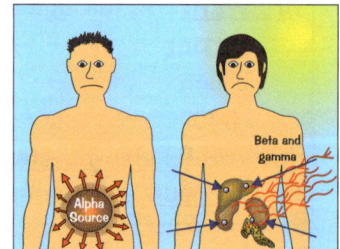

X-rays and Gamma Rays are Electromagnetic Waves

1) <u>X-rays</u> and <u>gamma rays</u> are both <u>high frequency</u>, <u>short wavelength electromagnetic</u> waves.

2) They have <u>similar wavelengths</u>, and so have <u>similar properties</u>, but are <u>made</u> in different ways:

   • <u>Gamma rays</u> are released from some <u>unstable atomic nuclei</u> when they decay (see p.104). Nuclear decay is completely <u>random</u>, so there's no way to <u>control</u> when they're released.
   • <u>X-rays</u> can be produced by firing <u>high-speed electrons</u> at a heavy metal like <u>tungsten</u>. These are much <u>easier to control</u> than gamma rays.

3) <u>X-rays</u> pass easily through <u>flesh</u> but not so easily through thicker and denser materials like <u>bones</u> or <u>metal</u>.

4) The <u>thicker</u> or <u>denser</u> the material, the <u>more x-ray</u> that's <u>absorbed</u>. So it's the <u>varying amount</u> of radiation that's <u>absorbed</u> (or not absorbed really) that makes an <u>x-ray image</u>.

Radiation — easy as α, β, γ...

Well actually this stuff is pretty darn difficult to get your head around. But I'm afraid you're just gonna have to pull those socks up and get down to it. There's no other way — <u>cover</u>, <u>scribble</u>, <u>check</u>. Do it now.

Medical Uses of Radiation

Ionising radiation has loads of uses in hospitals, and you have to know all about them. Whoop-ti-do.

1) Radiotherapy — the Treatment of Cancer Using Gamma Rays

1) Since high doses of gamma rays will kill all living cells, they can be used to treat cancers.
2) The gamma rays have to be directed carefully and at just the right dosage, so as to kill the cancer cells without damaging too many normal cells.
3) However, a fair bit of damage is inevitably done to normal cells, which makes the patient feel very ill. But if the cancer is successfully killed off in the end, then it's worth it.

TO TREAT CANCER:
1) The gamma rays are focused on the tumour using a wide beam.
2) This beam is rotated round the patient with the tumour at the centre.
3) This minimises the exposure of normal cells to radiation, and so reduces the chances of damaging the rest of the body.

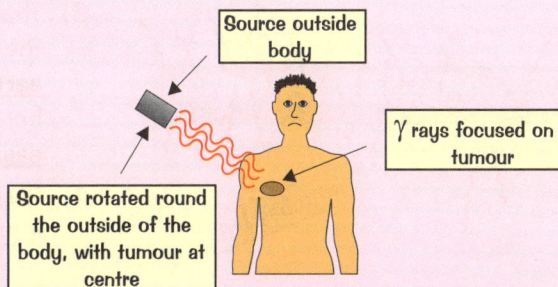

Source outside body

γ rays focused on tumour

Source rotated round the outside of the body, with tumour at centre

2) Tracers in Medicine — Short Half-life Gamma and Beta Emitters

1) Certain radioactive isotopes that emit gamma (and sometimes beta) radiation can be used as tracers in the body.
2) They should have a short half-life — around a few hours, so that the radioactivity inside the patient quickly disappears.
3) They can be injected inside the body, drunk or eaten or ingested.
4) They are allowed to spread through the body and their progress can be followed on the outside using a radiation detector.
5) One example is the use of iodine-123, which is absorbed by the thyroid gland. It gives out radiation which can be detected to indicate whether or not the thyroid gland is taking in the iodine as it should.
6) All isotopes which are taken into the body must be GAMMA or BETA (never alpha). This is because gamma and beta radiation can penetrate tissue and so are able to pass out of the body and be detected.
7) Alpha radiation can't penetrate tissue, so you couldn't detect the radiation on the outside of the body. Also alpha is more dangerous inside the body (see previous page).

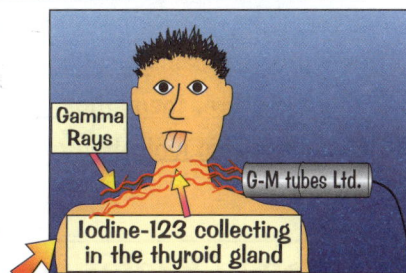

Gamma Rays

G-M tubes Ltd.

Iodine-123 collecting in the thyroid gland

3) Sterilisation of Surgical Instruments Using Gamma Rays

1) Medical instruments can be sterilised by exposing them to a high dose of gamma rays, which will kill all microbes.
2) The great advantage of using radiation instead of boiling is that it doesn't involve high temperatures, so heat-sensitive things like thermometers and plastic instruments can be totally sterilised without damaging them.

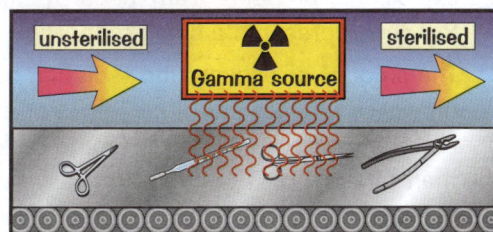

unsterilised | Gamma source | sterilised

Ionising radiation — just what the doctor ordered...

See — radiation isn't all bad. It also kills bad things, like disease-causing bacteria. Radiotherapy and chemotherapy (which uses chemicals instead of gamma rays) are commonly used to treat cancer. They both work in the same way — by killing lots and lots of cells, and trying to target the cancerous ones...

Uses of Radiation and Background Radiation

Radioactive materials aren't just used in hospitals (p.107) — you've got to know these uses too.

Tracers in Industry — For Finding Leaks

This is much the same technique as the medical tracers.

1) Radioactive isotopes can be used to track the movement of waste materials, find the route of underground pipe systems or detect leaks or blockages in pipes.

2) To check a pipe, you just squirt the radioactive isotope in, then go along the outside with a detector. If the radioactivity reduces or stops after a certain point, there must be a leak or blockage there. This is really useful for concealed or underground pipes — no need to dig up the road to find the leak.

G-M tubes Ltd.

3) The isotope used must be a gamma emitter, so that the radiation can be detected even through metal or earth which may be surrounding the pipe. Alpha and beta radiation wouldn't be much use because they are easily blocked by any surrounding material.

4) It should also have a short half-life so as not to cause a hazard if it collects somewhere.

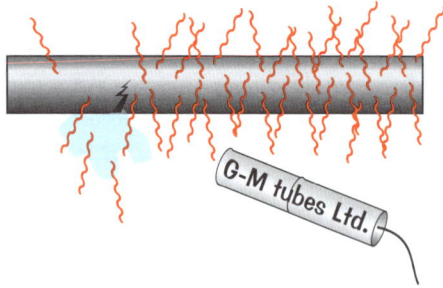

Smoke Detectors — Alpha Radiation

1) A weak alpha radioactive source is placed in the detector, close to two electrodes.
2) The source causes ionisation of the air particles which allows a current to flow.
3) If there is a fire, then smoke particles are hit by the alpha particles instead.
4) This causes less ionisation of the air particles — so the current is reduced causing the alarm to sound.

Background Radiation Comes from Many Sources

The background radiation we receive comes from:

1) Radioactivity of naturally occurring unstable isotopes which are all around us — in the air, in food, in building materials and in the rocks under our feet. A large proportion of background radiation comes from these natural sources.

2) Radiation from space, which is known as cosmic rays. These come mostly from the Sun.

3) Radiation due to human activity, e.g. fallout from nuclear explosions, or waste from industry and hospitals. But this represents a small proportion of the total.

4) The amount of background radiation can vary depending on where you are and your job. For example, what type of rock your house is built on (some rocks are more radioactive than others), or if you're in an aeroplane (because you're exposed to more cosmic rays), or if you work in an industry that uses radiation (nuclear power or medical related).

The RELATIVE PROPORTIONS of background radiation:

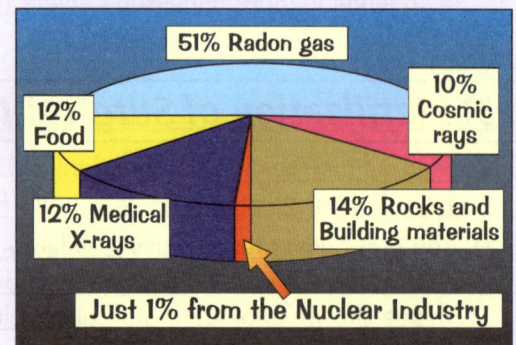

51% Radon gas
10% Cosmic rays
12% Food
12% Medical X-rays
14% Rocks and Building materials
Just 1% from the Nuclear Industry

No need to be alarmed, but there's radiation in your smoke detector...

Nuclear radiation is used for loads more things than tracers and smoke detectors. It can be dangerous if you're not careful with it, but mostly it's really handy. Please don't eat your smoke detector though. Bad idea.

Radioactive Dating

Yet another use of radiation is radioactive dating. Some of the naturally occurring radiation on earth can be useful for dating things — like rocks and fossils and stuff. It's pretty cool, if you're into that kind of thing.

Radioactive Dating of Rocks and Archaeological Specimens

1) The discovery of radioactivity and the idea of half-life gave scientists their first opportunity to accurately work out the age of some rocks and archaeological specimens.

2) By measuring the amount of a radioactive isotope left in a sample, and knowing its half-life, you can work out how long the thing has been around.

Radiocarbon Dating — Carbon-14 Calculations

1) Carbon-14 makes up about 1/10 000 000 (one ten-millionth) of the carbon in the air.

2) The level stays fairly constant in the atmosphere — it hasn't changed for thousands of years.

3) The same proportion of carbon-14 is also found in living things.

4) But when they die, they stop exchanging gases with the air outside and the carbon-14 is trapped inside, and it gradually decays with a half-life of 5730 years.

5) By measuring the proportion of carbon-14 found in some old axe handle, burial shroud, etc. you can calculate how long ago the item was living material using the known half-life.

Phil took radioactive dating a bit too far.

> **EXAMPLE:** An axe handle was found to contain 1 part in 40 000 000 carbon-14. How old is the axe?
>
> **ANSWER:** The carbon-14 was originally 1 part in 10 000 000.
> After one half-life it would be down to 1 part in 20 000 000.
> After two half-lives it would be down to 1 part in 40 000 000.
> Hence the axe handle is two carbon-14 half-lives old, i.e. 2 × 5730 = 11 460 years old.

You can use the same old stepwise method from page 105, going down one half-life at a time.

Dating Rocks — Relative Proportions Calculations

1) Uranium isotopes have very long half-lives and decay via a series of short-lived particles to produce stable isotopes of lead.

2) The relative proportions of uranium and lead isotopes in a sample of rock can therefore be used to date the rock, using the known half-life of the uranium. It's as simple as this:

Initially	After one half-life	After two half-lives
100% uranium	50% uranium	25% uranium
0% lead	50% lead	75% lead

Ratio of uranium to lead: (half-life of uranium-238 = 4.5 billion years)

Initially	After one half-life	After two half-lives
1:0	1:1	1:3

I tried dating a Geiger counter once, but we didn't click...

You measure radiation using a Geiger counter. You know, the more it clicks the more radiation you've found. Well, I thought it was funny. Anyway... Did you know that the oldest human ancestor dated by radioactive dating walked the Earth over 4.4 million years ago. Crazy times. Now give this question a try:

1) The remains of a skeleton were found to contain 1 part in 160 000 000 carbon-14. How old is the skeleton?*

* Answer on page 116.

Nuclear Power

One more use for radioactive materials — nuclear power. Keep going, you're nearly at the end of the module.

Nuclear Fission — The Splitting Up of Uranium Atoms

1) Nuclear power stations are powered by nuclear reactors.
2) In a nuclear reactor, a controlled chain reaction takes place in which uranium or plutonium atoms split up and release energy in the form of heat — this is nuclear fission.
3) This heat is then used to heat water to produce steam.
4) The steam turns a turbine which drives a generator that produces electricity.

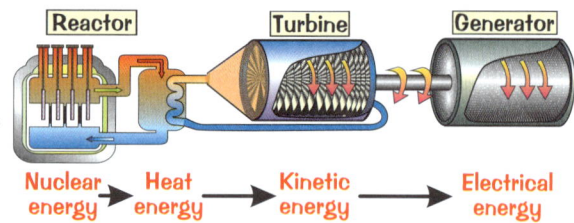

Reactor   Turbine   Generator

Nuclear → Heat → Kinetic → Electrical
energy   energy   energy   energy

The Splitting of Uranium-235 Needs Neutrons

Uranium-235 (i.e. a uranium atom with an atomic mass of 235) is used in some nuclear reactors and bombs.

1) Uranium-235 (U-235) is actually quite stable, so it needs to be made unstable before it'll split.
2) Materials can become radioactive when they absorb extra neutrons — so slow-moving neutrons are fired at the U-235 atom.
3) A neutron joins the nucleus to create U-236, which is unstable.
4) The U-236 then splits into two smaller nuclei, releasing loads of energy and producing radioactive waste.
5) The split nucleus also releases 2 or 3 fast-moving neutrons which go onto produce a chain reaction...

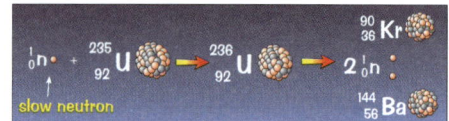

$${}_{0}^{1}n + {}_{92}^{235}U \rightarrow {}_{92}^{236}U \rightarrow 2\,{}_{0}^{1}n$$

slow neutron

${}_{36}^{90}Kr$

${}_{56}^{144}Ba$

You Can Split More than One Atom — Chain Reactions

1) To get a useful amount of energy, loads of U-235 atoms have to be split. So neutrons released from previous fissions are used to hit other U-235 atoms.
2) Each split uranium nucleus releases more than one neutron.
3) These neutrons cause further nuclei to split, releasing more neutrons, which cause more nuclei to split and release more neutrons... and so on and so on. This process is called a chain reaction.
4) Nuclear bombs are chain reactions that are out of control.
5) But in nuclear reactors the chain reaction is controlled using control rods...

Control Rods Control the Chain Reaction

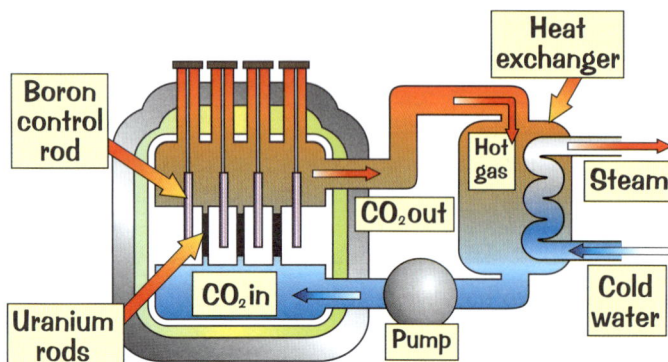

Heat exchanger

Boron control rod

Hot gas

CO_2 out

Steam

CO_2 in

Cold water

Uranium rods

Pump

This is a gas-cooled nuclear reactor — but there are many other kinds. The gas (CO_2) is used to take the heat away from the reactor so it can be used to make steam.

1) Free neutrons in the reactor "kick-start" the fission process.
2) Neutrons collide with surrounding uranium atoms, causing them to split and the temperature in the reactor to rise.
3) Control rods, often made of boron, limit the rate of fission by absorbing excess neutrons.
4) This stops the reaction going out of control but allows enough neutrons to hang around to keep the process going.

Uranium — gone fission, back after lunch...

Nuclear power doesn't produce any greenhouse gases, but it leaves behind radioactive waste instead. Hmm...

Nuclear Fusion

Loads of energy's released either when you break apart <u>really big nuclei</u> or join together <u>really small nuclei</u>. You can't do much with the ones in the middle, I'm afraid. (Don't ask, you don't want to know.)

Nuclear Fusion — The Joining of Small Atomic Nuclei

1) <u>Nuclear fusion</u> is the <u>opposite</u> of nuclear <u>fission</u>.

2) In nuclear fusion, two <u>light nuclei combine</u> to create a larger nucleus.

3) The example you need to know is <u>two atoms</u> of different <u>hydrogen</u> isotopes combining to form <u>helium</u>:

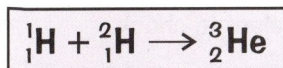

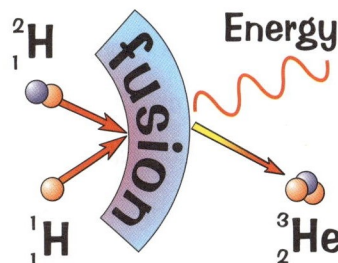

$$^2_1H + ^2_1H \rightarrow ^3_2He$$

4) Fusion releases <u>a lot</u> of energy (<u>more</u> than fission for a given mass) — all the energy released in <u>stars</u> comes from fusion at extremely <u>high temperatures</u> and <u>pressures</u>. So people are trying to develop <u>fusion reactors</u> to make <u>electricity</u>.

5) Fusion <u>doesn't</u> leave behind much radioactive <u>waste</u> and there's <u>plenty</u> of hydrogen about to use as <u>fuel</u>.

6) The <u>big problem</u> is that fusion only happens at <u>really high pressures</u> and <u>temperatures</u> (about <u>10 000 000 °C</u>).

7) <u>No material</u> can physically withstand that kind of temperature and pressure — so fusion reactors are <u>really hard</u> to <u>build</u>.

8) It's also hard to <u>safely control</u> the high temperatures and pressures.

9) There are a few <u>experimental</u> reactors around at the moment, the biggest one being <u>JET</u> (Joint European Torus), but <u>none</u> of them are <u>generating electricity yet</u>. It takes <u>more</u> power to get up to temperature than the reactor can produce.

10) <u>Research</u> into fusion power production is carried out by <u>international</u> groups to <u>share</u> the <u>costs</u>, <u>expertise</u>, experience and the <u>benefits</u> (when they eventually get it to work reliably).

> **FUSION BOMBS**
> - Fusion reactions also happen in <u>fusion bombs</u>.
> - You might have heard of them as <u>hydrogen</u>, or <u>H bombs</u>.
> - In fusion bombs, a <u>fission reaction</u> is used first to create the really <u>high temperatures</u> needed for fusion.

Cold Fusion — Hoax or Energy of the Future?

1) A new scientific theory has to go through a <u>validation</u> process before it's accepted.

2) An example of a theory which <u>hasn't</u> been accepted yet is '<u>cold fusion</u>'.

3) Cold fusion is <u>nuclear fusion</u> which occurs at around <u>room temperature</u>, rather than at millions of degrees Celsius.

4) In 1989, two scientists reported that they had succeeded in releasing energy from cold fusion, using a simple experiment. This caused a lot of <u>excitement</u> — cold fusion would make it possible to generate lots of electricity, easily and cheaply.

5) After the press conference, the experiments and data were <u>shared</u> with other scientists so they could <u>repeat</u> the experiments. But <u>few</u> managed to reproduce the results <u>reliably</u> — so it hasn't been accepted as a <u>realistic</u> method of energy production.

Revision Summary for Module P4

Some of this stuff can be just learnt and regurgitated — other parts actually need thinking about.
All the information's there, you've just got to sit down and put the effort in. The best thing to do is take
it a page at a time, break it down and make sure you've learnt every little thing. If you can answer these
questions, you should have no problem with anything the examiners throw at you. You'd better get going.

1)   What causes static charge to build up?

2)   Which particles move when static charge builds up?

3)   Give two examples each of static electricity being: a) a nuisance, b) dangerous.

4)   Explain how you can reduce the danger of getting a static electric shock.

5)   Give three examples of how static electricity can be helpful. Write all the details.

6)   Explain what current, voltage and resistance are in an electric circuit.

7)   Describe what earthing and double insulation are. Why are they useful?

8)* A computer has a power rating of 400 W and uses a 230 V mains supply.
     What rating of fuse should by used in the plug — 1 A, 3 A, 5 A or 13 A?

9)   What happens to the current flowing through a circuit if the resistance of a variable resistor is increased?

10) Explain how you could work out the resistance of a resistor in a circuit.

11) Define the frequency, wavelength and amplitude of a wave.

12) Explain why ultrasound rather than X-rays are used to take images of a foetus.

13)* Write down the nuclear equation for the alpha decay of: a) $^{234}_{92}$U,   b) $^{230}_{90}$Th,   c) $^{241}_{95}$Am.

14)* Write down the nuclear equation for the beta decay of: a) $^{234}_{90}$Th,   b) $^{90}_{38}$Sr,   c) $^{131}_{53}$I.

15) Give a proper definition of half-life.

16) Briefly describe what nuclear radiation does to living cells.

17) Why are alpha particles so good at ionising atoms?

18) What is the main difference between X-rays and gamma rays?

19) Describe in detail how radioactive sources are used in each of the following:
     a) treating cancer,   b) tracers in medicine.

20) Describe in detail how radioactive sources are used in each of the following:
     a) tracers in industry,   b) smoke alarms.

21)* An old bit of cloth was found to contain 1 part in 80 000 000 carbon-14.
     If carbon-14 decays with a half-life of 5730 years, find the age of the cloth.

22) What type of particle is uranium-235 bombarded with in a nuclear reactor to make it split?

23) Explain how a chain reaction is created in a nuclear reactor.

24) What is the difference between nuclear fission and nuclear fusion?

25) Briefly explain why cold fusion isn't accepted as a realistic method of energy production.

* Answers on page 116

Index

Answers

Revision Summary for Module C3 (page 43)

1) 14 H and 6 C

2)
```
    H  H  H
    |  |  |
H – C – C – C – H
    |  |  |
    H  H  H
```

4) $2Na + 2H_2O \rightarrow 2NaOH + H_2$

14) When using the concentrated acid it will take less time to produce the same amount of gas than when using the dilute acid — the rate of reaction is faster. The slope of the graph (time vs volume of gas) will be steeper for the acid which produces the faster rate of reaction.

15) a) 40
   b) 108
   c) $12 + (16 \times 2) = 44$
   d) $24 + 12 + (16 \times 3) = 84$
   e) $27 + 3 \times (16 + 1) = 78$
   f) $65 + 16 = 81$
   g) $(23 \times 2) + 12 + (16 \times 3)$ $= 106$
   h) $23 + 35.5 = 58.5$

16) a) 186.8 g
   b) 80.3 g
   c) 20.1 g

Forces and Acceleration (page 49)

1) Resultant force = mass × acceleration
   resultant force = $70 \times 1.2 = 84$ N
   resultant force = driving force – drag
   $84 = $ driving force $– 8$
   so, driving force $= 84 + 8$ $= 92$ N

Revision Summary for Module P3 (page 60)

1) u = 0 m/s, v = 0.08 m/s, t = 35 s
   Distance = $((u + v) \div 2) \times t$
   $= ((0 + 0.08) \div 2) \times 35$
   $= 1.4$ m

3) Acceleration = change in speed ÷ time
   $= (14 - 0) \div 0.4 = 35$ m/s^2

11) Force = mass × acceleration
   so, acceleration = force ÷ mass
   $= 30 \div 4 = 7.5$ m/s^2

16) Momentum = mass × velocity so,
   velocity = momentum ÷ mass
   $= 45 \div 6$
   $= 7.5$ m/s

17) Force = change in momentum ÷ time
   so, change in momentum
   = force × time
   $= 70 \times 0.5 = 35$ kg m/s

20) Work done = force × distance
   $= 535 \times 12$
   $= 6420$ J

21) G.P.E. = mass × g × height
   $= 12 \times 10 \times 4.5 = 540$ J

22) K.E. = ½ × mass × velocity^2
   $= ½ \times 78 \times 23^2 = 20\ 631$ J

24) Increase in K.E. = Loss of G.P.E.
   $= 150$ kJ

25) Increase in K.E. = Loss of G.P.E.,
   $½mv^2 = mgh$
   but mass stays the same, so can use $h = v^2 \div 2g$
   $v^2 = (h \times 2g) = (20 \times 2 \times 10)$
   $= 400$
   $v = \sqrt{400} = 20$ m/s

26) Work done must be in J =
   $540 \times 1000 = 540\ 000$ J.
   Time needs to be in seconds,
   $4.5 \times 60 = 270$ s
   Power = work done ÷ time
   $= 540\ 000$ J $\div 270$ s
   $= 2000$ W or J/s $(= 2$ kW$)$

27) Power = force × speed
   $= 500 \times 20$
   $= 10\ 000$ W or J/s $(= 10$ kW$)$

Revision Summary for Module B4 (page 80)

1) 80 ants × 4000 m^2 = 320 000 ants in the whole car park.

2) $(23 \times 28) \div 4 = 161$ woodlice.

Revision Summary for Module C4 (page 96)

24) a) bromine + lithium → lithium bromide
   $Br_2 + 2Li \rightarrow 2LiBr$
   b) chlorine + potassium → potassium chloride
   $Cl_2 + 2K \rightarrow 2KCL$
   c) iodine + sodium → sodium iodide
   $I_2 + 2Na \rightarrow 2NaI$

Plugs and Fuses (page 101)

1) Power = Voltage × Current,
   Current = Power ÷ Voltage
   $= 1200 \div 230 = 5.2$ A.
   So the kettle will need a 7 A fus

Resistance (page 102)

1) Resistance = voltage ÷ current
   $= 9 \div 3 = 3\ \Omega$

2) Resistance = voltage ÷ current
   so voltage = resistance × curre
   $= 2.5 \times 6.4 = 16$ V

Radioactive Dating (page 109)

1) Original amount of carbon-14 is 1 part in 10 000 000.
   So one half-life will be 1 part in 20 000 000. Two half-lives wi be 1 part in 40 000 000...
   Four half-lives will be 1 part in 160 000 000.
   $4 \times 5730 = 22\ 920$ years old

Revision Summary for Module P4 (page 112)

8) Power = voltage × current, so current = power ÷ voltage
   $= 400 \div 230 = 1.74$ A
   Need to use the fuse with the rating just above the current use
   — so need to use the 3 A fuse.

13) a) $^{234}_{92}U \rightarrow ^{230}_{90}Th + ^{4}_{2}\alpha$
   b) $^{230}_{90}Th \rightarrow ^{226}_{88}Ra + ^{4}_{2}\alpha$
   c) $^{241}_{95}Am \rightarrow ^{237}_{93}Np + ^{4}_{2}\alpha$

14) a) $^{234}_{90}Th \rightarrow ^{234}_{91}Pa + ^{0}_{-1}\beta$
   b) $^{90}_{38}Sr \rightarrow ^{90}_{39}Y + ^{0}_{-1}\beta$
   c) $^{131}_{53}I \rightarrow ^{131}_{54}Xe + ^{0}_{-1}\beta$
   You won't have to remember th symbols for the elements in an exam, so you can stop memoris that periodic table for now.

21) Originally amount of carbon-14 was 1 part in 10 000 000.
   So one half-life will be 1 part in 20 000 000. Two half-lives will be 1 part in 40 000 000.
   Three half-lives will be 1 part in 80 000 000.
   $3 \times 5730 = 17\ 190$ years old.

REBECCA CLARKE

HE THAT DWELLETH IN THE SECRET PLACE OF THE MOST HIGH

A Setting of Psalm 91
for Unaccompanied Mixed Choir (SSAATTBB) with Soloists (SAATB)

OXFORD
UNIVERSITY PRESS

Long renowned for her chamber music and songs, **Rebecca Clarke** (b. Harrow, England, 1886; d. New York City, 1979) was virtually unknown as a composer of choral music until posthumous publication of her *Ave Maria* (OUP, 1998) and *Chorus from Shelley's 'Hellas'* (OUP, 1999). Since then, her entire choral output has been performed and recorded, and is published herewith.

Clarke wrote choral music over virtually the whole of her career, from around the time she began composition studies with Sir Charles Stanford (himself a great choral composer) in 1907 through her final flowering in the 1940s, revising and recomposing as late as 1976. Taken as a whole, Clarke's choral music comprises a survey of some of the most characteristic types of English writing for voices, from the medieval carol (*There Is No Rose*) through lute-song (*Weep You No More, Sad Fountains*), madrigal (*Philomela*), glee (*Now Fie on Love*), and romantic partsong (*Music, When Soft Voices Die*), to a kind of visionary modernism couched in traditional forms (*He that Dwelleth in the Secret Place of the Most High*), illustrating Clarke's creative engagement with models as diverse as Dowland, Stanford, Vaughan Williams, and Bloch.

Clarke composed *He that Dwelleth in the Secret Place of the Most High* over a period of nearly a year beginning on 16 April 1920, when, according to her diary, she was "suddenly quite thrilled over a setting of another psalm" and worked on it "like mad" all day. Clarke was much occupied with the psalms during this period: she had worked on a setting of Psalm 97 (apparently never completed) in the summer of 1919, and she set Psalm 63 for voice and piano in December 1920, while also sketching out the first movement of her Trio. She finished *He that Dwelleth* on 7 March 1921, and on 23 March spent more than seven hours copying it out. The next day she showed both completed psalm-settings to Holst, who "was very nice, but criticized them very severely." Holst's comments may have provoked a few small changes in pencil near the beginning of Clarke's manuscript, but few of the changes are substantive and none of them is carried forward into the rest of the piece. Except for some cautionary accidentals, the pencil changes have been ignored in this edition.

The psalm-settings and the Trio are Clarke's most direct musical expression of her great admiration of Ernest Bloch. This is particularly clear in *He that Dwelleth*, with its cantorial tenor solos, its tremendous rhetorical drive, and the effective bitonality in the opening and closing sections caused by soloist and chorus singing essentially the same material at two different speeds.

I am deeply indebted to Celia Cobb of Gonville and Caius College, Cambridge, for her help in editing Clarke's manuscripts, and to the Choir of Gonville and Caius and its director Geoffrey Webber for their performance and beautiful recording of Clarke's complete choral works, which led to many improvements in the content and presentation of the printed music.

—*Christopher Johnson*

The front cover reproduces a detail from an untitled pencil drawing by the composer's sister Dora Clarke (later Middleton). The design on the back cover is adapted from Rebecca Clarke's Christmas card for 1933.